FINDING
MAGIC

by
MALCOLM "PUCK"
PUCKERING

FINDING MAGIC
By Malcolm Puckering

Layout and Design by Stina Henslee
Copyediting by John Lovick
Promotional pictures courtesy of Fredde Lieberman

ISBN-13: 978-0-692-16214-9

6 5 4 3 2 1

To
MALIAH and MIKAYLA
When they are eighteen

FOREWORD

Welcome to a love story!

No, it's not like the Ali MacGraw and Ryan O'Neal movie, rather it is a love of life... a journey toward a dream.

The world is full of many successful people. Success is many times accompanied by fame, financial achievements, or happiness. Some successes encompass all three, some only one or two. In the end, I think success is the end result of a passionate search for what you really love. Puck's story is just such a love story.

I remember the first time I met Puck. He talked of what he would like to do in life. I saw the drive, the passion, and the determination in his eyes. This is the type of person I consider a success. He did not disappoint me.

I have watched him grow in his achievements to reach a point in his life that has gained my respect and admiration and yet I realize that he is still progressing and has much more ahead of him.

Puck has also shared his failures with me as well as his successes. It's all a learning process and it's all in this book. Puck will take you through his life with stories that will make you laugh and others that will tug at your emotions.

A biography enables you to live the life of another through the use of words. This biography is an enjoyable inspiration to anyone who loves anything. Live your dreams. Embrace your passion. Let no one tell you that it can't be done.

This is the human spirit.

Enjoy this journey as I have after reading this book and knowing the man.

-Denny Haney

CHAPTER 1
Disturbed

As my eyes opened for what felt like the very first time, I found my view obstructed by the bottom of a mattress that made the top bunk. This room felt foreign to me and there was good reason for it. I was waking up in a house that was far from my home. I was only around three years old but already knew that my start in the world was beginning at a disadvantage. I remember going downstairs and seeing a family preparing breakfast. This family was my foster father, mother, and sisters. My foster mother was Gloria Gittens and I called her Aunt Gloria. She was an older woman with brown skin and a slender build. Aunt Gloria had four daughters who were all older than me and I don't remember much about my foster father as he passed away early on during my stay with them. There were also a number of fellow orphans that would come and go quite regularly. Even though I was a toddler it was apparent that the younger the child the easier it seemed to get adopted.

On occasion I would visit different homes to meet with prospective families. Looking back, this was more like an audition where I never seemed to get the gig. Sometimes adults talk about adult stuff in front of small children thinking we don't yet understand what they're saying. The word "disturbed" always seemed to pop up when my name was mentioned. I didn't know what that meant back then but had a feeling it couldn't be good otherwise my days there would surely have been much shorter.

Then there was Mrs. Siegel, a representative from the adoption agency. She would visit sometimes to check in and her job was to help find permanent homes for us. Mrs. Siegel seemed very nice and made me feel as though she was more than just a representative and really cared. We would stay in contact periodically as I grew up.

The daily climate in the foster home was strict as Aunt Gloria ran a tight ship. She was stern and I knew not to step out of line. If I did, the consequenc-

Aunt Gloria

es would be swift and sharp. This was the early '70s when children were to be seen and not heard. We knew our place and stayed out of grown folks' business and one look was all it took for us to straighten up. There was no wimpy-ass time out in those days.

The Gittens home was located in St. Albans, which is in Queens, New York. In the late '60s and early '70s, St. Albans was an ethnic, family-oriented neighborhood. All the adults looked out for one another, and this included us kids, as well. If you did something wrong and your neighbor saw it, they would chastise you themselves and then tell your parents, who would let you have it again. Some years later that friendly practice became known as the neighborhood watch program. This was way before kids had access to that 800 number you could call and complain that your parents were whupping your ass.

In the house next door to The Gittens was an older couple, Learmond and Evelyn Puckering. They were from a beautiful island in the British West Indies called Barbados. Learmond was a quiet man with OCD who was really frugal or, to put it in plain terms, *cheap*. Evelyn was a beautiful person and truly an angel on earth. She would visit Aunt Gloria and bring me jelly beans, which made me feel special among all the other children at the foster home. I think she had a soft spot for me since I was the oldest and had been there the longest. She had a grandson named Andre that stayed with them after school until his parents came to pick him up after they had finished work. He was five years older than me and we would play together after school sometimes and became pretty good friends.

Down the block was a girl my age named Janice. She was a skinny Puerto Rican kid with pigtails and was my best friend.

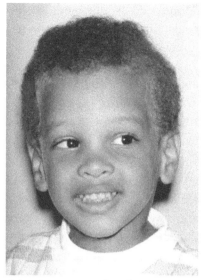

Adoption picture. Age 2

She taught me to play hopscotch, toss jacks, and even jump rope. All of these games were pretty girly but I enjoyed them nonetheless.

The neighborhood kids were rough and I guess they had to be to survive. For some reason being an orphan didn't garner any sympathy from them and in fact had the complete opposite effect. Making matters worse, I was light skinned with white features and blonde streaks in my Afro. My blonde streaks were in the same spot as the Bride of Frankenstein's and don't think for a second the kids on the block didn't point that shit out! I don't know why, but being light-skinned in those days just wasn't popular. The kids called me all kinds of names like High Yellow, Piss Yellow, Red Bone, Red Nigger, Yellow Nigger, and even House Nigger. I would come to learn later in life that light-skinned blacks tend to come in and out of style. I guess it all depends on who's hot on the music charts, sports, or on TV and in movies at the time. Although my skin tone and Anglo features seemed to be a hindrance back then I would learn later in life how to use them to my advantage.

Growing up in a foster home was tough for me, especially as I watched all the younger kids getting adopted while I remained unchosen. The older I got the less desirable I became. Maybe I was "disturbed" like the adults seemed to think. I also had a hard time being around groups and was deathly shy. So much so that I would sometimes hide to avoid meeting new people. One time when my foster family had company I hid deep in a closet behind some clothes and no one could find me for hours. Also, I was a cute kid and all the extra attention and cheek pinching made me very uncomfortable. It was kind of ironic to be so cute and still not able to score a family of my own.

Another thing that possibly contributed to my being "disturbed" was an early exposure to sex. Out of my four foster sisters I was closest with the youngest since she and I were nearest in age. One time she and I were in my room lying on the top bunk. She put her hand in my pants and touched my penis, which made me excited. She put my hand in her pants and had me touch her, too. She got undressed and then undressed me. She then put me on top of her and placed my penis on her vagina. Notice I said on top and not in, because my penis was so small at that age there was no way I could have penetrated anything. So by default I kinda, sorta lost my virginity at age five. I think she was around thirteen so we were both experimenting and as I grew older and looked back I never considered it abuse. She made me promise not to say anything about what we did but being a kid I quickly broke that promise and told our neighbors' grandson, Andre. He then told some of the neighborhood kids but luckily it never got back to Aunt Gloria, or any other adults that I knew of.

So with my newfound knowledge I decided to show my best friend Janice what I had learned. I took her to my room and on the same top bunk proceeded to place my penis on top of Janice's vagina. I then told her not to tell anyone. I guess "disturbed" was actually more like "damaged"!

CHAPTER 2
RAMBUNCTIOUS

It was just short of my sixth birthday and I was still at the foster home with no prospects in sight. I felt like I would never get adopted and then the tides turned. The neighbors' grandson Andre, whom I had become close with, asked his parents if they would adopt me. His parents Elsie and Learmond Puckering were in their thirties and had considered having another child. At their sons request they made a collective decision as a family to legally adopt me. This process was long and costly but eventually resulted in me becoming a Puckering. They even gave me a middle name "Graham". This was my new father's middle name and his father's before him. It felt great to be part of a real family and the best thing of all was Andre's grandparents were now my grandparents. That jelly-bean toting angelic woman was now my grandmother, too. Things couldn't get any better.

Mr. and Mrs. Puckering, or now mom and dad, lived in Springfield Gardens, not too far from St. Albans. Dad was an X-ray technician and mom was a registered nurse. They both worked for the Department of Health in Brooklyn and were a typical middle-class family with a typical middle-class home. Mom and dad had tons of friends and family, making house parties a regular occurrence. Our home was great and had a playroom with lots of toys and games for me and Andre in the attic. There was a large bar stocked to the hilt plus a piano and drum set in the basement. This home was made for

My new Dad

My new Mom

entertaining. It was decked out '70s style with a few long, beaded doorways, shag carpet, a breakfast nook, plastic covers on the furniture, runners in the hallways, and even some of those velvet posters with the black lights. We had a basketball hoop over the garage in the backyard and played b-ball often. My brother would always beat me badly as he was older and much taller. One time he was beating me so bad in a game of Around the World that I threw the ball and yelled, "Fuck!" really loud. This was a word I had heard many times from the neighborhood kids. Well as soon as the word left my mouth I heard my mother scream "Malcolm, get in here!" This came from her bedroom, which was on the backside of the house, close enough to hear her foul-mouth new addition to the family. I was petrified, to say the least. As per her request I went inside and made my way to my parents' bedroom. She told me to bring her the sewing case. This was a large red faux leather box she kept in the hallway closet. This box held all the things you needed to sew and mend, like buttons, thimbles, thread, needles, scissors, etc. As soon as I brought her the box she opened it and immediately went for the scissors. She told me to come closer and stick out my tongue. I did this hesitantly and she quickly grabbed hold of my tongue before I could pull it back into my mouth. She placed my tongue between the razor sharp shears and threatened to cut it off. She said if that word ever came from my mouth again the tongue was coming out! I'll never forget that day as long as I live as it scared the living shit out of me! At the time of this writing I am fifty-one and my mother is eighty-eight and I still find it hard to utter even the most tame word "damn" in her presence. Just shows that you will always be your parents' child no matter how old or successful you get.

My brother went to Saint Catherine's of Sienna, which was a school around the corner from my grandparents. They enrolled me there as well, starting in grade one. Saint Catherine's was a strict Catholic school and we had to wear dark grey pants with a white button down collared shirt, plaid tie, and hard black shoes. The only day we could dress down was on Wednesday, which was a half day of school and half day of chapel. The majority of the teachers were nuns who donned the typical Roman Catholic habit, which consisted of a tunic covered by a scapular and cowl, with hood. Those religious garments looked scary and what made them even more frightening was the fact our teachers/nuns were allowed to spank us if we got out of line. Outside the main building was a concrete playground where we had recess after lunch was finished. This playground had a long yellow line painted right down the middle separating it into two equal parts. One half was for girls only and the other just for boys. If a boy crossed the line and was caught playing in the girls' half, his punishment was to wear a bright pink bow in his hair for the remainder of the school day. I don't remember what the girls punishment was but there's no way it could have been more humiliating than what the boys were subjected to.

I had a hard time focusing in school and always seemed to get into trouble. One time I had been sent home with a note for my parents. The note was for being disruptive. I remember this so well because it was the first time I had seen my parents pissed off, especially my new mother. The teacher used a word to describe my behavior that really infuriated her. The word the teacher used was "rambunctious". All I know is that my mother got really angry and then commenced to whup my ass! She kept repeating that word "rambunctious" every time she swung the belt. It got so bad that my brother stepped in and begged my mom to stop. I guess this must have snapped her out of it and she stopped. That was not a good day and gave me a little glimpse into the future of what would happen if and when I screwed up.

As I stated earlier the nuns were allowed to spank us and our parents had given them written permission to do so. You've all heard the Bible verse "He that spareth his rod hateth his son: but he that loveth him chasteneth him bedtimes" or in laymen's terms, "Spare the rod, spoil the child." The nuns took that verse literally. Unfortunately this all went awry when one of them went too far. My brother had broken a classroom rule but instead of implementing an authorized spanking this nun chose to pull him by the hair. When my mother got wind of this she made an unexpected trip to the school and gave that nun a piece of her mind. This confused me a little because to my understanding a good whupping was just part of growing up, wasn't it?

My mother was always concerned that people would treat me different if they knew I was adopted. For some reason she felt there was a stigma attached to that word and always kept this a secret. So between the overzealous nuns and poor academic ratings at Saint Catherine's, accompanied by my mother's quest to keep my adoption confidential the search for a new home began.

CHAPTER 3
STRONG ISLAND

Two of my parents' closest friends were Leroy and Mary Reddick. They had a son Terrence and two daughters, Gail and Lorelei. We were all very close and treated each other as family. They became Aunt Mary and Uncle Leroy and their kids were considered our cousins. They lived in Cambria Heights and their home was known as a Kool-Aid house. A Kool-Aid house is a place in the neighborhood where everyone hung out and, yes, drank lots of Kool-Aid, preferably grape. We would spend quite a bit of time there and I loved being around my older cousins. To make things even better, Aunt Mary and Uncle Leroy where real laid back, so the rules in their home were very lax. This always made for a lot of fun and youthful experimentation. The adults would sit around drinking, eating, talking, and laughing which gave us plenty of time to run around unsupervised.

My cousin Terrence was a big muscular kid who was always doing crazy shit. He introduced me to a lot of questionable things at an early age. I was about seven and Terrence was maybe fifteen when he gave me my first sip of beer. That's if you call Olde English 800 beer. It's actually malt liquor and gets you buzzed really fast. One afternoon he bought a can for us at the corner bodega. You could buy beer and even cigarettes at any age back then if you said it was for your parents. Terrence bought the beer and asked for a paper bag with a straw. He said since I was seven-years old I needed to take seven sips really fast. I was a little hesitant but he was my older cousin and I didn't want to let him down. So I take the first sip and man, this stuff tastes bad. It's like someone mixed Coke, ginger ale, Nehi grape, and Sprite all together and then added a pinch of vomit. I took the second sip, followed by a third, all the way to my seventh. Almost instantly I felt light-headed. This was followed by a feeling I can only describe as "happy". It made me feel really happy and I started laughing for absolutely no reason. I just couldn't stop giggling. When we got back to his house he kept trying to calm me down, telling me to stop laughing and act normal so our parents wouldn't realize I was drunk. Imagine a seven-year-old kid fucked up on seven sips of Olde English 800. I told you Terrance was always doing crazy shit!

My mother's sister also lived in Cambria Heights. It was my Aunt Eileen, Uncle Victor, and my cousins Steven and David. I loved going to their house because they had an above-ground swimming pool. There weren't many homes in Queens with a pool so it was always a treat to visit them. My cousins were super cool too, especially Steven. Steven and my brother Andre were born the same day, one year apart. Steven loved to draw and was in a real gang. Gangs were big in New York and it was kinda like that movie *The Warriors*. Gang members wore matching jean jackets and used graffiti to mark their turf. Being an artist placed Steven in high demand.

The Lords were another of my parents' friends that also became family. There was Uncle Kestor, the Dentist, Aunt Elsa, the seamstress, and cousins Geoffrey and Angela. They really seemed to have it together amongst all the craziness in Queens.

It was great that my parents had so many family members and friends because we needed every last one to help us make the move from Queens to Long Island, or as we say in the hood "Strong Island". My parents bought a beautiful home in Roosevelt, a black middle-class neighborhood. Although Roosevelt was a small town it spawned a lot of very talented and famous people. This was the home of basketball great Julius "Dr. J" Erving, shock jock Howard Stern, rap legends Public Enemy with Flavor Flav, and Charlie and Eddie Murphy, to name a few.

Roosevelt was rural but still had a tough, ghetto side. We lived on the corner of Hudson and Brookside Avenue. Brookside ran mostly through Baldwin, our neighboring town. Because part of our home was on Brookside Ave. we were zoned in the Baldwin School district. That meant we wouldn't be going to Roosevelt schools. This was a big selling point for my parents to purchase this particular home. Baldwin schools were ranked very high academically and Roosevelt was not. Ironically, Roosevelt schools were mostly black and Baldwin mostly white, go figure.

I started at Brookside elementary in the second grade. The first day my mother walked me to school. This was around a thirty-minute walk if you took the streets and didn't try to jump a brook that made it a little shorter. There were adult crossing guards at all the large intersections to keep us safe. My mother would only walk me this one time to show me the way and then I was on my own for the rest of the year. I made that walk in all kinds of weather. If it was raining I wore a hooded raincoat and galoshes that went over my shoes. If it was snowing I wore a heavy coat with a snorkel hood, mittens, and tall green and orange rubber boots. When our parents told us stories of how they used to walk miles to school in treacherous weather we knew they weren't bullshitting!

Again, Baldwin was a mostly white school and I felt a little lost at first. Coming from St. Albans, I wasn't used to seeing that many white kids in one place and it was a slight adjustment. These kids didn't talk the way I was used to hearing and definitely didn't dress like it. I quickly made friends with the only other black kids in the class. It's funny how groups of like people seem to seek each other out. I don't consider this racist or prejudiced, but just adapting to what's familiar and comfortable. So there started my friendship with Tracy Abraham and Ronald Brinson. Both boys lived within a block of my home in Roosevelt. Tracy was really tall for his age and a little awkward on his feet. Watching him was kinda like watching a baby giraffe walking for the first time. Ronald was small but really strong and quick. We all loved sports and played everything from baseball to basketball together. We also loved riding our bikes around the neighborhood. I was allowed to play outside after school as long as my homework was done, chores were finished, and I changed out of my school clothes. We ate dinner at six and that was the time I had to be in the house. This was never a problem because we lived across the street from a church that rang its bells at 6 p.m. sharp. These bells could be heard for miles. As soon as I heard the first bong I started running home and if I timed it right could make it by the last bong.

We ate dinner every night as a family. We had a kitchen table that we would convene at to eat and talk about the day. We weren't allowed to play the radio or anything that would distract from this family time. The one thing I hated about dinner was having to clean my plate. This was necessary to become a member of the clean plate club, as my dad would say. This was a tall order for a kid that hated veggies, especially peas and my mother wouldn't let me leave the table till every last one was finished. Sometimes the family would be done eating, dishes washed, and watching TV while I remained at the table rolling those damn peas from side to side with my fork. Something about the texture would make my gag reflex kick in when I tried to swallow them. This was freaking torture! To top it off we had a plaque on the wall that said the "Puckering Family Dog House" on it. There were four wooden cut out dogs on pegs and one empty peg inside of a red doghouse. If you were on punishment or in trouble your dog cut out was placed on the doghouse peg. The four dogs had our names printed on them, which my dad printed with one of those embossing label maker guns. On the nights my peas stayed on the plate my pup hung in the doghouse.

When we didn't have peas for dinner I would finish with the family. My job after we ate was to dry and put away the dishes once my brother had washed them. This had to be done before we could play or watch any television. My brother would always mess with me because I was easily rattled. He'd wash the dishes as fast as he could, knowing I couldn't keep up. He did this to leave me there all alone while he ran off to enjoy the evening before bedtime. This really pissed me off and was only the beginning of the older brother crap I would have to endure. Everything between Andre and me was a contest and he seemed to really enjoy beating me. I don't remember us being that competitive when I was still in the foster home but I guess things changed once we were under the same roof. Our age

Puck's family dog house

difference probably played a good part in this, too. A twelve-year-old doesn't want to hang with his seven-year-old brother unless he's really bored. He would torture me, too. I remember him pinning me on my back and tickling me till I wet myself. He did this several times and would threaten to tell my parents that I peed my pants. There were plenty of purple nurples and Indian sun burns to go around, too. If you don't know what a purple nurple is, it's when you pinch and twist someone's nipple till it turns purple. An Indian sun burn is when you grab a persons wrist with both of your hands then squeeze and twist each of your hands in opposite directions. It burns like hell and gives the appearance of a red sunburn. Thinking back, that was a pretty racist name for such a juvenile game. So torturing the little brother was in full effect at the Puckering household.

Competition was a big problem and it would usually end with me getting in trouble. We had to bathe before going to bed and Andre and I shared the upstairs bathroom. My mother would tell us when it was time for us to bathe, which would signal that the race was on. Who would get undressed the quickest and make it to the bath first? The loser would have to sit and wait for the other to finish. Well the race had started and I could see that I was undressing the fastest. I quickly made my way to the bathroom with my brother hot on my heels. I made it though the door within seconds of Andre and I slammed the bathroom door on him. Well, there was a problem with this that I didn't foresee. I evidently slammed the door too hard and the tiles on the wall next to the door fell off and crashed to the bathroom floor, shattering to pieces. This was really loud and I could hear my mother making her way up the stairs. She opened the door and saw what I had done. Although in my mind it was an accident, for some reason my mother didn't see it the same way. Being naked for bath time really made that beating last way longer than usual. The welts on my bare ass made sitting painful for a couple of days. I stopped racing for the tub after that incident; lesson learned!

CHAPTER 4
DA VINCI

My parents loved to travel, and because they knew so many people they decided to create The Pucks' Travel Club. A travel club is a group of people who travel together and get discounts for bulk reservations. My parents were the owners and tour coordinators of this group. They planned everything including the airfare, accommodations, meals, tours, and shows. My parents' motto was "Go with Pucks' and leave the planning to us", and that's exactly what they did. They still had their jobs and the group was simply a labor of love they did on the side. They honestly made no profit with the exception of a few free vacations from time to time. First they would come up with a trip idea and in 1972 it was Hawaii. This trip would start with three days in Los Angeles, then seven in Honolulu, ending with three more in Las Vegas. They co-ordinated everything, including a day at Disney Land, a Luau on Waikiki Beach, and a show at Caesar's Palace. To advertise the big trip, my parents would send out brochures to everyone in the group. They had over a hundred members that consisted of mostly friends and family. Me and my brother Andre had jobs, too. Ours was to fold, stuff, and stamp all of the mailers. We would sit in front of the TV using metal dinner tray stands as desks. I guess we had to earn our keep if we wanted to go on these trips. They also threw a vacation-themed dinner dance every year before the big trip. These were usually held at posh country clubs, hotels, and banquet halls.

Cruising with Mom, Dad and Andre

The room would be decorated to look like the destination of the upcoming trip. They would hire Ron Anderson, who was the leader of a well-known band in the New York area. Everyone ate, drank, and danced the night away. I loved them too because all my cousins would be there and I would get all sugared up and run around like I had no damn sense. On the last day of school the teacher would ask what everyone was going to be doing for the summer break. I would puff my chest out and say, "I'm going to California, Hawaii, and Las Vegas." It felt great to brag but I don't think anyone really believed me, but they couldn't have been more wrong.

By the time I was in sixth grade I had visited a great many vacation spots in the US as well as several abroad. I even went on the Leonardo da Vinci. This was one of three sister ships in a luxury Italian cruise line that included the Raphael and the Michelangelo. One day in the kids club on the ship we had to wear costumes and then march in a parade around the ballroom for all the guests. My mother dressed me up like a pirate. She wrapped a colorful scarf around my head, clipped on one of her hoop earrings, and blackened one eye with some make up, and put a patch over the other one. Before the march we went to eat and, loving all things sugar, I was drawn to a cake on the buffet. I must have eaten four pieces before I started feeling funny. I had experienced this strange feeling once before while hanging with my cousin Terrance. Come to find out the cake was laced with rum. When we did the parade march my mother noticed I couldn't keep still or stop laughing. Well, she quickly found out that I was eating rum cake and immediately snatched me up and off to the cabin to sober up. For the second time in my eight years on earth I was bombed.

When it came to common sense I wasn't very bright and this tended to keep me in the doghouse. While in the cabin with my brother and cousin Dawn I did something really stupid. My parents always said I had a hard head and I thought they meant it literally. I grabbed a silver water picture from the nightstand and commenced to slam it on my head. Upon impact I heard something break inside. Turns out this pitcher was glass-lined and I had shattered it completely. When my parents came back and when they went to pour themselves some water, they got a pile of broken glass instead. What happened next was the customary ass whupping, followed by the traditional grounding. I just didn't quite think things though and paid for it daily.

It was 1974 and there was an announcement over the ship's loudspeakers. They said that President Richard Nixon had resigned. I didn't know much about politics at that time but everyone seemed to be in shock. That announcement cemented the memory of our vacation that year on The Leonardo da Vinci.

CHAPTER 5
LIVERWURST

I don't know if it was because of my early days in a foster home, or if I was just having a difficult time adjusting to my new family but I definitely had issues. One major issue was bed-wetting. I would have these dreams that I was jumping out of the bed, walking to the bathroom, lifting the seat, pulling down my pajama pants, then peeing into the toilet. It felt so real until I woke up in a puddle. It didn't matter if I didn't have anything to drink before bed or if I went to the bathroom beforehand. It just happened and there was nothing I could do to prevent it. This did not make my parents happy, especially since I was ruining my mattress. Every time this happened we'd strip the sheets, flip the mattress, and put on new sheets. The bed now had a huge round permanent yellow stain on both sides. As the years went on and "accidents" occurred I learned to hide it from everyone. I would wake up quietly, change my clothes, and put a towel over the wet spot then go back to sleep. One time, though, I didn't wake up. I was scared that since it was morning someone would find out. I changed pajamas and decided sneak down to the laundry room in the basement and get a can of Lysol to spray my bed so no one would smell the stale urine. I retrieved the can undetected and made my way to the mattress for Mission: Deodorize. I pointed spray nozzle and let it rip. To my dismay I had the nozzle facing the wrong direction and it was aimed directly toward my face. I unintentionally sprayed myself dead in the eyes. This stung really bad and I thought I was gonna go blind. I started screaming in pain, and my mother came running up the stairs. She asked what was wrong and I told her I sprayed myself in the face with Lysol. She rushed me to the bathroom and starting flushing my eyes. This was one of those times I really appreciated the fact my mother was an R.N. Once my vision was no longer in jeopardy my mother asked what in the world was I doing. I fessed up and told her I had wet the bed and was trying to hide the evidence, particularly the smell. She was pissed (pardon the pun) but didn't let me have it like I was expecting. I think the fact that I had just sprayed poison in my eyes scared her enough to give me a stay of execution this time around.

Aside from spraying Lysol in my eyes I did some other bizarre things. One of my chores, aside from drying and putting away the dishes, was to fold and put away the family's laundry. My father was in the Army Air Force during the Korean War and taught me to make a bed military style and also how to roll socks and fold clothes. I took pride in making my bed so tight I could bounce a quarter off my sheets. With these skills I was ready to attack the laundry. This was never a problem until Tracy or Ronald would come by to play. They'd knock on the door and ask my mom if I could come out, and then she would yell to me and ask if all my chores were done. Most of the times I would have to stay in because I wasn't finished folding and putting away the clothes. On one occasion I chose to lie. When my friends came by and my mother asked if I was finished with my chores I yelled, "yes" all the time knowing I wasn't finished with the laundry. I decided to hide the clothes under the bed till later and then fold them when I got back, thinking no one would be the wiser. Well, when I came back from playing we immediately ate dinner. I wanted to get the clothes from their hiding place but was scared that I'd get caught and my mother would know I had lied. So I left them under the bed to tackle the following day. The following day came and again I was still too scared, so they remained under the bed. A week went by and the laundry was still in its hiding spot. Eventually everyone in the house started running out of clothes. My mother started asking if I'd put them away in the wrong place in which I replied, "no" in fear of getting in trouble. This went on a few more days until my parents started searching the house for the clothes. Finally the jig was up and the clothes were found. By now they were

Dad, Andre, Me

so wrinkled that they had to be washed and dried all over again. I wish I could say I was forgiven and everything turned out all right but you know that wasn't the case. I got it bad this time but in all honesty, I deserved it.

This last one makes no logical sense whatsoever and really drives home the fact I had problems. We were considered middle class, but lived on a tight budget in order to make ends meet. We didn't have a new car or fancy clothes like some of my friends' families. In fact, the only time we got something new was for Easter or graduation when we'd get a suit and shoes from Alexander's department store. My dad shopped for groceries at Pathmark and we had plenty of No Frills food in the pantry. No Frills was the generic store brand. It had an all-white label with one red and one blue stripe at the bottom and the name of the food written in large black print. Instead of Cheerios we had Tasteos, instead of Froot Loops we had Fruity Rings; you get the idea. My friends would come by and make fun of me, saying we had poor people's food. To make matters worse, my mother worked for the Department of Health and would bring home food from the WIC program. This was government assistance food that was labeled USDA. This was even more embarrassing than No Frills, with the exception of the government-issued cheese.

The USDA cheese came in a long, white box and was around a foot long. You could cut it any way you wanted and it made the best grilled-cheese sandwiches. That's the only food item in our fridge no one ever made fun of. Everyone wanted a hunk of that stuff.

Because we didn't have a lot of spare money my brother and I had to bring our lunch to school. This sucked because most of the white kids got lunch money and the cafeteria food was pretty good. They had large hot pretzels, hamburgers and fries, bagels with cream cheese, potato knishes, and my favorite of all time, the black-and-white frosted cookie. I got to watch them eat those mouth-watering goodies while I brown-bagged it. My father always made sandwiches with perishable meats. His favorite sandwich to make for us was bologna and cheese or liverwurst. He would make them on white bread with mayonnaise, lettuce, and tomato. By lunchtime, the mayo had congealed, the meat was warm and sweaty, and the lettuce had wilted. He thought by wrapping it in aluminum foil it would stay cool and fresh. Dessert was always an apple or banana and the daily drink was milk served in a plastic thermos. This always smelled a little sour by the time you opened it. I never had the heart to tell him I hated those lunches because I knew how hard he worked and didn't want to hurt his feelings.

Because I couldn't bring myself to eat those bag lunches I would just leave them in my book bag and pray none of the lunch ladies would notice and say something about me not eating. Now I've got this sandwich in my book bag and could just throw it away and be done with it, but this wasn't how my brain worked. Remember I said that I had problems, and this pretty much proves it. I would end up taking that uneaten lunch all the way back home and then hide it in my room under the mattress. A banana or apple and a sandwich all wrapped in aluminum foil surrounded by a brown paper bag. I didn't want anyone to find the discarded food in any of the trash cans, so under my mattress it went. This went on for years and when there were too many bags under there and no one was around I would take out a few then go outside and stuff them into the sewer grate at the corner of our house. Eventually my mattress started to smell pretty bad. The good thing was, my parents rarely came upstairs. However my brother lived upstairs and noticed the stench of old food. He found my rotten stash and asked what the heck was I doing. I told him they were the lunches I hated to eat and I was afraid of getting caught throwing them away. He never told but used this as a blackmail tool. When he didn't feel like washing the dishes he'd threaten to tell our parents about the rotten sandwiches unless I did them. This went on for a while until my mother eventually found the lunches and that was the end of that.

To this day I still can't explain why I did what I did. Maybe it was simply the fear of getting caught but it was truly stupid and very weird.

CHAPTER 6
RORSCHACH

The town of Roosevelt had an array of colorful characters. Nassau Road was the main drag where the majority of stores and businesses were located. On weekends I loved going to Jerry's Barber Shop where every visit was an experience. The banter in the black barbershop can be informative, comical, and always entertaining. The old timers would debate with the young bucks about everything from sports to politics. I looked forward to every visit and continued going there as I grew into an adult. If you've ever seen the movie *Coming to America* with Eddie Murphy, you'll remember the very funny barbershop scenes. Well Eddie, being a former resident of Roosevelt, got a lot of the material for those scenes right there at Jerry's. Every time you asked Jerry about that movie he would let you know that Eddie owed him a check. Jerry's Barber Shop was the cornerstone of the community and should have been deemed a historic landmark.

Aside from an array of local bars and clubs we also had a roller rink for a short time. Roosevelt Roller Rink was the place to be and anyone who was anyone could be seen there nightly. Disco was still very big and the music and lights made for a highly visual experience. You'd see pimps and drug dealers decked out in the hottest outfits. Everywhere you looked were disco skaters dancing and doing all kinds of acrobatic tricks on eight wheels. My parents allowed me to go for afternoon skate sessions but never at night. My dad would drop me and my friends off and then pick us up when it was over. It wasn't open that long but left a lasting mark on "The Velt's" history!

Another interesting place on Nassau Road was the Roosevelt Mental Health Clinic. I got to know this one close up and personal because my parents sent me there after years of witnessing my odd behavior. I went every Wednesday after school for about an hour. My psychologist was Mr. Timothy Buttler, a young black man who came off as smart and hip. We would do all sorts of tests during my sessions like the Rorschach and role-playing, but mostly we'd just talk. Sometimes he'd take me to Centennial Park across the street and one time even to the roller rink with some of his other child patients. I remember him asking why I did a lot of the things that seemed to get me into trouble. I told him simply that I was afraid. I feared punishment so much that I got in more trouble just to avoid it. That's really profound when you think about it.

Every Sunday morning I went to church. My father's church was St. John's Episcopal back in Queens. I liked St. John's because we knew just about everyone there. I grew up with all the members and they were considered family. It was a small church and my dad was an usher. My brother and I would mess around a lot and one time we got in a crapload of trouble. We were at the altar, receiving communion, which was supposed to be taken seriously. This consisted of one round wafer and a sip of wine from the chalice. It was real wine and the whole church drank from the same cup. The priest just wiped away your lip prints and rotated it for the next person. That would never work today with our germaphobic society. Well, as Andre was getting his sip of wine I leaned over and whispered something funny in his ear. He started laughing and the wine came shooting out of his nose. The priest didn't know how to react and just moved on to me where I took my sip without incident. One of the members, an older woman named Ms. Evelyn saw what had just happened and was appalled at our behavior. We called her Evil Evelyn because she looked exactly like the Wicked Witch of the West from *The Wizard of Oz*. She was always so serious and seemed to hate us kids. When we got back to our seat she came over and told my dad about what we'd done at the altar. Without hesitation my father started beating us with his hymnal book right there in the pew. Playing around in the house of the Lord was unacceptable and we got the message loud and clear.

When we moved to Long Island my mother found a local Catholic church for me and my brother to attend while my dad commuted to St. John's. We would still get to go to my dad's church on holidays and special occasions, which we very much looked forward to.

The church she found for us was the Queen of the Most Holy Rosary, or QMHR for short, on Centennial Avenue. We went to Sunday school there and I also had my holy communion at that church. My mother didn't always attend but would send me and Andre. On those Sundays she stayed home, you could find her watching Reverend Robert Schuller and *The Hour of Power* mass on TV. She loved *The Hour of Power* and regularly sent money to Reverend Schuller's Crystal Cathedral in Garden Grove, California. I attended the 9:00 a.m. children's mass, while my brother went at 11:00 for the adults. My mother would always send an envelope for me to put in the offering plate. It was just two dollars, which I would usually keep and buy candy with at the corner store before heading home. Stealing from the church wasn't good, but I had no self-control when it came to candy. Sometimes I wouldn't even make it to church at all and instead go to my friend Tor's house to watch cartoons. Catholic church was really boring and I didn't enjoy it very much. I was used to my dad's church and that's the only one I really liked. One day I asked my mother if I could change from Catholic to Episcopalian so I could go to church with my father. The second the words left my mouth my mother punched me square in the nose. It was quick and hard causing my nose to immediately start bleeding all over my white church shirt. My mother said that when she got married she vowed to raise me as a Catholic and I would stay one till I was eighteen. She told me to change my shirt and go to church, which signaled the conversation was over. To avoid any family drama I never told my father what happened that morning. I believe my mother was hurt that I favored my dad's church over hers. I stayed at QMHR, but my taste for religion was tainted and as soon as I was old enough to decide for myself, I was no longer gonna go.

CHAPTER 7
NIGGER

L iving in Roosevelt and going to school at Baldwin was as different as night and day. You could still feel a lot of racial tension lingering from the '60s and I felt this probably more than anyone else because I lived in both of these worlds. Also, looking the way I did afforded me a peek behind the curtain into these vastly different cultures. I had a huge Afro and the white kids at school always wanted to touch it. It was if I had some magical lamp on my head that everyone wanted to rub and make a wish. The one cool thing about having an Afro was being able to hide things in it. I would put crayons, candy, and anything else that was small enough to fit. This became sort of a novelty to my white classmates and made me to feel like I was fitting in even if I was more like a human petting zoo.

Baldwin High was a stone's throw from my elementary school. One day while walking home with my buddy Ronald we were approached by three white high school boys. They were all wearing red and green matching jackets that had symbols on them we didn't recognize. I learned later that the symbols on their jackets were Greek and they were in a fraternity called Delta Gamma Rho. Some high school kids back then thought it would be cool to start fraternities, but in reality they were nothing more than gangs. These three white boys surrounded us and started to taunt me and Ronald. They called us niggers, coons, and even Alabama porch monkeys. I have to admit that last one was kinda funny and definitely a name I'd never heard before. They were carrying weapons and tried to intimidate us. One had brass knuckles and the other two had switchblade knives. These things were pretty easy to purchase in those days. This intimidation went on for a while until one of the teachers in my school saw them harassing us and yelled from a classroom window for the older boys to leave us alone. They got spooked and took off, leaving us standing there scared and con-

Afro

fused. The second I got home I told Andre and he got some of his friends and went back up there looking for them. They never did find those guys, but it felt good to know someone had my back.

Halloween was always one of the most fun times of the year. We would get into costume, grab a large brown grocery bag, and hit the streets to go trick or treating. We would pound the pavement for hours, going house to house, filling our bag with all sorts of sugary goodies. We also had a UNICEF box that our school gave us and some people would put coins in it to help the poor. All in all, a great time of year, but it did have its problems. The older boys would ride around on bikes and try to snatch our bags. I guess they were too lazy to go house to house and wanted their treats in a hurry. We would hold on really tight whenever we saw a group of older kids on bikes coming our way. One year when I was finished for the night and headed home, I was approached by some white kids on bikes. This was odd because we were in my neighborhood and they were definitely out of place there. They started circling me and that word resurfaced once again. They started calling me a nigger and told me to hand over my bag. They were pretty loud and my father, who was in the house not far away, must have heard all the commotion because he came bursting out of the house in a rage like I've never seen. He was running toward the boys and removing his belt. He started swinging his belt at the boys like a lion tamer. He was yelling at the top of his lungs, "Get the hell out of here!" The boys took off and I'm sure never ventured back into Roosevelt. My dad was my super hero and again it felt good to know someone had my back.

That night after dinner my dad sat me down to explain what prejudice was all about. He said that some people hate others simply because of the color of their skin. These people were ignorant and I shouldn't pay them any mind. He told me stories of when he was in the military during the war. There was still a lot of segregation at that time and blacks and whites had different bathrooms, water fountains, etc. He said once when he went into the blacks-only bathroom he saw that someone had smeared feces all over the walls. He said that kind of behavior was the norm back then. His advice to me was to simply ignore them and learn all I could in school so I could become something in the world. My dad was a very gentle man with the exception of that Halloween night, and I really looked up to him.

CHAPTER 8
ADVENTURE LAND

For my sixth birthday my dad took me and my cousin Maurice to a small amusement park in Huntington called Adventure Land. It wasn't very big, but it had the traditional Ferris wheel, carousel, and arcade-style games. While walking around, we noticed a show starting on a small stage. It was a magician, so we decided to move closer and watch the performance. At one point the magician asked for a volunteer from the audience. As he scanned the crowd I began feeling really nervous. Remember, I had a hard time with crowds, especially strangers. He looked in my direction and asked me to join him. My dad gave me a little nudge and I reluctantly joined this stranger onstage. I was scared standing out there in front of that large crowd with their eyes all trained on me. My hands were sweating and my legs shook uncontrollably and I started to sway back and forth to distract from my trembling legs. The magician asked me to hold a magic wand and wave it over an empty box. The moment he handed it to me the wand broke and went limp. Everyone laughed and I was mortified. He took the wand back and it became solid again. He said there was nothing wrong with the wand and handed it back, where it broke and went limp once again. Then he traded me an Oriental-style fan for the broken wand. The second I grabbed the fan it broke into four sections. The crowd roared! He took it back and automatically it was back to normal. He handed it to me again and, you guessed right, it fell apart. Now in my mind it felt like everyone was laughing at me. I already had a problem receiving too much attention and was almost in tears by this point. I guess he realized I was not enjoying the role of the magician's assistant and sent me back to my father. My dad saw that I was embarrassed and unhappy. The show was meant to be fun and this asshole had made his son the brunt of a bad joke.

We left the magic show and roamed around the park. My dad noticed a small stand that sold magic tricks and novelties. There was a guy there demonstrating some of the tricks. To cheer me up he said I could have any magic trick I wanted. I asked the guy to show me the one with the sponge rabbits. He proceeded to show me two sponge cutouts shaped like bunny rabbits. He said one was the mama rabbit and one was the papa rabbit. He placed the mama rabbit into my hand and told me to close and squeeze her tight. He then took the papa rabbit and did the same in his hand. He told me to say, "Go, papa, go," which I did. He opened his hand and the papa rabbit was gone. I couldn't believe it. He then told me to slowly open mine and there in my hand was the mama and papa rabbit, side by side. This was incredible and I was amazed. Just when I thought it was over, he told me to hold the mama and papa rabbit together tightly in my hand. He asked if I knew what happens when you put a mama and papa rabbit in a small dark place like a fist? I told him I had no idea. He advised me to slowly open my hand and find out. When I did, there were five small baby rabbits along with the mama and papa. They had babies! That simple trick sparked a fire that would stay ablaze the rest of my life.

As a child I spent a lot of time back in Queens visiting family, especially my grandparents. My grandfather was really cheap and staying with them could really suck at times. He would limit the time we could watch television to save on electricity. We could never make phone calls and he even made us reuse paper towels. That's right, if we used a paper towel he would make us flatten it and then lay it on the counter to dry so it could be used again. This drove my grandmother nuts because she loved to spoil us. I would spend the night quite often, as my grandmother liked having me around. I didn't mind because I got to see my old friends from the neighborhood. My brother was older and usually didn't have to stay, which gave me a lot of time alone with my grandparents. As a kid I was very inquisitive, or should I say nosey. I would go exploring through all of my grandparents' drawers and closets, looking for things I could turn into toys. To pass time I would play with my grandmother's hearing aids or my grandfather's dentures.

Grandma & Andre

Crazy as it sounds, this was a lot of fun.

On one expedition I ventured into my grandfather's closet where I found a shoe box hidden behind some shoes. It was filled with a bunch of long, white envelopes. I opened one of the envelopes and saw it had money in it. There were all denominations of bills, and plenty of them. Some of the envelopes were thick and some thin but all stuffed with money. I felt like I'd hit the jackpot! Immediately I started thinking of all the things I wanted to buy instead of how this would be stealing and was wrong. At first I only took a few bills amounting to around ten dollars. I then snuck out and hit the bodega at the corner and bought a bunch of candy with my newfound wealth. Every visit, I'd sneak out a few bills and buy some small things no one would notice me having. One visit I grabbed a handful, which added to around fifty dollars. I went to the corner and caught a bus to Jamaica Avenue where all the best stores were. At a giant record store called The Wiz I bought a new thing called a Sony Walkman. This was a small, blue aluminum box with headphones that played the local radio stations with full sound and extreme clarity. It was small enough to sneak home so I wasn't worried about getting caught. If I did I would just say I borrowed it from a friend. For my second purchase I went to the kung fu store. This was right next to the movie theater that played kung fu flicks all day long. This store had it all, nunchuks, Chinese stars, swords, you name it. I bought a gun. Now this wasn't a real gun and didn't fire anything, not even BBs. The box said it was a fabulous fake and was a mock gun that looked real. This was before they started making toy guns with the red tip so police knew it wasn't real and shoot your ass by accident! The gun was a little harder to hide so I got rid of the box and slipped it into the waistband of my pants and smuggled it into my grandparents' house. Making withdrawals from my grandfather's shoebox would continue for a couple years. I guess he just never noticed that his hidden stash was getting smaller. I was slowly going down the wrong path and the longer I stayed on, the harder it would be to get off.

CHAPTER 9
SHAG CARPET

After the visit with my dad to Adventure Land I wanted to be a magician. Magic was popular with major productions like *The Magic Show* on Broadway featuring Doug Henning, TV shows *The Magic Circus* with Mark Wilson and *The Magician* staring Bill Bixby. I told all the kids in my class that I was a magician and showed them the sponge rabbit trick I got from the amusement park. I didn't do it very well because it was above my skill level, but I performed it anyway. My second grade teacher got wind of my new hobby and asked if I would do a couple of tricks in the spring concert. The theme that year was "Spring Magic" and she thought it would be perfect. I was a little scared but ended up saying yes. I told my dad and he searched the local Yellow Pages for a magic shop. He found one close by in Baldwin named Creative Magic. This place was wonderful and had everything for the novice and professional magician. There were all sorts of posters hanging on the walls and tons of hand-painted props displayed lavishly on glass shelves. My dad told the man behind the counter that I was asked to perform some tricks at my school concert and what would he suggest for a kid my age. He showed us a bunch of small tricks but none of them really impressed me. I remembered seeing Mark Wilson's TV show where he made a solid black walking cane with silver tips magically transpose into two colorful handkerchiefs. I asked if he had that one and was overjoyed when he answered yes. He brought out a small

First show. Age 7

blue and black box that was labeled "Fantasio Vanishing Cane to Silks". He said that what I requested was inside. This box was only a few inches in every direction and I couldn't figure out how it could possibly be inside. Then he brought out two silk handkerchiefs and said that was all I needed to accomplish that trick. My dad bought it for me and also purchased the Siberian chain escape trick, as well as a top hat for me to wear. These tricks were not cheap and my dad made me promise not to tell my mother how much he had spent. If she found out, just like on the TV show *I Love Lucy*, he'd have a lot of 'splaining to do.

I took those tricks home and practiced them over and over in the mirror till I felt comfortable. When ready, I gave a small impromptu magic show for my family in the den. For the first time I felt what it was like to perform in front of an audience. My family applauded and I got an instant rush of adrenaline and yearned for more.

For the spring concert the teacher dressed all of my classmates in different colored capes made of crepe paper. I had a real black satin cape that I borrowed from a friend accompanied with the top hat my dad got me, which barely fit over my huge Afro. All of the kids were sitting on risers to my right and left. They sang a song from *The Magic Show* and then the principal introduced me. The auditorium was filled with all of my teachers and fellow students' families, which made me very nervous. I was introduced as "Malcolm the Magician" and as I walked out, the crowd started to clap. In an instant the butterflies went away and I began to feel euphoric. I knew right then and there that being onstage was something I wanted to do the rest of my life.

I needed more tricks, but my parents didn't have a lot of extra money to support such an expensive hobby. I decided to make another secret withdrawal from Bank Grandpa. On this visit I got greedy and grabbed one hundred dollars. So after school the following day I lied and told my parents I was going to a friend's house when in reality I was headed to the magic shop. I purchased two tricks that day, a French Arm Chopper and a Dove Pan. An Arm Chopper is a small guillotine that you placed your hand in up to the wrist. When you slammed the blade down your hand would fall into a small bag below, which looks as though you've cut off your hand. This was just an illusion, and your hand was later revealed to be safe and unharmed. The Dove Pan looked like something you took out from the bottom cabinet in your kitchen. First you remove the lid and squirt some lighter fluid in the pan. You then light it on fire and extinguish it by placing the lid back on. When you remove the lid a real live dove appears. Now I didn't have a dove, but my friend up the block had a teddy bear hamster. I borrowed his hamster and was ready to try out my new prop. The one thing I knew for sure was that playing with fire was a fast route to another ass kicking. Since no one was home I decided it was the perfect time to take a chance. I practiced in my bedroom, which was on the second floor. I needed to light the pan on fire, but didn't have any lighter fluid or matches. I remember watching my grandmother light the pilot light in the oven with a piece of tightly rolled paper towel and figured I'd do the same. She would roll the paper towel about six inches long then light the tip on fire from the stove-top burners. This way she had some distance between the flame and her hand to avoid getting burnt. I went downstairs to the kitchen and rolled up some paper towel like I'd seen her do and then lit it off of the stove. Now the dove pan was on the second floor and the stove was on the first so I needed to haul ass up the stairs before it went out. Once upstairs I would drop the burning paper into the pan, cover it and magically make my friend's hamster appear. Well, this ended up working much better in my mind. I lit the paper towel and started my way carefully up the stairs to my bedroom. About three-quarters of the way up the stairs the paper started to fall apart and cherry-red embers were floating all around me. I tried to swat at them but there were too many. One landed on the stairs and started to burn the flammable shag carpet. It literally caught fire and I started stomping furiously over and over until I eventually put out the small blaze. The smell was horrible and the nylon-based carpet had become black and crispy. I had really screwed up this time and thought I might not survive this one.

Lucky for me, my parents rarely came upstairs. My brother saw the burnt carpet but kept my secret and didn't even blackmail me. I figured he knew that this time was really bad and he was scared for me. Every time I was upstairs and my parents called me I would come running to avoid them coming upstairs and finding the toasted carpet. One day my luck ran out and I heard my mother coming up the stairs. She stepped on the crispy charcoal-colored carpet and heard the crunch beneath her feet. She looked down and saw the burnt rug and knew without hesitation it had to be me. She went into my closet, which was at the top of the stairs and grabbed my red and white metal-tipped belt. This belt was '70s style and looked like something the Jackson 5 wore. She called me from my room and began whipping my butt. For fear of my life, I started running and she gave chase. I headed down the stairs as my mother swung the belt, which wrapped around my head smacking me right in the eye. The pain was awful but I kept running and she continued after me. When she finally caught up and got a look at the damage the blow had done to my eye, she stopped dead in her tracks. My eye had swelled up like a bullfrog and was bleeding a little from the corner. I was looking like Rocky Balboa in the third round. She dropped the belt and rushed me to the kitchen where she got some ice to stop the swelling. Thank goodness this didn't impair my vision. I could tell by looking at my mother that she was scared. She seemed genuinely frightened that this time she'd gone too far. In her defense I could have burned the house down and the punishment really was appropriate. My parents kept me out of school for the next couple days till the swelling went down. I still had a slight black eye when I returned to classes and made up a story that made me look really cool. Daredevil Evel Knievel was hugely popular, so I told all the kids I hurt my eye when I crashed my bike doing a wheelie. When life gives you lemons, make up a story.

CHAPTER 10
DIRT BOMB

My fifth grade class was putting on a play called "Take me to your Marshal". It was about a Martian that lands on Earth and interacts with the humans. What makes this interesting is that he talks and acts like an old spaghetti-western cowboy. Reason being is that on Mars they received one electronic signal from Earth and it just happened to be a country and western television station. Everything he learned about Earth, humans, and the English language came from what he saw on that channel. All the kids in my class tried out for different roles in the play. The lead character, of course, was the Martian and that was the part I read for. I was still very shy and had a crapload of butterflies with everyone watching. I spoke with a heavy cowboy accent or what I thought to be one. I channeled my inner John Wayne and went for it. The line that sealed the deal for me was "Well by doggies, that ain't right." Funny how I still remember that line after all these years. Well I nailed it and the class was in stitches, securing me the part. Getting that crowd's admiration gave me that euphoric feeling again and it was great! My costume was a shiny green robe with a space helmet that in reality was nothing more than a football helmet covered in aluminum foil. This was finished off with a metal crochet needle taped to the top, simulating an antenna.

One of my friends also got a part and the teacher suggested we get together after school to rehearse our lines. That evening I asked my parents if it was OK to invite him over to practice lines, and they replied yes. The following day I told my friend and he said that he couldn't come to my house, but I could go to his. I asked why the change in plans and he told me that his parents didn't want him going into Roosevelt. That's when I realized my neighborhood had a bad reputation with our white neighbors. I

Students in Mrs. Betty Roe's fifth grade class at Brookside School recently gave a play called "Take Me To Your Marshall" in which a space man visited Earth. Participating were [Back row] Anthon Sewer, Keith McCartney, Larry Mileo, [Front row] Malcolm Puckering, Scott Ballard and Christina Puglisi.

First press clipping

understand now that this was simply fear stemmed from ignorance but back then I was just confused. We ended up going over our lines in the cafeteria during lunch but I was disappointed. The play was a success and my family had a blast watching me getting laughs with my redneck accent. This was just another experience that was steering me closer to the world of entertainment.

My elementary school stopped at the sixth grade and then we moved to another school for junior high. There were two different schools for us to choose from, Baldwin Junior High, known as the old junior high and Baldwin Harbor Junior High, which was newer but a lot farther away. Both schools required taking a bus, which I looked forward to. My brother went to the old junior high, where he ran track and played basketball, making him very popular. I wanted to go there too because that's where all of my friends were. Also, there were more black kids there, unlike the Harbor Junior High that was mostly white and Jewish. To my disappointment, my parents decided on the Harbor Junior High. Their decision was based on the fact it was newer and they felt had more to offer. They also preferred me to be in an all-white school. My mother always said we should learn how to adapt in the white world and The Harbor offered the chance to do just that. I was devastated and begged them to change their minds but my requests were denied. That fall I mounted a bus full of white kids headed to The Harbor.

I went in with a good attitude, because fighting it wasn't going to change anything. The majority of the kids at this school came from upper-middle-class to wealthy households. They had an air of entitlement and I felt out of place. I did encounter a handful of black kids who were stuck there just like me. I gravitated toward them and made quick friends. Although this was the '80s, the popular boys dressed like they were from the '50s. They all looked like Fonzie from *Happy Days* with their faded jeans, white T-shirts, leather biker jackets, and black combat boots. I

Marching Band

didn't get it especially, since everyone dressed in slacks, hard shoes, and collared shirts in my neighborhood. These kids were known as the "Dirt Bombs" although I have no understanding why. They smoked cigarettes and walked around like they owned the school. The two most popular Dirt Bombs were Mike and Mark Marciano. They were identical twins and real hell-raisers. On my first day I was running in the hall, trying to beat the bell when Mike jumped out and kicked me really hard in the stomach and said, "Stay out of my way, nigger." I fell to the ground dropping all my books while everyone just looked and laughed. This kid could seriously have used a hug. I had art class with his twin brother Mark and we were seated at the same table. Believe it or not he was actually friendly toward me. It seemed like with Mark on my side everyone else would just maybe follow his lead and be nice. This was all a bit premature because when he got around his brother and fellow Dirt Bombs he called me nigger, too.

I had always loved classical and jazz music and joined the orchestra. My father had played drums in a jazz band when he was younger and we had a small trap set in the basement. We also had a piano, but I preferred those loud-ass drums. In the orchestra I played percussion, which included the timpani, temple blocks, drum set, vibra-phones, chimes, and even the triangle. I had no idea playing drums would incorporate so many other instruments. My teacher was a tall white gentleman with a Colonel Sanders-style mustache and goatee named Dr. Zurcher. He was uber-talented and could play anything he put his hands on. I loved his classes and he made it fun to learn. I also joined the marching band and participated in an improvisa-tion class. The improv class was really cool. We would meet during lunchtime in the auditorium. Dr. Zurcher would play a rhythm on the piano and everyone else would join in. He'd point to us one at a time and that was our signal to solo. This was the total essence of jazz and really freeing. During the summer break from school I was allowed to take some of the school instruments home. I grabbed the drum kit so I could make my set at home look huge, like those rock bands. I also borrowed the electric keyboard. I had a few other friends in the neighborhood that played instruments and we decided to start a cover band. My buddy Ronald played saxophone, Alex keyboards, Tracy trumpet, Conrad bass, Michael guitar, and me on drums. Our band was called Atomic Funk and we played whatever was popular at the time. In full disclosure we could really only play one song and that was "Chic Cheer" by the band Chic. Our music never made it out of the basement but did make for a fun summer and helped keep my butt out of trouble.

It was around this time that I met a person who would become one of my best friends. For whatever reason I wasn't really hanging out with Ronald who I'd been friends with since moving to Long Island. He was hanging with another kid name Norman Spears. Norman was a tall, dark, complicated kid with large, crooked teeth. I don't know why, but he didn't like me very much and was always trying to get Ronald and me to fight one another. Norman was older and Ronald pretty much did whatever he said. Norman was also friends with a new kid in town named Malcolm Williams. Malcolm had re-cently moved to Freeport from Lakeview. I was walking home from school one day when I saw all three of them hanging out. Norman called me over and I knew this wasn't going to be good. When I reached them Norman said that I had stolen this new kid Malcolm's name and suggested we fight over it. Now this in and of itself is a ridiculous notion because whoever is older technically had the name first. We were young and dumb at the time and started fighting over our name. To this day I truly don't remember who won but whenever that story comes up I always claim victory. After our brief scuffle Malcolm stopped hanging with Norman and we became friends.

Malcolm, like me, was small for his age and we kinda resembled each other. We were both light-skined and had large, brown Afros, although mine still had the blonde highlights. He lived in Freeport about a fifteen-minute walk from my house with his parents and three siblings. He had twin sister named Linda that everyone called Lindy. She was really pretty and all the boys had the hots for her. His older sister Dana was in high school with my brother Andre. And lastly, a younger brother named Chris. His parents were Donalda and Malcolm Sr. We became really close and spent a lot of time hanging out together. We shared a lot in common, especially when it came to sports and music. His parents were pretty cool and I liked spending time at his house. He didn't have a curfew and could curse in front of his parents without getting his ass kicked. Coincidentally, Malcolm's father had gone to Morris High in the Bronx with my mother. At Morris they had a famous classmate, Colin Powell who would later become Secretary of State. An even crazier coincidence was Mal's mother went to high school with my dad. At their house when his mother would yell "Malcolm" even though there were three of us we could always tell from her inflection which one she meant. We were around each other so much that everyone began to refer to us as Mal & Mal or The Mals. It was almost like we were one person. Malcolm introduced me to his other friends and we became close, as well. There was Rich Levy who was the crazy one of the bunch. He wasn't scared of anything and a real individual with no problem standing out or being different. Then there was Joe Murray, the cool one, or Joe Kool as he became known. Joe was smooth with the girls and his clothes were always matching. He played little league baseball and had a basketball court in his backyard. Joe had two uncles from Jamaica who lived at his house. Although they were his uncles, they were only a year or two older than him. The oldest was Claude and youngest was Dave. Claude was calm and collected and always had your back. He could fix anything too, especially cars. His brother Dave was the polar opposite of his older sibling. Dave was the loud in-your-face-kinda guy. He was fun-loving and also a technical and mechanical genius. Lastly there was Brian who fancied himself a ladies man and was the youngest, so we called him Baby B. Rich, Joe, Claude, and Dave were all Jamaican and Brian's family was from Guyana. My family was a mix of Barbados and Grenada while Malcolm was the odd man out, the only one without a West Indian or Caribbean background. No crew was tighter then us and we were boys for life!

CHAPTER 11
STEEL DRUM

I n 1977 we had a really hot summer in New York City and there was a major blackout. The power outage lasted almost twenty-four hours and droves of people took to the streets and looted local businesses. People stole televisions, furniture, and anything they could drag through the broken storefront widows. DJs were becoming popular at that time so turntables, mixers, and speakers became major targets. Had the blackout not happened there probably would never have been so many neighborhood kids claiming to be disc jockeys. Hip-hop was still pretty new and becoming more and more popular each year. By the early '80s, the b-boy culture was at its height.

For Christmas, one of my classmates got two Technique SL-B1 turntables and a Newmark 1100 Mixer. He didn't know a lot about being a DJ and only had a few records to practice with. I told Malcolm that we should get all our records together and go to his house to spin some discs. We ended up going to his house every day after school and were getting pretty good. My classmate's house was a 40-minute walk, so I came up with an idea to borrow his equipment so that Mal and I could spin records without the long trek. I asked my friend and he agreed to let us borrow his stuff. We stole a shopping cart from the Pathmark grocery store and filled it with the two turntables, mixer, speakers, and all our records. Once at my house we set up the equipment in the guest room upstairs next to me and my brother.

We would practice every day until we felt confident enough to show everyone our skills. We did a few small gigs at some local house parties and even once at my father's church back in Queens. My father liked what we were doing and bought us some more records, which really helped out. Now we never told my classmate about any of these gigs, even though we were using his equipment. When I saw him at school he would ask when we would be returning his stuff. I would always make up some lame-ass excuse as to why I couldn't bring it back. We had hijacked his Christmas present and this was wrong on so many levels. Well, finally after almost a year of holding onto my classmate's equipment, his father got involved and we reluctantly returned everything. I felt guilty, but my lust for spinning those records prevented me from doing the right thing. I was becoming everything I hated and losing all sense of decency.

Sometime later we ended up getting our own turntables and mixer. We even added Mal's twin sister to our crew. We called her DJ Lindy B; the B stood for "Beauty". I know that sounds pretty corny but back in the day that shit was hot. By this time the focus of the hip-hop group was heading away from the DJ and moving toward the MC. MC stood for the Master of Ceremonies, which would later become known as the rapper. Black radio stations were starting to play rap records from groups like the Sugar Hill Gang and Grandmaster Flash & the Furious Five. With this growing popularity, Mal and I now wanted to be rappers. We wrote some rhymes and rapped them over the records Lindy would spin. This was just a hobby at the time and mostly for our own amusement because magic was still my passion.

My father really seemed to enjoy watching me perform magic and encouraged me to keep it up. He even brokered a few small shows for me at some of the local nightclubs. These clubs didn't have liquor license issues like today and you could work there even if you were under age. I was billed as "Puck the Young Magician". The clubs usually had a live band and my father would ask the pianist to play some background music while I performed. The pianist usually played "That Old Black Magic" which accompanied me as I made things appear, disappear, and transpose. The biggest show I did at that age was for Harlem Graphic Arts and was held at The United State Office Building in Harlem. This was the largest crowd I'd ever been in front of and gave me a little taste of things to come.

Performing Age 13   First promotional picture

On a vacation to Barbados with the travel club I performed an impromptu show on the hotel balcony for our members. Afterward they passed a hat and I made almost $30. I took that money and bought a steel drum. The drum came with a music book and I learned to play the song "Never on a Sunday". On the plane ride home with my steel drum in tow I began practicing that song over and over as the passengers begged my father to make me stop. My dad was too proud and just let me do my thing. Looking back, I believe he was living vicariously though me since he once had aspirations of being a musician but gave it up to support his family.

I was never really a good student and my grades reflected this. I got mostly Cs, Ds, and Fs. My parents weren't happy about this and stayed on me to do better. It wasn't that I was dumb, I just had a problem focusing. I got bored easily and spent a lot of time daydreaming. In class I would zone out and think about the drums, playing records, and doing magic. Our report cards were handwritten and one semester my grades were so bad that I got a matching-color pen and changed my red Fs to blue Bs. My father saw right though this forgery and spanked my ass. This may sound crazy, but I welcomed my father's whuppings. This kept the belt out of my mother's hands where the blows landed everywhere, arms, legs, back, wherever! My dad's spankings were surgical and the belt always landed right on target, which was my high yellow ass.

Sometimes I would get notes from the school requesting a parent-teacher conference to discuss my grades. I would always give these to my dad who would attend the meetings solo, never telling my mother. I don't really know what drove him to save me half the time but I thanked him for it constantly. When I was on punishment for my grades my dad would sometimes sneak me to magic shows and conventions. He would tell my mother he was taking me with him to visit family in Queens but really take me to the theater.

Dad on Drums

Aside from the summer vacations, The Pucks' Travel Club also coordinated one-day trips. One of my favorite destinations was the Jones Beach Theater and we went annually. This was a unique theater that was right on the water. The sets floated and would rotate to reveal all the different scenes. We saw a lot of classic musicals there like *Oklahoma!, Showboat, The King and I, Fiddler on the Roof, The Sound of Music, Carousel,* you name it. Guy Lombardo, the famous bandleader known for his New Year's Eve TV shows, would make a pre-show appearance. He would drive his boat out beforehand and then his orchestra would play dance music in a huge tent afterward. I gained a real love of theater watching these wonderful musicals. My parents always tried to expose us to the arts and these experiences had a lasting impression on me. My brother and I were lucky and I was adding to an arsenal of tools that would become beneficial as I got older.

CHAPTER 12
GEE, MISTER. THANKS!

I loved the holidays, especially Christmas time. We always put up a tree and decorated the house inside and out. My dad and I usually did this together and I looked forward to it each year. Money was always a concern, so we would get one big gift that we really wanted and the rest of our presents were mostly clothes and things we needed. I can still remember the big gift from each Christmas as I grew up. One year it was a blue Schwinn Stingray bicycle. I loved that damn bike until someone stole it from me. Stealing bikes was big and you had to lock it up tight and sometimes even that wasn't enough. Mal and I went to San Remo's Pizza Parlor one afternoon during Christmas break. They had a few video games there including our favorite, Space Invaders. My Schwinn Stingray had a banana seat, so we rode there on the same bike. We left my bike outside unlocked but kept it within view. I remember seeing a group of kids checking out my new wheels when all of a sudden one of them jumped on my bike and took off. We ran after them but on foot it was of no use. The other kids in the group were still at San Remo's watching it all go down. The thief's buddies had bicycles too but they were old and crappy. I grabbed one of the kid's bicycles and told him I would give it back if he got his friend to come back and return mine. I gave him a time to meet us back at San Remo's to make the exchange. In the mean time Mal and I rode this kid's shitty bike back to my house so I could get my fake gun, the one I bought on Jamaica Avenue. We wanted to have it just in case they came back with reinforcements and we were outnumbered. It was only a toy, but they wouldn't be able to tell, so we could use it to bluff them. We went back at the designated time but they never showed up. This sucked and I was stuck with this crappy bike while my brand new Stingray was gone forever.

I was really upset, but still had some quarters left so went back inside San Remo's to play more video games. While we were playing I saw a kid ride up with a bike that looked almost like mine. Aside from a few minor details it was damn-near identical. The kid dropped it outside on the sidewalk then came inside and started watching us play. He was a cute, little white kid with big cheeks and a brown bowl cut. He told us that he wished he could play, but didn't have any money. All of a sudden a light bulb went off in my head. I told the kid that I had dropped a quarter behind the machine and if he could find it he could keep it. He looked at me and said, "Gee, mister. Thanks!" To this day I feel really bad about what happened next. As he was searching behind the machine for the phantom quarter we ran outside and I jumped on his bike while Mal got on the crappy bike and we hauled ass outta there. I could hear the kid yelling in the distance but there was no way he was gonna catch us. We had done to him what had been done to us just a short time earlier. It should have felt good to replace my stolen bike but I kept hearing that kid's words in my head, "Gee, mister. Thanks!" Mal and I were officially scum bags and no good was going to come from this giant lack of judgment.

We went straight to Malcolm's house and hid the bike in his backyard. Mal's little brother Chris was eavesdropping and heard us talking about what we had done. He told Mal's father who immediately ran outside and started beating us over the heads, telling us to get rid of it. We ended up selling the bike to a neighborhood kid who promised to pay us in weekly installments, but that money never came. This sucked, but in all fairness we deserved to lose, and lose we did.

CHAPTER 13
DIGITAL DERBY

For as long as I could remember, my brother was always very athletic. He played stickball, basketball, foot races, handball, baseball, and football. We had a large empty lot a few blocks from our home where all the kids would hang out. It was fenced in and had a big sign on the gate that said, "Private Property—No Trespassing". We would hop the fence and put teams together for pickup games. The older kids were really competitive and took these games seriously. Every once in a while someone would get hurt, especially when it came to football. It was supposed to be two-hand touch, but that wasn't always the case. My brother was always the star athlete and I enjoyed watching him and his friends play.

Andre was my brother's middle name and that's what the family called him. His first name was Leonard and everyone outside of the family called him by the nickname Lenny. As Andre got older Lenny became "Puck" and I, being his little brother, was now referred to as "Little Puck". I looked up to Andre and wore this nickname like a badge of honor. My brother excelled at all sports but when he got to junior high and high school, he focused mainly on basketball and track & field. He was always big for his age, around 6' 2" by high school and around 220 pounds. He would be featured in the local papers from time to time for his achievements on the basketball and track teams. I would go to his games and be so proud watching him slam dunk on fast breaks. On the track team he held the high school record for the triple jump and 440-yard dash. His room was full of medals, trophies, letters, and certificates. Andre was also a good student and very popular with his classmates and teachers. I had big shoes to fill and usually came up short.

When Andre finished high school he received a track scholarship to Florida A & M University in Tallahassee. The day he left for his freshman year I cried like a baby as we said goodbye at the airport. This was the first time we had been

Digital Derby Christmas gift

separated since I became a Puckering. When my parents and I got back home our house seemed so big and empty. I couldn't wait for Thanksgiving and Christmas break when he would be home again.

Christmas quickly came, which was usually a really happy time for us, with the exception of 1980. This particular Christmas changed my life forever. My brother was home from college and I had gotten the greatest toy ever. It was an early video-style handheld game called Digital Derby. I would compete with my dad and brother to see who would get in the least amount of accidents while receiving the highest score. On New Year's Eve my mother told my brother that he needed to drive her to work because my father wasn't feeling well. She worked in Crowne Heights, Brooklyn, which was at least a forty-five-minute drive each way. She didn't want my brother driving back alone and told me I had to go with them. I pleaded to stay home because I wanted to be with my father and play my new game, but she said no. So off to Brooklyn we went.

We dropped my mother off and had finally made it back home. My brother opened the front door and we headed down the hallway toward the kitchen. When we got to the kitchen we found our father lying there on the floor. He was awake but incoherent. It was like he was paralyzed or something, because his eyes were open but he couldn't speak or gesture. My brother started freaking out and began to panic. For some odd reason I was very calm. I told my brother to call 911 and then my mother's job. While he did that I went outside to wait for the ambulance. The ambulance arrived quickly and the paramedics rushed to my father's side. They checked his vitals and then put him on a stretcher and headed for the ambulance. They were in such a rush that they broke our storm door right off the hinges. My brother and I followed behind the ambulance as it made its way to Lydia E. Hall Hospital in Freeport. We didn't know at the time but this hospital had a horrible reputation but unfortunately was the closest to our home. At the hospital my brother and I were escorted to the waiting room. Some time passed and a doctor came in and took my brother away. A few minutes later a nurse came and took me into another room. The nurse told me that my father was very ill and that he had died and was no longer with us. She pulled me close, wrapping her arms around me and squeezed tightly. All I could think about was this stranger hugging me and I wasn't even crying. In fact I was emotionless. I had just lost my hero but still I was dead inside and felt nothing! Then I heard my mother screaming in the waiting room. She had gotten a ride to the hospital and had just received the devastating news. When I saw her she was in a wheelchair and screaming hysterically. She grabbed and squeezed me just as the nurse had done moments earlier. I still didn't know how to react or feel. Part of me thought if I hadn't gone with my brother to drop my mother off he'd still be alive. Maybe I could have called the ambulance much earlier. I had no idea how long he had been lying there helpless on the floor. It was New Year's Eve 1980, going into 1981, and for the second time in my life I was fatherless. All of our family and friends came over that evening to mourn with us. It's funny how a family member's passing brings everyone out of the woodwork. I saw aunts, uncles, and cousins I hadn't seen in years. My father was beloved by all and no one ever had a bad word to say about him. He would give you the shirt off his back if you asked. My mother would argue he was too generous when it came to his friends and called him a pushover. To me, he wasn't a pushover at all, he was simply a wonderful and caring man.

My father's wake and funeral were held at Gilmore's Funeral Home back in Queens. The turnout was tremendous and the funeral director was forced to open the remainder of the room dividers to accommodate all the guests. I was sitting next to my mother and she was a mess. She was crying and screaming uncontrollably. At one point she grabbed my arm and squeezed so tight that I literally passed out from the pain. When my eyes opened I found myself surrounded by my cousins who immediately began to comfort me. They did this in the only way we knew how in our family and that was with humor! They cracked jokes and made this bad situation seem almost tolerable. My best friend Malcolm was there, too. He was wearing a suit and tie with sneakers, which I found kind of funny. He told me that his shoes were at his aunt's house in White Plains and it was either sneakers or be a no-show. We laughed and this helped ease the tension, as well. I was lucky to have so many wonderful people to help comfort me in this time of deep sorrow.

Being young, I was usually kept in the dark when it came to my parents' business. Some months after the funeral, I overheard my mother in her bedroom talking on the phone. She was saying that my father was depressed and this was why she had my brother drive her to work that day. She also said ever since he was a teenager my father went through occasional bouts of depression. I was fourteen years old and yet this was something I'd never noticed. To me he always seemed jovial and fine. Evidently my father suffered from bipolar disorder, which caused him to have extremely elevated and depressed moods. She also said he'd been hospitalized several times due to his mental illness. During the holidays his mood swings were more pronounced and that's why she had him stay home that New Year's Eve.

As if it couldn't get worse, about a year after his passing I stumbled upon some paperwork from an insurance company. It stated that my father's death was ruled a suicide. He was said to have died from an intentional overdose of prescription medication. Hearing this sent me on a downward spiral because I really loved my dad and didn't know how I was going to get along without him.

CHAPTER 14
LEAVES

Christmas break was over and my brother headed back to college and I headed to junior high. At school, everyone was being overly nice and my band class even made a huge sympathy card for me that everyone signed. My guidance counselor met with me and offered his assistance if I needed it. I felt okay and still hadn't come to the realization that my dad was gone. I didn't cry, not even once since receiving the news. By submerging my feelings and skipping the grieving process unbeknownst to me I was hurting myself. Instead of grieving I found other ways to deal with my loss, which were far from productive. The first thing that suffered were my grades. I already had a hard time in school and now without my dad around to protect me, they were rapidly dropping. Also, I was selfishly taking advantage of everyone's sympathy. I understood all too well how people would give me a pass due to my recent family tragedy and I relentlessly exploited this.

It was still cold outside and the leaves were finally off the trees. I hated when the leaves fell, because it was my job to rake and bag them. We had a huge yard and this would take hours. My homeboy Mal was lucky, because in his neighborhood they didn't have to bag their leaves. Instead he could just rake them into a pile by the front of his house and the county truck would come and take them away. We were talking outside his house one fall afternoon when I started screwing around. I had a book of matches and began shooting them at his leaf pile. If you don't know how to shoot a match it's pretty easy. First you pull out one match and place the head against the striker with just your index finger. Next you apply some pressure and flick your finger forward, which lights the match and shoots it outward. With practice you can get pretty good at hitting what you aim at. My target was that big-ass pile of leaves. As I shot a match, Mal would run and stomp it out. I'd shoot another and again he'd run and quickly stomp it out. I kept doing this until Mal got overwhelmed and was unable to stomp them all. One caught onto some of the dry leaves and started a small blaze. It started getting bigger and that's when I got really scared. Some of these burning leaves were being swept up in the light breeze and floating off the pile toward some nearby homes. I panicked and took off. I got home and tried to act normal, as if nothing had happened. About an hour after I got there our phone rang and my mom picked it up. It was Malcolm's mother asking her to come over and bring me along to discuss something important. I had a good idea what this invitation was about, but unaware of how bad it really was. As we approached Malcolm's block we saw fire trucks pulling out. Evidently the fire had gotten so big that they had to call the fire department to extinguish it. Thank goodness none of the homes on the block were affected. We went into Mal's house and sat down in his living room. His mother asked if I had seen how the leaves caught fire when I was there earlier? She had already asked Malcolm and I guess he hadn't ratted me out so she didn't really know. She suspected I had something to do with it but had no proof, so I flat out lied and said that I had no idea. I told Mrs. Williams that when I left to go home I hadn't seen any fire. At that point, Malcolm's older sister Dana chimed in and said there was no way I would have done such a thing. Dana was a real straight arrow and her endorsement was enough to vindicate me. Just that quick, the interrogation was over and I had just dodged a bullet that could have landed me in Juvie. What the hell was I thinking?

Now that my father was gone and my brother away in school, it was just me and my mother all alone in the house. My mother was still a wreck and this really started to wear on me. For some reason she decided not to sleep in her bedroom anymore. I guess she was avoiding the memories of my dad and their shared bed. Every night I had to bring down my twin-sized mattress and lay it on the floor in the den. On that small den floor she would make me sleep with her every night. I hated it because I was fourteen and the last thing I wanted was to have to sleep with my mother like a baby. After several months of this torture I told my mother that I wanted to sleep in my own room. She agreed that that was best and we made our way back to our own bedrooms.

As long as I could remember I never saw my mother drive a car. My dad had done all of the driving to and from work as well as everywhere else we needed to go. Now that it was just the two of us, I had to help out. In the winter everyone would go outside and start their cars then go back inside to finish getting ready. This would get the car nice and toasty as well as defrost the windows. I don't know if it was just the times we were in but no one really worried about someone stealing their vehicles. We kept our car in an attached single-car garage. We had a tan Ford LTD with a brown vinyl top that barely fit in that narrow garage. It became my job to start the car, warm it up, and back it out of the garage. I did this each day before she left for work. At first it was fun driving the short distance each morning, especially since I wouldn't have my license for another three years, but after a while it became a dreaded chore. It was way too early in the morning and really cold outside. So one morning when my mother called for me to get the car I copped an attitude. The kind of attitude where you open and close doors really hard. I was wearing pajamas and a robe, but still freezing. Still pissed off and half asleep, I put the car in reverse and slammed my foot on the gas. The car moved so fast that I couldn't steer properly and ended up catching the front bumper on the right side of the garage, damn near pulling the whole side of the house down. After hearing the loud bang, my mother came running outside to see what happened. She was furious; not because I had an accident, but because she knew my bad attitude was the cause. After that day she never asked me to pull the car out again. She said my bad attitude was going to be my downfall.

Being a pyromaniac wasn't the only trouble I got into. While growing up, we always had a burglar alarm on our house. Our alarm used a small round key to arm and disarm it. All of the windows had silver foil tape on the glass and magnets on all the doors. Although we had never been robbed, my mother was always cautious and kept the system on even as we slept. Now that I was older my mother had finally given me a key to let myself in after school. I stayed by myself until she got home from work, which was only a few hours later. One time the alarm wasn't working. My mother had called the alarm company but it was going to take a couple days for them to come out and fix it. She told me that I was not to go anywhere after school because she didn't want the house to be empty with the alarm off. That day all of my boys were meeting at Mal's house to play with his new Atari game console. I wanted to be there so bad, but knew I wasn't supposed to leave the house until my mother got home. I decided that since she'd be home in a couple hours the house would be fine so I left to be with my friends. About an hour into playing Atari, Malcolm's doorbell rang. He went to see who it was and then told me it was my mother. She had the belt in her hand and asked if I was there. As soon as I got to the door she reached in and started swinging at me, but Malcolm got in between us and told her that she wasn't going to beat me in his house. Honoring his request she told me to come outside. When I did, she snatched me by the collar and dragged me off to the car. I could see all my friends, Joe, Rich, and Mal watching from the living room window. They were laughing and I was humiliated and embarrassed. She took off for home, screaming at me the entire ride. When we arrived home she said that I was gonna get my ass whipped when she got me inside. I was terrified and that's when my fight or flight instinct kicked in. In a millisecond I chose flight and opened the car door, proceeding to run in the opposite direction of our house. My mother was yelling for me to get my butt back there but I just kept running. She wouldn't see me for three whole days and for the first of many times to come, I was a teenage runaway.

CHAPTER 15
SKETTI

I ran for almost thirty minutes, all the while looking over my shoulder for that tan and brown Ford LTD. My mother just let me run, figuring I'd show up when I got tired and hungry, but that wasn't going to happen. I was too scared to go back home and sleep or food wasn't going to change that. I literally walked the streets for hours, debating what to do. Should I go back and face the music or stand my ground and show her I wasn't going to take it anymore? Eventually I ended up at my friend Joe's house. He had been at Mal's earlier and saw the whole thing go down. What he didn't know was what happened after my mom got me back to the house. I knocked on his bedroom window and he snuck me in through his back sliding glass door. His parents where really strict and since it was a school night, we had to be extremely quiet so they wouldn't know I was there. I told him that I ran away and asked if he could let me stay at his house until I figured out what to do. He agreed to let me stay and set up a lawn chair for me in the tool room of his garage. He brought out a blanket and pillow as well as some peanut butter and jelly sandwiches for me to eat. I was starving and those PBJs really hit the spot. I slept the night in that dark garage as the seriousness of what I had just done started to sink in. It was a long night and I didn't want it to end because I needed more time to think about my next move.

Joe woke me up after he got ready for school and I snuck out without being detected. I couldn't go to school in case my mother informed them I had run away. Joe lived around the corner from Coes Neck Park in Baldwin, so I decided to hang out there till the school day was over. In the kiddie section of the park was a giant tower shaped like a rocket ship. It was around thirty-feet high and made of steel. There were three levels you could climb through, making it the perfect place to hide; and best of all I could see the whole park from the top. The place was empty most of the day with the exception of a few old-timers playing tennis or chess. This would be my home for the following eight hours. When school finally let out, Joe brought the whole gang to the park. I told them I was going to stay away as long as possible to teach my mother a lesson. I knew that she would start getting worried and that just might be enough to save my tail when I finally went back.

That night I needed another place to crash and this time I asked my friend Sean for help. Sean was from Trinidad and we called him Bago, which was short for the lengthy Trinidad and Tobago. He said I could hide at his house, but I had to keep out of site. We went to his house while his parents were still at work and devised a plan to stash me away. In his basement there was a large room that had a TV, stereo, as well as two nice couches. The biggest couch was about a foot away from a wall and that's when we got an idea. I could hide behind the couch and if I was quiet, no one would know I was there. Right before his parents got home from work he set me up with a blanket, pillow, and a box of graham crackers for dinner. I stayed behind that couch from 5 p.m. to 7 a.m. without making a peep. In the late evening, I had an unexpected visit from Sean's parents. Around 10 p.m. his mother and father decided to go into the basement to watch some TV. Of all the places to relax they chose the couch I was hiding behind. I was scared they were going to catch me and I stayed as still as possible. I was barely breathing and only taking short breaths that I let out really slowly, as not to be heard. It was torture, but a couple hours later they retired for the evening and I could breath normal again. In the morning I snuck out only to spend another long day of solitude at Coes Neck Park.

For my third night, Mal offered to let me hide at his house. He had a small bedroom downstairs by their mudroom and told me that I could sleep there. I was looking pretty rough by this point and hadn't showered or even had a decent meal. I was dehydrated, too, and this was making me delirious. Mal snuck me some spaghetti and meatballs from the family dinner that evening and I attacked that food like David Hasselhoff on a bender. Mal later told me I was rambling and all he could make out was the word "sketti", which I repeated over and over. I must have been really loud because Mal's father heard us and came down stairs to investigate. He found us and asked what was going on and we confessed. Although his father was pissed off, he said I could stay the night and then go home the following morning. That night I slept on a comfortable couch in Mal's den while pondering the unavoidable punishment that was soon to be my destiny.

The following day I went back home while my mother was at work. I was nervous about seeing her but knew nothing could be worse than living like a vagrant. My mother got home and I could see the relief in her eyes. She was upset, but didn't beat me. She explained that she was upset about me leaving the house unprotected and that running away was not the right thing to do. She put me on punishment but I didn't really care at that point and was just glad to sleep in my own bed.

Living under the same roof with my mother could be tough. We had always bumped heads but my father and brother were there to act as a buffer. A couple of years before my father passed away he gave me some great advice that I never forgot. He said that it's useless to argue with my mother because that was one battle I could never win. He said, "Just let it go in one ear and out the other." That worked well for my father who was non-confrontational in nature but for me I had a hard time staying quiet. As I got older I really tried to ignore my mother's verbal attacks, but the tension between us continued to escalate. Our relationship was a pressure cooker and it was only a matter of time before it blew.

Around six months after I ran away another incident occurred. I had gotten in trouble again and my mother dealt with it in the usual way by utilizing the belt. It was summer break and she didn't trust me to stay home by myself anymore and decided to drop me at my grandparents' house for the day. Needless to say I wasn't happy about this and decided to run away again, but this time with no plans to return. Once my mother dropped me off I went to my grandfather's closet and grabbed around $500, the largest amount I'd ever taken. I thought this should be enough to keep me afloat for a while. I knew my grandfather would notice this time around but I didn't care anymore. I'd had enough and just wanted out of my mother's house.

I told my grandmother I was going to visit a friend who lived around the corner. Once I left the house I made my way to the Jamaica Avenue Bus Terminal and hopped on the N6 to Long Island. Upon arriving I went directly to Mal's house because I knew he was home alone. Mal's parents had carpooled that day and left their second car, a green Chevy Malibu in the driveway. Neither of us was old enough to drive, but we didn't let this deter us. Mal grabbed the spare keys and we stole the family vehicle and went to Roosevelt Field, a mega shopping mall in Westbury. I had a pocketful of cash and my first purchase was a Nike sports duffle bag. Next I bought some clothes and toiletries. Last, I got a CO_2-cartridge pellet gun from a sporting goods store. I really had no need for the pellet gun, but thought it might come in handy while I was on the streets. I packed everything in the duffle bag and then we hit McDonalds and ate like kings!

When we got back to Mal's house, his twin sister Lindy was there with her boyfriend Chip. Chip's real name was Claude and he lived in Uniondale, which was a neighboring town. Chip was one of the coolest kids around. He was in a DJ crew, knew martial arts, and had the swagger and confidence of a person much older. Everyone respected him and we all wanted to be like Chip! I told him that my mother was abusive and I had run away from home. I always considered Chip to be like an older brother and asked his advice. He offered to talk with his parents and see if they would take me in. After they heard my story, his parents felt sorry for me and said I could stay with them for a while. My plan was to turn my mother in to Child Protective Services for abuse and then see about finding another family to take me in. This all sounded good in theory, but not very realistic.

Staying at Chip's house was great! They treated me like family and I got to hang out with the big boys. Chip would take me to parties and even let me drink beer with him and his friends. I secretly wished his family would adopt me and I could have that kind of freedom all the time. That wasn't going to happen and I was about to get a quick dose of reality.

Mal, Joe, Rich, and Brian came by Chip's house to take me to Child Protective Services, which was in Hempstead. They all had bikes, so I hopped on Mal's handlebars and off we went. This was around a 30-minute ride and we looked like a small biker gang as we rode through town. We were all singing that song "Tainted Love" by Soft Cell. There's a line in the song that says "Sometimes I feel I've got to run away" and we thought that was a fitting theme song. Once at the office we all went inside and I told the receptionist that I wanted to speak with someone about child abuse. She had us sit in the waiting area and went into an office to explain my situation to the caseworker. After a few minutes I was called into the office but my friends remained in the waiting area. I told the caseworker that my mother had beaten me several times and that I ran away because I was scared for my life. She told me that what I had done was illegal and you just can't run away if you're having problems at home. She said the proper procedure would have been to inform them or the police and then someone would have come out to investigate. She then told me her office was obligated by law to contact my mother as well as the local authorities. She did just that and kept me there until the police arrived. They questioned me for a while and then took me home. When we got there I had to stay in the car while they spoke privately with my mother. I could hear her tell them that I had stolen money from my grandparents and used it to run away. She did admit to hitting me but said it was not in excess and definitely not abuse. The police filed a report but since I had no marks or bruises at the time, they just dropped me off.

My mother was furious that I had told Child Protective Services she was abusing me. She said no government agency was going to tell her how to discipline her child. To be honest I don't think she really believed what she was saying because after that incident she never put her hands on me again. She threatened to all the time, but never followed through. My mother was scared and that was good enough for me.

CHAPTER 16
PELLET GUN

Due to my horrendous grades I barely made it out of junior high. I had to go to summer school where I passed by the skin of my teeth. I didn't get to go to graduation with my classmates but was allowed to advance after spending summer vacation in a classroom. There was only one high school in Baldwin and I was looking forward to being reunited with my boys Mal, Joe, Rich, Brian, Claude, and Dave. My sophomore year started out well and for the first time I was feeling pretty good about school.

The assistant principal Mr. Didden had previously worked at my junior high. He remembered that I did magic and asked if I would be interested in teaching a magic class. This would be on Saturday afternoons for elementary school kids. At first I didn't know what to say because I hadn't touched or performed any magic since my dad's passing, when I was fourteen. That was something he and I shared and the thrill of performing had gone when he died. I gave it some thought and decided it might be fun and said yes. He asked how much it would cost for me to purchase all the supplies needed, so I checked with the local magic shop. They suggested I teach three beginner level tricks that were impressive yet easy enough for the kids to master. I asked the cost to supply fifteen students and was told it would be around $15 per kid and they would throw in my teaching supplies for free. So we were looking at approximately $225 to cover everyone. Being a sneaky shit I told Mr. Didden it was going to be

$350. He gave me the cash and I went to the shop to pick up the tricks whilst giving myself a nice $125 bonus in the process. What I hadn't considered was Mr. Didden asking for me to submit the receipt. Every time he asked I would make up an excuse, saying I left it at home or needed to look for it. Eventually he forgot and stopped asking.

Magic class met for two hours every Saturday afternoon. These kids were pretty young and teaching them was harder than I had anticipated. I was around their age or younger when I began doing magic, but for some reason these kids just weren't as coordinated as I was back then. I got really frustrated and, without thinking, would sometimes curse out loud. I didn't even realize I was doing this until Mr. Didden called me to his office after a parent had complained. They said their child told them I was using bad words in class. I ended up getting fired and was replaced by another magician who was older and more mature. I just couldn't seem to get out of my own damn way!

My friend Brian's sister Debbie was really cute and I had had a crush on her for years. Being that I was a year younger, plus her brother's friend, worked against me and she wasn't the slightest bit interested. One day we got into an argument and she threatened to have her boyfriend come to the school and beat me up. Her boyfriend was already out of high school and a pretty big guy. I was intimidated, so during lunch I went home and got my pellet gun for protection. I wasn't very bright and showed it to a few of my fellow students. Word spread and Debbie eventually heard about it. As this information was passed from student to student it got distorted and my pellet gun had now evolved into a real gun. Debbie was scared for her boyfriend and told our principal, Dr. Lynch. He came right to my class and asked me to go with him. We went to his office and he asked if I had a gun in my bag. I told him yes but that it was only a pellet gun. He made me take it out and put it on his desk. This was a big pellet gun and it looked really menacing. I could see the fear on Dr. Lynch's face and knew right then and there I was in a shitload of trouble. He called the police and made me wait in his office for them to arrive. When the police got there, they confiscated the pellet gun and placed me under arrest. Unbeknownst to me it's illegal to bring a weapon onto school grounds and is an arrestable offense. They made me do a perp walk right past the cafeteria where I saw all the kids and teachers watching as I was escorted in handcuffs arm in arm by the police. That was the last time I would walk the halls of Baldwin Senior High.

I was in the back seat of the police car and had no idea where we were headed. The ride was fairly long and ended on the steps of The Family Court building in Mineola. I was shuffled into a small concrete room with a metal bench and a large steel door. I stayed there for a couple of hours until I was transferred to a courtroom. As I entered the courtroom I was surprised to see my mother seated in the back of the room. I was told she had filed what's called a PINS petition on me. PINS stands for Person in Need of Supervision. This is set up by the courts to help parents who can no longer bear the responsibility of raising their child and need the courts to intervene. This meant I would not be going home anytime soon. They provided me a law guardian, which is what they call a lawyer for kids. The judge was an older, white woman who looked a bit like Judge Judy from TV. I stood before her and she began going over my case. The more she read the more upset she seemed to get. By the end she was yelling at me like a parent yelling at their kid. She recommended I be sent to a foster detention home pending further review. The home she sent me to was in Malverne and run by Mr. and Mrs. Brown, an older black couple in their late sixties. Mr. Brown was pretty chill and it took a lot to piss him off. Mrs. Brown was the opposite and not nearly as patient. Their daughter lived there as well and was a single mother with twin toddler boys named Darian and Darius. Aside from myself, there were usually one to two other court-ordered kids in the home. We were all there temporarily until the court either sent us back home or found permanent placement for us. At the time I arrived there was a very promiscuous young black girl and a street-wise teenage boy named Leon living there. I mostly hung out with Leon because we were closer in age and he was a cool kid. We went to the local high school in Malvern and all the kids knew we came from Mr. Brown's foster detention home. This had its advantages, because the girls seem to like the bad boy image.

Even though we were in a structured home with lots of rules we still found ways to do the wrong thing. Unlike today, cigarettes were in style and my roommate Leon smoked Newports. He gave me my first cigarette and I liked it. As if that wasn't enough, we would also combine our lunch money and buy a 40-ounce bottle of Olde English 800 or Colt 45 malt liquor every day after school. I was a follower and easily influenced by others, so Leon was probably not the greatest person to be hanging with.

On some Friday nights, Mr. Brown would take us to a nearby roller rink in Hempstead called Subway. It was called Subway because the entire structure was underground. There was a small entrance-way on the street level with a set of stairs leading down. Downstairs was the roller rink, a bowling alley, food counter, and nightclub all secretly hidden below the street. I loved this place and knew a few people who worked there. These were some of the guys I had met as a runaway while staying at Chip's house. They were all older, but still treated me like one of the gang. There was William, a small, light-skinned guy with brown hair. We looked a lot alike and would tell everyone we were brothers. He had a baby face and didn't look anywhere near his age. This worked well for him, especially since he had a thing for young girls. Many years later after we'd lost touch I saw him on the news. In a jealous rage he killed his young girlfriend by slashing her throat. He had such a calm demeanor and no one could have predicted this. Next was Charles, who was the house DJ. Charles was known all over Long Island as one of the hottest DJs around. He was tall and light-skinned with a very pronounced case of vitiligo. This gave his skin light- and dark-spotted patches that kind of resembled a Dalmatian. He was cool as hell and a really good brother. Then there was Chris Bonaparte, whom I was closest with. Chris was a former high school star athlete and also a martial artist. He was a member of the Guardian Angels and known for knocking people out. He became my big brother and always had my back. Also in attendance were Jay and Deb. They were a couple and always hugging and kissing in the back room. Lastly was Wardell. He had a serious reputation for being a badass. One night while he was driving home high off his ass, he accidentally hit a guy, dragging him to his death. He left the scene of the crime and then turned himself in the following day when he was sober. The guy he hit was sitting on a television in the middle of the street. Wardell didn't see him and since it was unintentional, didn't spend that much time in jail. After getting out it seemed like he was trying to get his life together.

The manager of Subway was a skinny, middle-aged white guy with curly, blonde hair named Jack. Jack was in his thirties and usually wore tight, designer jeans, a striped, collared shirt, and a black leather vest with boots. He was blatantly gay and always seemed nervous like a chihuahua. Most of the employees at the roller rink were tough black guys and maybe that's what made Jack so uneasy. Subway's owner was a gangster named Billy and he didn't much try to hide it.

I liked hanging out at Subway and asked Chris if he could help me get a job there. He got Jack to hire me, so all I had to do was convince Mr. Brown. I asked if it would be OK to work at the roller rink part-time a few days a week after school. He said it was cool with him, but needed to clear it with my law guardian. A few days later the verdict was in and I was lacing up my skates for my first real job.

My work responsibilities rotated daily. I would bounce between the skate rental counter, manning the concession stand, or patrolling the rink floor. Patrolling the rink was my favorite because I got to practice my skating. We would yell at people for skating too fast and help them get up when they fell. I got really good and could do spins, kicks, and all kind of crazy tricks. I had my own pair of skates, as did all my friends who worked there. We all had black lace up skates with white All American Dream Wheels. We also wore orange nylon construction worker vests that displayed the Subway logo on them. Girls loved us and there were times when I was talking to two or three at the same time.

Most of the employees smoked weed and this is where I got my first introduction to marijuana. I already smoked cigarettes, so I thought: How much worse could it be? This was pretty naive and my first time was not a good experience. First off, I was a complete novice and second, they failed to tell me the joint we smoked was laced with PCP, or angel dust, as it was known on the streets. I only had a couple puffs and was gone. It felt like I was out of my body and then I got sick. At one point I tried to jump out of the DJ booth, which was twenty or so feet from the rink floor below. Charles grabbed me just in time and protected me from hurting myself. I never really acquired a taste or enjoyed the high from marijuana and therefore rarely indulged.

Once while cleaning the bathrooms between skate sessions, I found a set of car keys. The keychain had a Chrysler logo and said Avis on it, so I assumed it was a rental car. I showed the keys to Chris and William, asking what to do with them. They grabbed the keys from me and went up to the parking lot to look for a Chrysler. The keys ended up fitting a brand new Chrysler New Yorker. After finding it, we all jumped and drove it behind the Hempstead Motor Inn, which was next door. Once it was hidden, we returned to work like nothing happened. Later, during our shift, Jack asked if anyone had found a set of car keys in which we all replied, "No". After work, we went behind the hotel and saw the car was still there. We jumped in and took the car for a joy ride all the way to Coney Island in Brooklyn. We kept that car over a week until the police eventually found it. We never kept anything identifying inside the car and always parked it a good distance from our job. Thank goodness we weren't anywhere near the car when they found it or we'd all have gone to jail.

At the Browns, I shared a small bedroom in the basement with Leon. I liked it down there because we had our own TV area with two comfortable sofas. The stairs that led to the basement were hard linoleum with aluminum strips on the front edges. At the top of the stairs was one of those accordion style wooden gates typically used to contain pets. We were told to keep the gate latched at all times because their grandsons sometimes roamed around upstairs in their walkers. One night I heard a series of loud bangs followed by a child screaming. Someone had left the gate open and one of the twins had fallen down the staircase all the way to the bottom. I ran over and could see that the baby bleeding from his head and scream-ing in pain. Mr. Brown came running downstairs and grabbed the baby. He didn't say a word and just ran upstairs, got his car keys, and rushed the toddler to the ER. Mrs. Brown came downstairs and started screaming hysterically at me, saying I had left the gate open and this was all my fault. I hadn't been upstairs since getting home earlier and had remembered locking the gate. I tried to plead my case but she kept yelling and I decided it was time for me to go. As soon as she went upstairs I packed some things and then snuck out the back door and was out. I never saw the Browns again, nor did I ever find out the extent of their grandson's injuries, but I hoped they weren't serious.

CHAPTER 17

I GOT YOUR ASS!

After running away from the Browns, I walked to a pay-phone and called Chris from the roller rink. He borrowed his mother's car and took me to his house where I stayed the night. The following day, having nowhere to go I returned to work at Subway. By now, the word was out I had run away from the detention home and everyone had my back, even Jack. If anyone came looking for me they would stall them while I hid out of sight. Luckily no one ever came looking and we never had to put that plan into action.

Subway attracted a lot of degenerates and I got to know quite a few of them pretty well. Being on the run, I needed to find places to stay on a nightly basis, which at times felt like I was on some kind of Underground Railroad for teenage delinquents. One of these shady individuals I got to know was a guy named Kenny. He was in his early thirties with no job and still living at home. Kenny volunteered to let me stay a few nights at his house, which I thought was pretty cool. Kenny had a reputation for being a petty criminal but I made a conscious decision to overlook how he chose to earn a dollar. We were broke and spent that first night thinking of ways to get some money. The following day Kenny went to a bank and opened a checking account with five dollars and a fake ID. They gave him a starter checkbook to use until the printed ones came in. The address on the fake ID was bogus, so he was all good. He wrote out a starter check for $50 and signed it with the fake name he used on the ID. Now all we needed to do was turn this check into cash. Neighborhood liquor stores would cash checks for their regular customers and after banking hours there was no way to verify if the check was good or not. Kenny got the yellow pages and found a listing for a store that wasn't too far away. He called and asked for the store owner. He gave the false name and asked the owner if he remembered him, saying he was a regular customer. I couldn't believe it but the owner actually said, "Oh yeah, I remember you. What do you need?" I found this to be hilarious since he just had conjured that name out of thin air. Kenny told him that he was going to be sending his son over to cash a check for $50 and could he take care of him? The owner said, "No problem," and that's where I came in. I played the part of the make-believe son and would be delivering that rubber check to the liquor store. I got to the store and recited everything Kenny told me verbatim. I said that my father had called earlier about me bringing a check up to be cashed and then handed it to him. Without hesitation, he cashed it and told me to give my father his regards. This was unbelievably easy and now we had some money. We did this two more times at different stores and then decided to stop while we were ahead and not push our luck.

The money didn't last long and a few days later we were scheming again. This time Kenny told me about a house he had robbed a year earlier. The house was owned by a dentist who had an office in the basement. He lived there with his wife and mildly retarded, twenty-something-year-old son. Kenny said they were Seventh Day Adventists and went to church in the evenings, but left the son home alone. He explained that when he robbed them last time he got the son to open the door while his parents were out by telling him he was a family friend. The son let him in and then Kenny robbed the place while the son watched, unaware of what was happening.

Kenny said it would be a piece of cake and we would do it that night. We got to the house around the time the parents were to be at church. We went up the steps and knocked on the door but to our surprise the wife opened up and not the son. I thought to myself, let's just abandon the mission and get the hell out of there. Kenny wasn't on the same wavelength and was determined to follow through with the robbery, even though the wife was home. He told her that he had an appointment with her husband but we could tell by her reaction she wasn't buying it. Once Kenny realized she knew something was wrong, he pushed his way into the house, leaving me standing outside on the steps. She started screaming at the top of her lungs and then Kenny did the unthinkable. He began punching this poor woman in the face. I was in shock and couldn't believe he could be so violent, especially to a woman. Next I saw the son running toward us and he was yelling, "I got your ass, I got your ass!" Everything was going wrong, so we took off running and in his haste Kenny ran into the side of the door and fell to the ground. The son jumped over him and started chasing only me. I ran as fast as I could as he continued yelling, "I got your ass, I got your ass!" I kept running until the yelling started to get lower and lower and finally silence. Either I had outrun him or he had given up and went back for Kenny. I continued running until I got to Kenny's house and hid out in his backyard. Around thirty minutes later Kenny showed up with a huge cut down the side of his face from where he had run into the door. Right there, I parted ways with Kenny and went back to Subway Roller Rink to collect my thoughts. All I could think at the time was, "What the hell was I doing and how long could I keep this up?!"

When I got to Subway I talked with Chris, William, and Wardell, telling them about what had just happened. I said there was no way I could stay another night at Kenny's after seeing him beat that woman. I had around $30 left from the check scam and used it to get a cheap room next door at The Hempstead Motor Inn. This hotel was a dump and you could rent rooms for as little as four hours at a time. They called it the short-stay package, which even included closed-circuit porn on the TV. It was really sleazy but would have to do since I was running out of options. I went down to the lobby to get some food from the vending machine where I was approached by a guy who struck up a conversation with me. He was tall and thin with brown skin and an Afro haircut. He wore a Spitfire Kangol hat and had on leather pants and a silk shirt. He asked if I was there with anyone and I said, "No" but that I worked next door at the roller rink. That's when he told me he was a pimp and asked if I wanted to make a little cash. He said that he would pay me $100 if I did him a small favor. There was a girls group home nearby and the staff would take them to the roller rink on Wednesdays. He wanted me to speak with some of the girls and talk them into running away. I would tell them to run away from the group home after lights out and then come to the hotel where my friend would give them money and a place to stay. Most of these girls were young and naive and a couple of them actually did it. Once he got his hands on them they would be pampered and then when their guard was down, he'd turn them out. He paid me for my part and I used the money to stay at the hotel.

One night, while talking in his room, he asked if I had ever been with a woman. To sound cool I lied and told him yes. Then he asked if I'd ever been with a man, which immediately sent up a red flag and made me feel uncomfortable. I said, "No" and quickly excused myself, running straight to my room, locking the door behind me. This line of questioning kept me up that night and all I could think about was this guy raping me. The next morning I left the hotel really early and walked an hour to Malvern High, the last school I attended before running away from the Browns. When the school opened I went to the office and spoke with the principal. I told her I wanted to turn myself in and asked if she could call the police to come get me. I was so tired of looking over my shoulder and being scared all the time. This decision would turn out to be one of the smartest things I could do.

The police took me right from Malverne High to the courthouse. I was greeted by my law guardian, who told me I wouldn't be going back to Mr. Brown's and instead be sent somewhere more secure. Just like before, it would be temporary until the courts found a permanent place for me. The judge sent me to a secure facility for juvenile delinquents called Saint Mary's Children's Home in Syosset, New York. This place was pretty intense and I felt like the only sane kid there. Saint Mary's was a two-story building and we were housed on the second floor, which consisted of six or so two-man bedrooms and a communal shower. Downstairs was the kitchen, dining room, classroom, and a recreation room with a TV. There were always two adults on duty who were all pretty cool as long as you didn't try them. The kids at St. Mary's were all screwed up. Some were there for robbery, assault, and even one for attempted murder. There was

even a girl trapped in a man's body. He was really feminine and always hitting on me. This guy was around six-feet-tall and weighed
200 pounds, easy. He was from Westbury and told everyone he was
the "Queen from the 'Bury". They said he was there for trying to
stab his stepfather and I made sure to stay on his good side.

We went to school in the same building and in our free time watched
TV and played cards or board games. We weren't allowed outside
except for once a week when they loaded up the van and took us to
a drive-in movie. At the movies we would park and have to watch
from inside the locked van.

The only visitor I ever got there was my law guardian, who would
come once a week to discuss my case. As a juvenile, we were required
to appear in family court every ten days. This was hell on my mother
who would have to take off work to attend. On one of these many
appearances, my law guardian said she was trying to get me placed
at a local group home called Nassau House. If I went there I'd go
to the local public high school and still be able to see my friends.
When my mother got word of this she lost it. She wanted me as far
away from my Subway Roller Rink friends as possible. She did some
research and found a place upstate called George Jr. Republic. Aside
from having a stellar reputation, it was also far away from all the bad
influences of Long Island. Her only hurdle was getting the courts
to approve it and finding the money to pay for it. This place cost
almost 20K per year and she didn't have that kind of money. Plus,
even if the court approved me I would still have to pass an in-depth
interview and IQ test to be admitted. She didn't let that stop her and
petitioned the court while looking for government aid to help offset
the tuition.

My mother's efforts paid off and she got the judge to approve her
request for me to be sent to George Jr. Republic, pending an admissions interview. She also got the state to help with the tuition
costs, should they accept me. Only thing left was for me to pass the
interview and IQ test. I was taken from St. Mary's by van to an office
building in the city about an hour's drive from Syosset. There I met
with a representative from GJR. The interviewer was an attractive
young woman and we talked for roughly an hour. She asked why I
was at St. Mary's and what I wanted to achieve if given the chance

Junior Republic

Admissions Office
TELEPHONE
607-844-8153

March 30, 1982

Dear Malcolm,

Congratulations upon your acceptance to the Junior Republic!

Here is the handbook which I promised you would receive. This was
written by staff and citizens, and may offer some tips for your early
days on campus.

I greatly enjoyed meeting with you, Malcolm. While you obviously
have many strengths, I noticed that there were also a few feelings
you have which are confusing to you. We strongly believe that you
are ready to face some difficult issues and are ready to examine
and put behind you feelings of anger and pain, so we are eager for
you to be a citizen of our community.

We hope to see you sometime in April. Until then, good luck in
practicing your magic and remember no doves, bunnies, or chopping
blades are allowed at the Republic! See you soon!

Sincerely,

Bill Crimmins
Miss Crimmins

SMC:mg

Enc: NCH

GJR acceptance letter

to turn my life around. She also asked if I had any interests or hobbies and I automatically began telling her about my love for the art
of magic. She seemed to like the idea that I wanted to get my life
together. I also took a test that would be used to evaluate my intelligence. In a nutshell they wanted to know if I had any violent ten-
dencies and if there was a good likelihood for rehabilitation. After
the interview I was taken back to St. Mary's to await their decision,
which I was told could take weeks. Finally the news had come in and
I was called to the dining room table where my law guardian was
there to give me the final outcome. My mind wandered and I started
fantasizing about when I was at the interview. I thought about the
colorful brochures that boasted about all the things GJR had to offer.
They had a huge gymnasium with an indoor swimming pool and
acres of farmland with cows and horses. They offered lots of activities and the residences looked new and modern. There was a lake
with canoes and paddleboats and they even had their own camp-
grounds with lean-tos and fire pits. I wanted to go there so bad and
I couldn't stop thinking about it. I was snapped out of my daydream
when my law guardian told me that I had been accepted. She said I
would be going to court the following week and they would be flying

me upstate to my new home that same day. I was more than ready to get out of St. Mary's and start fixing my life at George Jr. Republic.

When I got to the courthouse the following week I was escorted to the holding area. On our way to this room, we passed my mother and brother who were sitting on a bench outside the courtroom. Upon seeing them I got really nervous and didn't know how to act. I decided to just walk by without acknowledging them or saying a single word. My brother came running over and grabbed my shirt by the chest and told me I was an ungrateful fuck and when I turned eighteen to change my last name because they wanted nothing more to do with me. Then he let me go and went back to my mother who was crying by now. I was still having feeling of anger and resentment toward my mother, but what he said was sobering and really hurt. Maybe I should have spoken, I really don't know. One thing's for sure though, things had to change.

CHAPTER 18

NOTHING WITHOUT LABOR

I was all packed and on my way to George Jr. Republic in Freeville, New York. The counselors put me on an airplane and the stewardess escorted me to my seat. Last time I remembered being on a plane was with The Pucks' Travel Club, but this time I wasn't going on vacation. When we landed I was greeted by two people, a man around thirty and a kid who looked to be about my age. They helped me with my bags, then we jumped in a station wagon and made our way to the campus. On the way there they told me a little about "The Republic" as they called it. George Jr. Republic was founded in 1895 by William R. George as a fresh-air camp for kids from New York City. Later it was transformed into a home for troubled youth. The boy was assigned as my big brother to help me get adjusted. He seemed like a decent kid and I had a lot of questions for him. He explained where I would be living and what to expect on my first day.

When we arrived I was impressed with how enormous the campus was. There were a lot of houses that I was told were called cottages. Although there were both boys and girls on campus the cottages were non-coed. There were nine cottages in all and each housed anywhere from seven to twenty kids. I was going to be living at the Lodge Cottage located on the very edge of campus. The Lodge had previously been a local hotel that GJR had purchased. Although the residence was really big it still had a warm and cozy feel to it.

The decor was rustic with a fireplace and a huge galley kitchen. Upstairs were around eight rooms with two beds each and some bathrooms. Every cottage was supervised by adults called houseparents. The houseparents were usually a married couple ranging in age from their twenties to sixties. They resided in the house whether they were on or off duty. We also had associate houseparents to relieve the regular houseparents on their off-days and vacations.

GJR Brochure

My houseparents were the Russos and we called them Ma and Pop. Ma Russo had thick, long, black hair and olive-colored skin. She was medium height and a little on the heavy side. Pop was a small dark-skinned Italian guy with short, black hair that hung over his forehead. All of the cottages were different and had their own unique personality. One was filled with jocks, another nerds, and mine was where all the cool and popular kids were housed. Ma and Pop Russo were hippies and the rules were a lot more laid-back than in some of the other cottages. So, in simple terms, I had lucked out. My big brother took me to the other side of campus to the clothing shop. We walked and it had to have taken us twenty-five minutes to get there. I did say this place was huge! At the clothing shop, they took my measurements and then loaded me up with a boatload of clothes for all occasions and seasons. I got work boots, Wrangler jeans, corduroy pants, dress shirts, T-shirts, ties, sports coats, socks, underwear, gloves, hats, shoes, and a heavy coat. Next stop was the bank where I was set up with a checking account. They started me off with a $20 advance to use at the commissary. At the commissary I bought hygiene products and even cigarettes. We were allowed to smoke, which was nuts because none of us were of legal age. Somehow The Republic was able to acquire permission from the US Government to use cigarettes as a therapeutic tool in our rehabilitation. Smoking was a huge privilege and there were a lot of rules about when and where you could do it.

George Jr. Republic was exactly that, a "republic". We were self-sufficient and pretty much independent from the rest of the country. The Republic had its own currency and grew a lot of the food we ate. There was a cornfield, an apple orchard, and maple syrup trees. We had goats, chickens, pigs, and black Angus cows. The Republic rarely used outside labor and we built and fixed most everything ourselves. There was an upholstery shop, carpentry shop, horticulture shop, small engines and mechanic shop, print shop, seamstress shop, dry cleaners and laundry, dining hall, and more.

The motto at The Republic was "Nothing without Labor" and you had to earn everything you received. You could go to school or work at one of the shops and learn a skill. You also had the option to do both if you chose. You earned a paycheck for each job you worked and at school too, receiving bonuses for high marks. With the money earned you were responsible for paying rent, buying supplies, toiletries, and for all your meals and social activities.

William R. George aka "Daddy George" also believed that by giving youths responsibilities they would grow and mature into well-adjusted and productive adults. To prove this premise he implemented a self-government, so we could police ourselves. We had a full government with all three branches. The executive branch consisted of a president, vice-president, secretary of state, and secretary of the treasury. The legislative branch was made up of all the residents called "citizens" and we held town meetings and voted regularly. The judicial branch had a bar association and gave classes. There were lawyers, magistrates, and even a chief justice. Everything centered around our own constitution where our rules and laws were clearly documented. Lastly, we had a jail system with a warden and jail keepers.

Every aspect of GJR was supervised by adults. They would act as consultants to help guide us, only stepping in if it became too much for us to handle. I know this all sounds crazy, but it really worked. If you broke a law any citizen or staff member could write you up on an affidavit. Next you went to court and pleaded your case before the magistrate. There was a full-scale court house fashioned with an

Carpentry Shop

authentic bench and judges' chambers. The magistrate wore a gown and was fully knowledgeable about the law and the GJR constitution. If found guilty, you received your sentence. This could be a fine, probation, or worst-case scenario, jail time. Our jail was virtual and meant that you lost all privileges. You also were pulled from your job and performed hard labor all day without pay. There were always plenty of tough jobs to be done around campus and if you were in jail it was all yours. To put it mildly, jail really sucked!

They gave me a list of jobs when I arrived and I chose the carpentry shop. The carpentry shop was run by two men, Leroy and Mr. Kiefer. Leroy was a short, round old man with silver hair. He was always jolly and a lot of fun to be around. Mr. Kiefer had a potbelly, but was tough and solid as a rock. He was a little younger than Leroy and had one of those noses that looked like he'd been in a few too many scuffles. They were both very knowledgeable about carpentry and construction. The shop was fully equipped with lumber and all the necessary benches and power tools. Both Leroy and Mr. Kiefer had pickup trucks with wooden boxes attached to each side where they kept all the tools we used outside the shop. Our mission was to repair and build things all around campus and I learned a lot. We did roofing, demolition, Formica work, plumbing, built stairs, laid sheetrock, and basically anything that called for a carpenter. Mr. Kiefer and I grew close and he became a trusted friend and mentor. He would listen to my problems and I could tell him anything, even if it risked getting in trouble. I trusted him immensely and he kept my secrets.

The campus was spread out and it took some time to learn my way around. All of our meals were served at the Ewald dining room with the exception of Sunday when we ate in our cottages. For breakfast and lunch we had to dress in slacks, collared shirts, and shoes. At dinner we added sport coats and ties. Ewald was a modern building with a large lobby on the first floor that had some couches and cozy chairs. There was a giant fireplace and large floor-to-ceiling windows that showcased the meticulously manicured landscape outside. We would sit in the lobby until the meal chimes rang then make our way upstairs to the dining room. The dining room was elegant and had around twenty long tables with ten place settings at each. Every setting consisted of a placemat, napkin, a water glass, and polished silverware. We had to use proper table etiquette and manners while in the dining room. No elbows on the table, utilizing the proper utensils pertaining to each course, chewing with your mouth closed, and no talking with your mouth full. If you didn't follow these rules you were asked to leave the table and sit on the side till everyone was finished eating. They would box up your meal and you had to wait until you got back to the cottage to eat it. By this time the food was cold and not very enjoyable. The meals were brought to each table by citizen servers. Being a Ewald server or dishwasher was another job you could have and most citizens worked there to earn extra money. The meals were pretty elaborate and we ate quite well. When you paid your rent a part of that money was used to cover your meals. There was an option to pay a little extra and add "first class" to your meal package. This got you seconds and even thirds on the main course. I wanted to make extra cash and picked up some shifts at Ewald. I started as a server and learned all I could about food service and the restaurant business. Eventually I was promoted and became the dining room supervisor, where I earned even more. I was gaining invaluable skills that I was hoping to implement after I left The Republic. Everything we did there was structured to prepare us for life in the real world.

Now living at The Republic wasn't all work. We had a lot of fun activities and events to keep us from getting bored. I spent most of my free time at the Boscowitz sports complex. This was another modern building that housed the gymnasium, weight room, indoor swimming pool, and boys and girls locker rooms with showers. In both locker rooms was a uniform closet staffed by a fellow citizen. There you could request gym clothes, swimsuits, and towels, which were washed and restocked for us daily. I would always get a pair of shorts, grey crop-top T-shirt, jockstrap, and a towel. I spent a lot of time on the basketball court, playing pickup games. This is where I met the majority of my good friends there. The boy that I became closest with was Norman from New Rochelle, in Westchester. Norman had brown skin, a low black Afro, and lots of muscles. He was well-read, and had a quick wit and devilish smile. He was president at the time and we hit it off instantly.

About six months into my stay I got word that the Lodge Cottage was closing. The Russos were going to be taking over Stevens Cottage, but it was a small house and they couldn't take us all with them. Being one of the newest I didn't make the cut and had to find another cottage. Remember, all of the cottages had their own unique personality. Norman lived in the Choate Cottage, which was known to be kind of strict and for having the best athletes. The architecture of the Choate Cottage was very interesting. The center building was a pentagon with a 360-degree fireplace dead center. The bedrooms and showers were in three separate hallways that were attached to this pentagon. From an aerial view it looked like a three-legged spider. Two of these legs were bedrooms and bathrooms for the citizens. Each hallway had four bedrooms with two to three beds in each. There were two communal bathrooms that didn't have any partitions or stalls between toilets, which took a little getting used to. The third leg had a kitchen and the houseparents' living quarters. The houseparents at Choate were the Thorpes. Pop Thorpe was a large man, both tall and wide. He was probably in his late fifties and the type of guy you didn't want to piss off. He had a confidence about him and everyone vied for his approval. Ma Thorpe was around the same age as Pop and was short and round. She and Pop made a good team and although they were tough, always put us first.

The cottages would regularly compete against one another in different sporting events. Flag football, softball, indoor soccer, etc. Pop was very competitive and this is why all the best athletes ended up in Choate. I wanted to live there but had to go through an interview with Ma and Pop first. They wanted to see if I would be a good fit for Choate and if Choate would be a good fit for me. It did help some that Norman lived there and had personally vouched for me. Pop made it known that they ran a much tighter ship than my previous houseparents, the Russos. They told me that I would be required to participate in all cottage sports competitions, which I had no problem with. My interview went well and they offered me a room at Choate. I moved in shortly after and my buddy Norman became my new roommate. This cottage was going to push me to my limits and I was going to be the better for it.

CHAPTER 19
YOUNG ADULT

Ma and Pop Thorpe were always trying to get us to take advantage of everything The Republic had to offer. I showed some interest in the citizen judicial system and they pushed for me to take bar classes. The adult advisor to the citizen government was Mr. Valenti. He was in his sixties and had a dark complexion and a gray military-style buzz cut. Following their recommendation, I enrolled and took bar classes. The curriculum lasted about a month and I studied long and hard. I passed with top grades and was later sworn in as a magistrate. This job held a lot of responsibilities and would prove to be very challenging, as I had to walk a very fine line as a judge. At times I would have to pass judgment on my friends while trying to keep them from hating me. If my sentence was too lenient I would have to deal with the adult staff members who would get pissed off. This was a constant balancing act between the citizens and staff. Over time I figured it out and excelled in this demanding position. I was never one to rest on my laurels and was later appointed president of the bar association then chief justice in charge of the entire judicial branch. Mr. Valenti taught me so much and my knowledge on the law was expanding.

The Republic had gotten a large donation one year and purchased some computers. Now the PC was still pretty new and it was a big deal to have one. They purchased the Apple 2C personal computer with a dot matrix printer. Mr. Valenti took some classes and became quite proficient with them. He passed that knowledge on to me and I began using the computers to organize the justice department.

Now we worked, played sports, went to school, but we also socialized. This was a coed campus and there was no shortage of pretty girls. We were young but way more advanced than the average kids our age. We had been though a lot in our short lives and were pretty savvy. Being a magistrate had a lot of perks and the best one

On the Bench

was having my own private judges' chambers. This was the only room on the entire campus for the citizens that had a door you could lock and I held the only key. I would sneak girls into my chambers and we'd kiss till our jaws locked up. On occasion, I'd get to second base but that's usually where it ended. I had several girlfriends and for once in my life was considered one of the popular kids.

We had high school varsity soccer and basketball teams and I played on both. These teams were a lot of fun, especially since we got to leave campus and play other schools in the area. On the way home we always stopped at McDonald's, which we all looked forward to. The other schools were intimidated by us because, after all, we were juvenile delinquents. I was one of the captains of our varsity basketball team along with John Tolbert who was my good friend. We had a good squad but our final season ended early and not because of our record. On one of our away games we screwed up royally. Next to the visiting team's locker room was a glass case that had a jewelry box displaying twelve sample graduation rings. Each of the rings had a different birthstone for each month of the year and was made of gold. One of my teammates jimmied the lock and stole the box of rings. We all knew about it and he gave each one of us a ring, which we took back home with us after the game.

The basketball team

The next day we were all called to the gym and told that the school we played the night before had accused us of stealing. They asked if we took the rings and the gymnasium went silent. Then out of nowhere my buddy John spoke up and took full responsibility for the entire thing. He admitted to taking the rings and said no one else on the team had any knowledge of it. Later on we secretly gathered up all the rings and got them to John, who turned them in to our coach. They were returned to the school and that was the end of our season. Out of everyone on the team I had the most to lose. I could have lost my position in the court, supervisor job in the dining room, foremanship in the carpentry shop, and more. Now Ma and Pop Thorpe were no dummies and knew we all had something to do with it even though John took the rap. Although I didn't go to jail like my friend, they made it abundantly clear I was in the doghouse at Choate. After that incident I focused on staying out of trouble and was rewarded generously for my effort.

There were three levels of citizenship at The Republic and each one earned you more freedom and privileges. These were really hard to achieve and very few citizens did. The first status was called "mature citizen" or MC for short. With this status you were allowed to stay up a couple hours later than everyone else, purchase more cigarettes, visit friends in other cottages, and some other elite privileges. Second was "young adult" or YA. As a YA the sky was the limit. You had no bedtime, could smoke anytime and anywhere you wanted, rent cars, and even take college courses off campus if you wanted. The third and highest level was graduation from The Republic, but I'll explain that one a little later on.

My initial court placement at The Republic was for eighteen months. When it was almost time for me to go home my mother petitioned the courts to have my time extended another year, taking me to my eighteenth birthday. My mother wanted me to be of legal age when I left so if I acted up again she wouldn't be legally responsible for me. It was during that additional year I made MC status and then the coveted YA. This was big and there were only three YAs on a campus of around 200 kids. They were me, my friend John Tolbert, and a girl named Maria Diponzio. The three of us were really tight and spent a lot of time together enjoying all the extra privileges.

All citizens were assigned a social doctor. Social doctors were a cross between a high school guidance counselor and a psychologist. They helped to guide our journeys at The Republic while preparing us for our introduction back into the real world. My social doctor was Mr. Gardner. He was a tall, awkward man who walked with a slight hunch and spoke like he had a mouthful of marbles. He was kind of nerdy but, all in all, a good man. As a YA I could take classes off campus. Now I hadn't taken full advantage of school while at The Republic and opted instead to learn skills like carpentry, restaurant management, and the citizen government. My plan was to eventually take my GED and then try to go to college. Mr. Gardner suggested I take some early admission classes at Tompkins Cortland Community College to test the waters. TC3, as the locals called it, was only a twenty-five minute drive from The Republic. Taking his advice I signed up for six credit hours, split between psychology and English composition. My fellow YA, Maria also enrolled, which made it easier having someone there my age. I really applied myself like never before and studied hard.

Since neither I nor Maria had a driver's license we had to be dropped off and picked up daily. I decided to use my YA status and get my driver's license so I could rent cars from The Republic and drive

Maria and myself to classes. I asked Mr. Gardner if he would teach me to drive and he agreed. I got my driver's permit and then the lessons began. He had a brown Honda hatchback with a five-speed manual transmission. Learning to drive a stick was hard at first but he was very patient with me. I know this had to be hard on him, especially with all the gear grinding, but he never showed any sign of frustration. We practiced one hour every day until I was ready to take my road test. He accompanied me to the DMV and I took the test using his car. I passed and got my license at seventeen.

Every year we got to go home for two weeks in the summer and two weeks for Christmas. During these breaks I worked to mend the broken relationships with my mother and brother. As I progressed I could sense the trust starting to come back. I couldn't wait to go home and see my friends, too. Mal, Joe, Rich, Brian, Dave, and Claude. Catching up was great and it was as if no time had passed between us. As soon as I got comfortable though, my break was over and it was back to The Republic.

Things couldn't be going better. I was popular, had great jobs, was taking college courses, had my driver's license, and was rebuilding the relationships with my family. By this time my brother had transferred from Florida A&M to Northeastern University in Boston. Mr. Gardner was planning a trip to Boston to visit his family and I asked if he could get The Republic to let him take me along so I could visit my brother. He checked with the powers that be and since Andre was twenty-two and considered an adult said it would be OK. It was only for a weekend but this would end up being one hell of an experience.

The ride to Boston from upstate New York was long, but with license in hand, I got to help with some of the driving. I'm sure this attribute was a factor when Mr. Gardner made his decision whether or not to take me. During the ride we talked about a lot of things to include my ever-evolving relationship with my family as well as my future aspirations and goals. This helped pass the hours until we got to Boston. I had never been there and was excited. When we arrived he dropped me at my brother's apartment, which was located right off campus.

Andre had two roommates, Tony and Michael. Tony was his best friend from childhood and lived around the corner from us in Roosevelt. He was Puerto Rican and as kids we nicknamed him "The

Rican". Now that he was older it was just plain Tony. Tony had two distinct personalities, just like the comic book character Hulk. When he was sober, Tony was pretty calm and reserved but once he drank would become a wild man. He was a strong guy, so anyone with half a brain avoided pissing him off when he was tanked. His other roommate was a small, white boy named Michael. Michael played hockey and was your average college-town boy. Mr. Garner walked me up to their apartment and met my brother. He told him to look out for me and that he'd be back on Sunday. Andre told him that I was in good hands and then Mr. Garner nodded in acceptance and left. He wasn't gone a minute when my brother brought out a shot glass, bounced a quarter off the kitchen table, landed the coin in the glass, pointed at me using his elbow and said, "Drink!" I didn't know what he meant until I saw him fill the glass with some Tanqueray gin. Now keep in mind I had only tried straight liquor once before and that hadn't gone so well. At our home in Roosevelt our parents always kept a stocked bar.

One day while they were at work my buddy Mal and I experimented with a bottle of their Old Grand-Dad bourbon whiskey. We had seen people do shots of liquor on television and noticed they always had some kind of chaser to help it go down easier. All we had in the fridge was a carton of milk so that's what we used. I poured each of us a shot of the Old Grand-Dad and a chaser glass of milk. The plan was to drink the whiskey really fast then chase it down with the ice-cold milk. We took turns doing this and I was up first. I drank my shot down in one swallow and it really burned. Next I gulped down the milk, which cooled and soothed my throat. I told Mal that it wasn't too bad and now it was his turn. Mal put the glass of Old Grand-Dad to his lips and quickly jerked his head back like they did in those old western saloons. He was moving too fast and the whiskey bypassed his mouth and went directly into his eyes. He started jumping around and hollering at the top of his lungs. I didn't know what to do, so I splashed the milk in his face. I thought since it helped my throat it might do the same for his now-swollen eyes. Eventually his eyes stopped burning and we had a hilarious story that we could tell at parties.

Now back to Boston. My brother had tricked me into a college game of quarters. The premise of this drinking game is to bounce a quarter off a table and have it land in a shot glass. If successful on your first attempt you can make anyone at the table take a shot. There are a lot of other rules, but that's the general idea. I was trying to prove that I could hang with the big boys but was losing badly! Andre's roommate Michael was drunk, too, and started sticking steak knives into the apartment's walls. I was going behind him and removing them, or so I thought. When I looked at my hand all I saw was red. Evidently my hand had run across the blades in the act of removing them and was bleeding. My cut wasn't bad enough for stitches so they just bandaged me up and the game continued. That was about all I could remember from that night.

The following day I woke up completely naked, which was the first indication something had gone terribly wrong. They told me that after I had cut myself on the steak knives I got sick and had thrown up all over myself and the apartment. My brother's girlfriend had come by and saw me passed out on the kitchen floor stewing in my own vomit. She went into nurturing mode and cleaned me up, which would account for my attire or lack thereof. After being filled in on the happenings from the previous night I ate some breakfast and began to feel a little better. My brother and his roommates started drinking again but cut me off, which I happily welcomed. I was finished and wouldn't drink again for over a year. The rest of the weekend was tame, which left me in good shape by the time Mr. Gardner came to get me. This was the first time my brother had ever let me hang out with him and his friends. I guess he had finally stopped seeing me as a little kid. We bonded that weekend which was worth every minute of that Saturday morning hangover.

CHAPTER 20
GRADUATION

Staying out of trouble was often difficult for me. I would be doing well for a good stretch of time and then fuck it all up. One of those times almost cost me everything I'd worked for. The highest honor you could get at The Republic was called "graduation". Now this wasn't an academic graduation, but a graduation from a teen to an adult. To be considered you had to apply and then a panel of staff from various areas at The Republic would evaluate your growth. You also had to write a book about yourself highlighting your time there. This book was your body of work and included all the lessons learned and how your life had evolved at The Republic. It would take months of deliberations before the panel would issue their decision. Graduation was celebrated annually and during my stay I witnessed two ceremonies as a non-participant. This one particular year there were around twelve graduates. A few of them had already been released and were back home living in the real world. They had to travel back to Freeville in order to participate in this elaborate ceremony and celebration. Two of the graduates that returned that year were LaToya and Alyse who happened to be friends of mine. I was still allowed to rent cars so fellow YA and friend John and I took LaToya and Alyse to see a movie off campus.

Although being a YA offered a lot of freedom and privileges we still had a curfew to be back on the grounds. At the movies I sat with Alyse while John sat in another row with LaToya. My teenage hormones were raging and we ended up kissed and petting the entire movie. It was so intense that I still can't tell you what we went to see that night. Alyse was eighteen and very well-developed. She was wearing black leather pants and a white silk blouse. My hands were all over her and she didn't stop me. I was still a virgin and had never gone all the way but was extremely turned on. I was like a dog chasing a bus and not quite knowing what to do now that I'd caught it. Well the movie finished and it was almost time to head back and make our curfew. Still horny, John suggested we find a motel and rent a room. I knew we'd miss curfew but at that point there wasn't much blood left in my head so I didn't give a shit. We drove around town and found a small motel, which the girls paid for since John and I only had Republic currency. The room they gave us had one bed which John and LaToya jumped on, sending me and Alyse to the floor with a blanket and some pillows. I didn't care where I was laying because I was about to bust my cherry. John and LaToya wasted no time and when I looked up at the bed could see them having sex. They weren't virgins like me and were going at it like pros. Alyse wasn't a virgin, so I acted like I wasn't either. I pretended to know what I was doing and faked my way though foreplay before closing the deal. Being my first time, I lasted less than a minute. The reset was almost instantaneous and went back in, lasting about ninety seconds this time around. For the next thirty minutes we stayed there on the floor talking until our porn-star roommates were finally done. Afterward we drove back to face the music and even though we were in big trouble for breaking curfew I couldn't seem to wipe the stupid smile from my face. I had finally lost my virginity and it felt awesome!

When we got back to campus I dropped John and the girls off, then headed home to face Ma and Pop. As I made my way down the walkway I could see Pop through the window. He was sitting at the dining room table smoking a cigarette. His arms were crossed and resting on his potbelly and he did not look happy. As I entered the room Pop asked me what happened and that's when Ma came in and sat next to him. They were pissed! I told them that we went to grab something to eat after the movie and lost track of time. I could tell they didn't believe me because the neighboring towns of Dryden and Groton were very rural and restaurants didn't stay open that late. I stuck with my story as they expressed their disappointment

Card from Mrs Siegel

in me. Ma and Pop told me how they had gone to bat for me on so many occasions and how I had let them down. They concluded by suspending my YA privileges indefinitely. They would still let me attend TC3 but I would have to be dropped off and picked up as before. This was like being executive platinum on American Airlines, which entitled you to fly first class and then instantly being downgraded and banished to coach. The next day was really tough, having to face my fellow citizens that looked up to me. That hurt more than the loss of privileges. I gracefully accepted my punishment and set my sights on climbing back and regaining my YA status.

With the loss of privileges I found myself with more time on my hands, which made my mind wander. I started to think about being adopted and wanted to know who my birth parents were and if they were still alive. When I left the foster home as a child I'd received a birthday card from Ms. Siegel, the representative from the adoption agency. In the card she told me how happy she was that I had a new family to love me and added her address and asked that I reach out from time to time and let her know how I was doing. It was now more then eleven years since getting that card and I had no idea if she was at the same address. I decided to take a chance and wrote her a letter. In it I told her all about my life and where I was at presently. I mentioned that I was curious to get information about my birth parents and asked if she could help me. About a month later I received a response. At The Republic all of our mail was routed through your social doctor, where it was searched for contraband and read. After inspection, they would then determine if it was appropriate for you to receive. Mr. Gardner read the letter and felt it was fine so it was delivered to me at the cottage. The return address on the envelope said The Louise Wise Adoption Agency. My palms got sweaty as I began to read it.

Dear Malcolm:

Mrs. Siegel forwarded your letter to me. I was so sorry to hear about your father's death and all the problems you have had since then. However, I was also glad to learn that you are at the George Jr. Republic. It is a very fine place and your letter makes it sound as if they have been of great help to you and that you are beginning to get things together for yourself. I know that working out family problems is hard, but at least you have a good idea of how you and your mother can improve your relationship.

I can well understand your natural curiosity about your birth parents. The New York State Adoption Law permits me to share with you the descriptive information in our records, but not the identifying material.

Your birth mother was a 21-year-old white, Jewish woman. She was the oldest of three children. She had a younger sister and brother. When you were born her parents were in their early fifties. Your maternal grandfather was a high school graduate who worked for his father and then his brother, each of whom owned their own small businesses. The grandparents were American born.

Your birth mother was said to be of medium height with brown hair and blue eyes. She was interested in sports and after high school supported herself off and on at clerical work. She also had some talent as an artist.

Your birth father was a 40-year-old black man who was married, but separated from his wife. He and your birth mother lived together for almost a year. He is described as tall and slender, with a medium complexion. He was a talented musician (pianist) and composer.

Your mother's parents were working class people whose finances were always a problem. Family difficulties were further complicated by the fact that your maternal grandfather was never able to establish himself or his family independently from his own domineering and controlling father. All these tensions in the household led your birth mother to become quite rebellious and to have problems dealing with figures of authority. (Your letter suggests that you can understand this kind of situation.) She left her home after graduation from high school and supported herself as best she could in a variety of jobs.

Since your birth father was already married, there was no possibility that your birth parents could, themselves, marry. Further, your birth father was reluctant to take on the responsibilities of parenthood. Your birth mother realized that she too was not mature enough for marriage, nor able to provide you with the security or stability of family living that she wanted you to have. Their relationship ended during your birth mother's pregnancy.

Despite the fact that your birth mother really wanted you to have the security she couldn't provide, she was conflicted about relinquishing you and unable to come to a firm decision to take the final step of legally surrendering you. The legal requirements are complicated and at times seemed overwhelming to your birth mother so that she periodically disappeared.

As I read the record it seemed apparent that she eventually had to avoid this painful decision yet allowing your future to be decided by the courts. This is not uncommon and usually happens when a mother is caught in the dilemma of concern for her child and yet hopes unrealistically to make a home for him. It is easier to let someone else make the decision.

All of this is so complicated that it is hard to deal with by mail. Perhaps when you leave George Jr. Republic and return to your adoptive mother's home you will want to come to see me so that we can meet and talk about your feelings.

In the meantime I know that you will continue to make the most of what George Jr. Republic offers. You are probably restless but if you can remain there as long as the staff feels it is wise, you will undoubtedly continue to add to the improvement you've already made.

If you want to write I will be glad to hear from you.

Sincerely,

Barbara F. Miller

Consultant, Post Adoption Services

I went through a series of emotions while reading this very well thought-out and written letter. At that moment so many questions from my past had been answered yet so many more were being formed. I decided to let it rest for the time being and concentrate on getting my shit together.

After several months of keeping my nose clean and staying out of trouble I earned my YA status back. I swore never to put my privileges in jeopardy again. To keep myself busy I dove head first into my studies. I left my longstanding job with Mr. Kiefer in the carpentry shop as well as my second job in the dining room. I began taking a few high school classes when I wasn't off campus at TC3 working on my six credit hours. I even had one teacher whose specific job was helping me to prepare for the GED exam. The plan was to finish at TC3 and immediately take my GED before leaving The Republic. My friend Norman, the one that had vouched for me to move into the Choate Cottage had left The Republic and was now attending The State University of New York at Oswego. Oswego was a four-year school located a little further upstate on Lake Ontario. I was still in contact with him and he suggested I apply there because SUNY schools, as they were called, had a special program set up for a handful of students with GEDs. If accepted into the program, you had to take a few classes in the summer and if you got at least a 2.0, would be accepted as a full-time student in the fall. It sounded good to me and I sent in an application.

Preparing for the GED was brutal. The last high school grade I had completed was ninth. I was going to have four years of high school crammed into a six-hour test. It felt like all I did was study, eat, and sleep. I only had a short time left at The Republic and desperately needed to pass to avoid going back home without a plan. Aside from all the studying I was also writing my bio book for consideration of Graduation from The Republic. My process for writing this book was to simply take a long, honest look in the mirror and then put pen to paper. I finished a thirty-page book about my ups, downs, losses, and achievements in just one sitting. It was so therapeutic to see my journey on paper. I submitted my book and waited to see if I'd be approved.

I finished my English composition and psychology classes at TC3 and then took the GED exam as scheduled. I was now waiting on four pieces of mail with decisions that were of great importance to me. Graduation from The Republic, GED scores, TC3 grades, and an Oswego acceptance or denial letter. The first to come were my grades from the early admission classes. I had passed both college courses with a 3.0 and 3.5 grade point average. One down, three to go. The second was from Oswego, which said I had been approved for admission contingent on my passing the GED examination. Two down, two to go. I had only been in Ma and Pop's apartment section of the cottage maybe twice since arriving, so I didn't know what was up when they asked me to their residence. They sat me down on the couch to share some news with me. They both looked very somber and their eyes were watering. They proceeded to tell me that they had received the decision on my graduation application and book. Looking at their faces, I braced for the worse. Then in unison they said, "You're graduating!" I thought they had watery eyes because they were sad but they were the tears of proud parents. The ceremony was going to be held several months after my release so I would have to come back to get my diploma. This was fine with me and I couldn't have been happier with the news.

The time had come and after a little over two-and-a-half years I was finally going home for good. Leaving The Republic was bittersweet because on one hand I was going to be free of all the institutional rules and regulations but on the other hand was going to miss the structure and relationships I had built. Ma and Pop had a going-away party for me and I made the rounds to say my farewells. I said goodbye to Mr. Kiefer, my confidant and mentor; Mr. Valenti, my educator; Mr. Gardner, my preparer; and Ma and Pop Thorpe, my protectors and cheerleaders; as well as all the wonderful friends I had made over the years. The teacher that helped me to prepare for the GED had family in Long Island and offered to drive me all the way home. This would be an upgrade from the cramped seat of a Greyhound bus. The whole ride we talked about my plans for the future. She talked to me in a way I wasn't yet used to. She was treating me like an adult and not a citizen of George Jr. This was really cool to finally be seen as a real young adult. Eventually we arrived at my house and said our goodbyes. I rang the bell and my mother greeted me at the door. We hugged and she told me how proud she was of all I had achieved. Then she handed me an envelope that was addressed to me from The New York State Department of Education, it was my GED scores. I had a lot riding on these. I ripped open the envelope and pulled out the letter. There stamped in big letters right at the top corner it read, PASSED! I then proudly told my mother that I was going to college!

CHAPTER 21
OSWEGO

G raduation time had come and I boarded a Greyhound bus and headed back to The Republic. It was going to feel so different being back on campus as a free man. I looked forward to seeing everyone and closing that chapter of my life in such a positive way. Ma and Pop set up my old room and had a beautiful reception waiting for me. They made lots of food and decorated the living room for this special occasion. On a sad note I found out that Pop was sick and had lung cancer. He smoked a couple of packs a day and it had caught up with him. He lost his hair and was visibly thinner than when I last saw him. We talked about his disease and he begged me to stop smoking. He described the horrors he had been subjected to with all the treatments and procedures. He was in pretty bad shape but was being upbeat, as he didn't want anything to ruin my special weekend. It was hard for me to see this powerful man so broken but I tried to keep a smile on my face and enjoy the festivities.

After that wonderful reception I made my way around campus visiting with everyone I knew who was still there. I also met a lot of new citizens who had arrived after my departure. They had heard stories about my achievements as well as my exploits and treated me like a rock star. It was all so freaking surreal. The weekend included a dinner for all the graduates and even a fireworks display. It all went by so fast and the graduation ceremony was finally here. This wasn't like the usual high school graduation where you make your way across the stage and grab your diploma. Since there were only a handful of us, they took their time and shined the spotlight on each graduate individually. All the graduates were given a "Citation of the Graduate" which was read aloud by the staff member we were closest with. Mine was read by Mr. Kiefer, whom I had known since my first week at The Republic. The following made me immensely emotional as it became clear that I had undergone a metamorphic change from that initial admissions interview to this celebratory day. A change that would benefit me well in the future.

CITATION OF THE GRADUATE

MALCOLM GRAHAM PUCKERING, you have met in honorable fashion the requirements for graduation from the George Junior Republic.

In the spring of 1982 you chuckled with disbelief in your admissions interview as the Citizen Government was described to you, and you stand here today having participated in that very government to the fullest. You moved from Full Keeper to Parole Officer to Bar Member to Magistrate to President of the Bar Association to Chief Magistrate. In these positions you have been described as receptive to guidance from others, but also as an independent thinker who makes his own decisions.

Also in the spring of 1982 in your admissions interview you vowed to work with horses and nothing else at The Republic. On your second day here you went to the carpentry crew and have remained there ever since, moving to the position of Foreman. Both here and in your position of Supervisor at Ewald you are seen as being able to function in a position of authority over others without sacrificing your relationships with them.

In Choate House you have been a Big Brother, both formally and in-formally and despite your busy schedule have contributed immeasurably to the spirit of the cottage. A large number of newer Citizens cite con-versations with you as having been important to their adjustment here.

You were not, however, too busy to have fun, and you have participated extensively in recreation. You were a contestant in the Tisdale Run, competed in the Triathlon, were on the soccer team and were a co-cap-tain of the basketball team.

Your future has recently become a pressing concern and you have since made great strides in school. You took two college courses and prepared for and took your GED examination.

You received community recognition with the awarding of Young Adult Status.

In the spring of 1982, you were a magician who could make things happen at the flick of your wand. You have indeed made things happen at The Republic but not because of any magic. You made things happen because of your determination, your ability to learn from your mistakes, your respectful way of exerting leadership, your wonderful wit, your good mind, and your caring attitude toward others. You write, "I probably won't be here to see that I did help, but as long as I did that's all that matters." That you should stand here today shows that we recognize the fact that you helped, that you helped abundantly. We are the richer for having known you.

Malcolm, you have earned this recognition marked in these certificates and symbolized by the accolade of the George Junior Republic.

Godspeed and our best wishes go with you.

Gabriel Viada

Associate Executive Director

Frank C. Speno

Executive Director

Then we were given our diplomas and a medallion. The medallions were gold-plated one-dollar coins that had The Republic's founder William R. George's face on it. These coins were used as the official currency of George Jr. Republic before they started utilizing checkbooks. Next was the awarding of the Donald T. Urquhart scholarship. This was a cash award given to the graduate who showed the highest quality of citizenship and growth. When they called my name and said that I was this year's recipient I was overwhelmed. This was going to really help with my supplies and books at Oswego.

When the ceremony was over I became soberingly aware this would be my final goodbye to the place that had helped me so much. I was on a fast track to self-destruction and George Jr. Republic derailed that train and put me on a new path toward growth and productivity. I owed so much to the philosophy of William "Daddy" George and would be forever grateful that my mother had fought so hard to send me there.

When I arrived back in Roosevelt everything moved so quickly. I spent as much time as I could with my mother and friends while preparing for my upcoming trip to Oswego. I would be at Oswego for the summer, taking two classes to prove I had what it took to become a full-time college student. Once again I boarded a bus and headed upstate but this time without adults supervising my every move. Upon arriving I was assigned an advisor who explained the summer program, classes, dorms, meals, and all other pertinent information. I was given a room in Funnelle Hall, which was smack dead in the center of campus. Funnelle was next to Hart Hall, which was an identical building and they were attached by a tunnel in the center that housed the Cooper Dining Center. Each building housed around 400 students. The first things that caught my attention were the doors on the front of the dorms. They had two main entrances in the front of the buildings. One was a revolving door like you'd see at a Manhattan hotel and the other was a door that opened weird. Instead of just swinging out to open, these doors swung in and then out. I would soon learn that they were intentionally made this way to resist strong winds. Oswego's campus was on Lake Ontario and the winds coming off the water were extremely strong in the winter. In fact if you were under 110 pounds they would excuse you from classes on very windy days. They even had poles with ropes all around campus to help you walk when the weather was extreme. Thank goodness it was summer and the campus couldn't have been more beautiful. Oswego was ranked on a list of the top ten places to watch the sunset in New York state. The sun going down on Lake Ontario was spectacular and I spent many dawns sitting on the grass experiencing its brilliance.

I shared a dorm room with a boy named Hector. He was of Colombian decent and had a heavy Spanish accent. He was a little older than me and had some rough edges but seemed to be a good guy. Hector's Spanish would come in handy as there were around twenty female students from Puerto Rico on campus that summer. Our dorm was coed and this was a new experience for me. We had separate bathrooms but it wasn't rare to find a girl in the boys' bathroom when the showers were full in theirs. It didn't take long for me to adjust and I was really enjoying my new found freedom as a college student. The two classes I took were anthropology and English literature. It was only six credit hours and left a lot of free time to socialize. Being away from home and unchained from the structure of The Republic I went a little overboard. The drinking age at that time was only nineteen years old. Back then New York driver's licenses only listed your name, address, height, weight, eye and hair color, with no picture. If you had a friend who was of drinking age you only needed to be similar in stature and appearance and memorize their address and birthday to use it. Sometimes the bouncer or store clerk would try to trick you by asking for your zodiac sign so it was always good to know that as well. With a borrowed license we would buy alcohol from the local liquor store. The drink we liked was Southern Comfort mixed with Sprite. This was really sweet but got you nice and buzzed. We'd get a bottle, along with some plastic cups, and ice then head to the lakefront to sit in the grass and get drunk. Drinking would more times than not lead to sex. College was everything I expected and more. Even though we spent a lot of time drinking and messing around I still managed to stay on top of my classwork. When classes were done I received passing grades along with an acceptance letter to come back in the fall as a full-time student. It was a great summer and I had achieved my goal.

My old roommate Norman from Choate Cottage was in his sophomore year at Oswego. He was renting a car and driving up for the fall semester with his girlfriend. He invited me to join them and I jumped at the chance to hang out with my old friend while skipping a bus ride in the process. Norman picked me up at my home and we drove to downtown Brooklyn to get his girlfriend. Her name was Tracy and they had met at Oswego. Tracy was a slim, light-skinned girl with straight, black hair. We looked very similar and if you had just met us for the first time would think we were related. She was very cute and didn't speak like someone who lived in the Wyckoff Projects in Brooklyn. She spoke with a slow, country-style of speech that was soothing and non-confrontational. On the ride up I got reacquainted with Norman while simultaneously getting acquainted with my new friend Tracy.

When we got to campus I received my dorm assignment. They had put me in Riggs Hall, which was the only all-boys dorm on the edge of campus while Norman and Tracy were in Funnelle, where I'd spent the summer. I wasn't happy about this and Norman told me that he'd speak with housing and see if he could get me switched. I spent a week in Riggs when Norman informed me that not only was I being switched to Funnelle, but we were going to be roommates again. This was great news and I looked forward to being back in Funnelle.

Since I had not been accepted into Oswego with SAT scores and a regular high school diploma they placed me on EOP. EOP stands for the Equal Opportunity Program. This is a program for students who need extra support financially and academically. We would get financial help from the state for everything from classes and books to housing. They even gave us a cash stipend every month for incidentals. If our grades faltered our advisor would assign us tutors, which were also included. I was going to need every bit of help now that I was a full-time student. I had not yet established a major but was gravitating toward psychology. I really enjoyed Psychology 101 at TC3 and thought with my tumultuous childhood I could maybe become a child psychologist and help other troubled youths. Lord knows I had a lot of experience on the subject.

Norman and I didn't always get along and rooming together had its ups and downs. He had a really strong personality and could be aggressive at times. I did however get along great with his girlfriend, Tracy, who was in our room so much I considered her a second roommate. Although she was pretty there was no physical attraction between us. We shared more of a sibling-type connection and she was becoming like a sister and I could tell her just about anything. Now even though Norman and I had been through the same rehabilitation at George Jr. he was still very wild. There were always drugs around and he offered them to me regularly. We would smoke weed, pop mescaline, and sniff cocaine, which would become my drug of choice. I never really liked the high from smoking weed and attributed this to that bad experience at Subway Roller Rink back in the day. Mescaline was a hallucinogen and taking those could be scary. The movie *Purple Rain* starring Prince was very popular and I had purchased the iconic poster of Prince and Apollonia sitting on his purple motorcycle and had it displayed proudly on the wall of our dorm room. One night after popping a mescaline tab I started tripping and that famous poster came to life right in front of my eyes. I hallucinated that Prince was talking to me and giving me shit for staring at Apollonia. That was enough for me and I never did mescaline again. When Norman introduced me to cocaine I was scared to try it. He convinced me that it was safe and I would like it. He was right about me liking it and I started using the drug whenever it was around. I didn't do it all the time at first because it wasn't readily available in rural Oswego. Also, it was expensive and aside from our monthly stipends, we were broke. On the upside, we got a lot of late-night studying done when it was around because the coke would keep us up all night. Thinking back, this was probably not the best way to justify my drug abuse. Luckily all the partying didn't affect my grades too much and I passed my first semester. Norman didn't tell us but he was on academic probation and needed to bring his grades up to avoid getting kicked out. He failed to do so and was not going to be returning with me and Tracy after the winter break.

During Christmas break I had another experience that let me know the racism I'd endured as a kid was still alive and kicking. One evening on a visit to the local Pathmark grocery store I ran into Malcolm's father, Mr. Williams. At the time I was wearing a black fedora hat made by Stetson. This was the same hat popularized by rap legends Run DMC. When Mal's dad saw the hat he suggested that I not wear it because he considered it a gangster-style hat and felt it was trouble. In fact his exact words were "Lose the hat, it's trouble!" Well being young and dumb I continued to wear that hat. Later that night I walked around the corner to visit a friend. I got to her doorstep and rang the doorbell. Just at that moment I heard a powerful voice behind me yell, "Police, now put your fucking hands behind your head and lay on the ground!" I turned to see who this was and found myself looking down the barrel of a large handgun. I immediately followed his instructions and hit the ground. My friend's mother opened the door and asked what the problem was. The officer told her to get back in the house and mind her business. Next I heard a helicopter overhead and it was shining a spotlight on us. The officer waved it off and the helicopter left. I asked what I did and received no response. By this time, a police car rolled up and another officer got out and came over to us. They handcuffed me behind my back really tight and if felt like my wrists were going to break. They lifted me up, dragged me to their car, and tossed me into the back seat. They threw me so hard that my head slammed against the door on the opposite side of the vehicle. One of the officers started grabbing and turning me in all directions. He was searching for something, which I later found out was blood.

Evidently someone had robbed a home in the neighborhood and had cut themselves hopping a fence as they made their getaway. The description the witness at the scene gave was that of a black youth wearing jeans, white sneakers, a black leather jacket, and black hat. Malcolm's father was right, the hat was trouble! To be honest that's not much of a description and describes my whole freaking neighborhood. This was profiling at its best and I hadn't even been read my rights. While looking me over they found my wallet, which contained my driver's license as well as college ID from Oswego. Once they realized I was not the guy they were looking for I was uncuffed and sent walking as if nothing had transpired. On my walk home I was still shaking from fear while my eyes watered in anger.

Once in my house I told my mother what had happened. She grabbed the back of my shirt and walked me back over to the officer's car that was still down the block. My mother started questing them about what had happened and was told to go away before they arrested her. She let them know that you can't just arrest someone and then let them go without reading their rights and processing them. She also told them that we would be reporting them for misconduct and abuse. When we got home she called the family lawyer and explained what had just taken place. Our lawyer, knowing my past history with detention homes and George Jr., suggested we let it go as it would be their word against ours and I had history of juvenile delinquency. So the police were off the hook and I had learned to ditch the fucking hat. I was looking forward to getting back to college and away from those crooked-ass cops.

When Tracy and I returned after the holidays I had a room to myself. Tracy never really liked her roommate so I suggested since Norman was gone that she move in with me. This worked out great because Tracy had a TV and a small fridge so I was good to go. To make things even better we would combine our monthly stipend and fill the fridge with tons of snacks, food, and drinks. My contribution was an electric hot plate my mother gave me for Christmas and we learned how to turn Top Ramen into a gourmet meal. We weren't supposed to cook in our rooms so we'd put a wet towel under the door so we wouldn't alert the resident assistant. This was a little trick I learned from smoking weed with Norman.

We had a lot of groups on campus and I joined the Black Student Union. This was quite small considering there were only a hundred and twenty-five black students on a campus of around seven thousand. We would organize social events and lecturers that spoke directly to us as black youths. One of the biggest speakers we had was Alex Haley. Alex was most known for his book *Roots*, which was turned into a historic made-for-television miniseries. The story of *Roots* was based on Alex Haley's real-life family tree. He spoke about how he started as a writer, penning love letters for his fellow mates in the Coast Guard. Later he began to research and trace his family tree. He also mentioned that at times he helped adopted people research and find their birth parents. I hadn't thought about finding my biological family in quite some time, but hearing this piqued my interest. After the lecture I had the opportunity to speak with Alex one on one. I asked him about the topic of adoption and the process of seeking out one's birth parents. He asked if I was adopted and I told him that I was. I expected him to give me the steps needed to start the legwork but instead he told me about the possible downfalls. A few of the people he helped unite with their birth parents had very negative experiences. One was rejected by the biological parent immediately upon their introduction. Alex said that sometimes the guilt a parent harbors after giving up a child is too much to bear. When they find themselves face to face with that guilt they don't exactly know how to deal with it and most choose to run. In another case the adopted person and biological parent began to spend time together building a relationship. Since the adopted person went in naively, he was unaware of his birth parent's criminal past. In the end the parent's past came to light and their relationship crumbled. I believe Alex was trying to warn me that seeking out my biological parents could possibly turn out to be very disappointing. With that advice I decided once again to abandon the idea of finding my birth parents.

The winter semester was a lot harder academically then the fall. I was having a tough time keeping the minimum 2.0 average needed to stay at Oswego. They assigned tutors for me but without any adult supervision I was giving in to all the wrong temptations. I had spent so many years in institutions that I lacked the self-control to stay focused on my studies. I was crashing and needed to figure out how to fix it. I decided that withdrawing from school would be my best bet. It was already too late in the semester to pick up my grades and if I ended the year with failing marks it would hurt my transcript. By withdrawing before the end of the semester I would get all incompletes, which wouldn't show as a negative mark should I re-enroll or transfer. Now I had to figure out how to break this news to my mother.

CHAPTER 22
PEACOCK ALLEY

I called my mother collect and told her that I was very unhappy at school. She said that college was hard and I needed to stick it out, which was followed by a lecture on how tough my life would be without a degree. And as if that wasn't enough, she added an additional deterrent, stating I couldn't come home and expect to live for free. Against all of her warnings and advice I stuck to my guns and told her I wanted out. I planned to come home and apply to another State University of New York with the EOP program. The school I had in mind was SUNY New Paltz, which was a lot closer to home than Oswego. It had a good reputation and I was confident they would accept me since I withdrew before I could ruin my transcript. I expressed this to her and without having much of a choice agreed to let me come home until I could get into another school.

I broke the news to Tracy, who was still rooming with me. Since I was going to be leaving she would have to go back to her assigned room. She wasn't happy about this and reluctantly moved out. The next morning I rented a car to drive back home to Roosevelt. While loading the car Tracy came down to see me. I thought she was just coming to say "goodbye", but instead told me that she was going with me. Evidently she and her roommate had some issues and decided if I was leaving she was too. I was more than happy to have the company, so she grabbed her stuff and we left together.

Joe, Claude, Mal, Brian, Dave

When I got home my mother sat me down and gave the ground rules. Since I was eighteen she didn't have to let me stay so I listened and listened well. First off I would be expected to pay $40 rent every week, which added to $160 a month. I would also be responsible to split the phone bill, which was itemized back then and could get really expensive. I think she did this to keep me from talking too long and making long distance calls. I told her that I was cool with that and would immediately start looking for a job while simultaneously applying to New Paltz.

At this time Mal was attending the University of New Haven, in Connecticut taking courses in hotel management. The semester I left college, he was doing a work-study program at Disney World in Orlando. While in Florida, he was dating a girl he met there named Nancy. Nancy had a really nice condo and they invited me and all the fellas down for a visit. I didn't have any money to go when I inadvertently received an unexpected gift in the mail. When I dropped out of Oswego I still had some unused funds from the Tuition Assistance Program aka TAP. Since I left at the beginning of the semester there was money that hadn't been spent and I was issued a refund from financial aid. The check they sent was almost $700 and I knew just how to spend it; I was going to Disney World! We all stayed in the condo, along with Nancy's roommate Sherry and were having the time of our lives. We spent the days lounging by their pool and evenings at the local nightclubs. What we weren't aware of was the amount of attention we were drawing to ourselves. The condo community Nancy and Sherry lived in was all-white and we stuck out like sore thumbs. Unbeknownst to us, our cohabiting with white girls was far from welcome and starting a stir with the residents. One night upon returning to the condo after a night of fun, we were smacked in the face with the sad reality of our presence. Stuck on the front door of the condo was a bright orange sticker around four inches square with black lettering. It read, "You have been visited by The Knights of The Ku Klux Klan." On the doormat directly below the sticker was a single business card. The card was from Glenn Miller and The Knights of The Ku Klux Klan. There were also two pictures on the card. One was a Klansman on a horse and the other a Confederate Flag. We couldn't believe this shit was happening in our day and time. This was something we thought had died in the '60s, but apparently we were mistaken. We took it all with a grain of salt and for the most part ignored their so-called warning.

Another evening while driving back to the condo, we were pulled over by the police. We were driving Nancy's car and the girls were not with us. The police offered no reason as to the stop and told us to get out of the car. Now these cops had thick, Southern accents and reminded us of *Smokey and the Bandit* or *The Dukes of Hazzard*. We were hesitant to get out of the car, especially after the sticker we'd received prior. The cop reiterated for us to get out of the car and said if we didn't, we'd be getting in his car. To avoid confrontation we got out of the vehicle as instructed. He took our licenses but didn't run them through any computer, but just glanced them over. He warned us about staying with white woman and told us we needed to go back home to New York. We were surprised he knew where we were staying and who we were staying with. This was obviously a small town and we needed to watch our backs. He let us go with that unconventional warning and the whole drive back we talked about how backward and behind the times Orlando was.

I guess because we were young, the threats and warnings from these racist-ass rednecks didn't seem to sink in. We continued to stay with Nancy and Sherry until our scheduled departure, which was one week away. Maybe we should have taken heed but we weren't that smart and it would take one more run-in for us to get the point. Mal and I loved pot pies and decided to hit the Piggly Wiggly grocery store and get some for dinner. Instead of driving together, we borrowed both girls' cars and raced each other to the store. This was an idiotic thing to do, especially when you factor in how well-known we'd become. So we're driving over the speed limit, weaving in and out of each other all in the quest to satisfy our pot-pie craving. I looked in my rearview mirror and saw some flashing lights in the distance. As I continued to drive, they were getting closer and it became apparent that those lights were for me. After all I'd been exposed to the previous weeks, I chose to run rather than pull over and chance meeting another racist cop. I floored it and as I passed Mal's car I got his attention and pointed back to the cop car. I was gesturing for him to speed up and follow me but I guess he didn't get the message. Running from the cops was something I would never have done in New York, but with the thought of being strung up in some wooded area I took my chances.

I went back to the girls' house and waited for Mal, but he never returned. We jumped in the car and headed back to where I'd seen him last. When we arrived, we could see that the cops had gotten him. He was in the back seat of their squad car in handcuffs. The girls told the cops that it was their car and asked what happened. The police said he was speeding, as well as driving with a suspended license. The girls were allowed to take the car, but we were told Mal was going to jail. We followed them to the jail to make sure they didn't make any unscheduled detours and were relieved when they pulled up to the county jail. We ended up sleeping in the waiting area till morning when he would see a judge. He was given bail, but didn't have any money, so we needed to find a way to raise it for him. In the waiting area we met a bail bondsman. He gave us his card, which read "Miami Vice Bail Bonds" with a picture of an alligator wearing a T-shirt and blazer. We didn't have any money to secure the bail but he suggested we give him our jewelry as collateral. I had two gold rope chains with nameplates and offered those in exchange for posting Mal's bail. He agreed and within a couple hours Mal was released.

When Mal got out we headed home immediately. By now I had spent all of the money I had gotten back from financial aid and didn't have the airfare to return home. Mal's parents sent his fare, but there was nothing extra for me. There was an airline at the time called PEOPLExpress. The best way to describe them was to picture a bus with wings. I say this because you paid for your ticket in the air rather than when you made the reservation. While in mid-flight they would come down the isle with a cash box and credit-card machine. Knowing how they operated I decided to board and when they got to me make up a story about losing my wallet. I figured they couldn't throw me off and when we landed I'd just make a run for it. All I cared about was getting the hell out of Orlando, even if it meant getting in more trouble. To get up the courage to go ahead with this, we smoked some weed. I still wasn't a big fan of the drug but needed something to give me the balls to embark on this risky venture. When the flight attendant made her way to me and Mal, I started the charade by searching unsuccessfully for my wallet. I gave her the bullshit story that I'd lost it and was caught off guard by her response. Instead of the sympathetic comment I was expecting she sarcastically said, "Come on, cuz. You really expect me to believe you lost your wallet?" She capped off this attitude, stating I would be arrested when the plane landed in New York. At that very moment a passenger sitting behind me heard what had transpired and offered to put my fare on his credit card if I gave him my contact info and promised to pay it back. I accepted his generous offer and was relieved I would no longer have to make a break for it. I finally made it home after nearly a month of living on the edge. My future plans consisted of staying my ass in New York for a while.

Now that I was back, finding a job was not easy, especially when you have no experience or job history. All the things I learned at The Republic couldn't be used on a résumé, without exposing my past so I chose to keep it to myself. I found a temp agency in the newspaper called Man Power and they got a few manual labor jobs for me to work. This helped a little, but wasn't steady enough. Just when things looked hopeless, Malcolm's father said he had a hookup for me. Mal's dad worked at a car dealership and knew a lot of people in the industry. He got me a job with a private detailing company that had a contract with the dealership he worked for. When new cars were purchased, we drove them to our garage and did all the prep work. We did rustproofing and undercoating, detailing, and simonizing. They taught me everything I needed to do and I caught on pretty quick. Everything we provided there was itemized and I was paid for each service rendered. It was a hard job, but the faster I worked the more money I could make. The owner was an older, white guy named Jerry and he had several of these shops spread out between Long Island and Queens. There were only two to three employees at any given time and Jerry would quite often leave us there alone. A guy named Kevin was the supervisor and in charge when Jerry was away. Kevin was a twenty-something, skinny, black kid with shifty eyes. I never understood why Jerry trusted him so much, but it was really none of my business. Sometimes when we were alone Kevin would get a six-pack of beer and some cocaine and we would get high while working on the cars. Kevin was from Terrace Avenue, which was one of the worst neighborhoods in all of Long Island. It was right behind the Hempstead Bus Terminal and was a rough street, lined with low-rent housing projects. Kevin was trouble and always thinking of ways to scam money off of Jerry. The shop was closed on weekends and Kevin had a key. He and I would open up on Saturday mornings and work on our friends' and families' cars. We did all the work at a huge discount and kept all the profits for ourselves. Jerry never noticed the missing supplies and we made good money every weekend. Kevin knew a lot of really shady people from Terrace and they would visit often. One standout was a young girl that went by "Mama" and I have no freaking idea how she got that nickname. She was a hooker and turned tricks to support her drug habit. One night Mama came by as we were closing up and asked if we wanted to get some coke, to which we quickly replied yes. Without permission Kevin took one of the cars that was left overnight at the shop. We drove to Terrace with Mama so she could get the drugs for us. We went into her building and the halls were lined with some of the sketchiest characters I'd ever seen. I was a little nervous, but everyone seemed to know Mama, so I stuck close. We got to the apartment where Mama said the drugs were and went inside. I looked around and saw around eight people sitting on the floor, smoking crack. Now I had never done crack and was not comfortable being around it. I liked powder cocaine, which didn't carry the negative stigma that crack did. I told Mama that I only wanted powder and she said to just give her the money and she'd be back shortly with the drugs. She went into a room and was in there for almost twenty minutes. The whole time I'm standing against a wall in the living room with Kevin and a bunch of strung-out crack heads. The room was filled with thick, yellow smoke and the smell was really strong. When Mama finally emerged she grabbed my hand and took me into the bathroom. She pulled out a glass pipe and dropped a small piece of crack cocaine into it. I told her the money I gave her was for powder cocaine and I didn't want any crack. She said that was all they had and it was the crack or nothing. She put the pipe to my lips and lit the rock with a lighter telling me to take a long, steady pull. Feeling trapped and uncomfortable, I followed her instructions. When I exhaled, my body felt really light and was one of the best feelings I had ever experienced from a substance. This was way too good and I felt like I could easily get hooked. I had heard stories of crack heads selling everything they had, even themselves for a hit. I didn't want to be that person and knew I couldn't take another pull. I told Mama I was gonna send Kevin in and when I left the bathroom, headed right for the front door and bolted. I remember seeing some thugs in the hallway and overheard them whispering about robbing me. I just kept running till I was out of the building and didn't stop until I was two towns away. What really sucked was that the $40 I gave Mama for the drugs was for my weekly rent. The next morning, when my mother asked for the rent I told her I was robbed. She didn't believe my bullshit but let me slide and I doubled up the next week. When I went back to work at Jerry's, Kevin and I never spoke about what happened and that was the last time we hung outside of the garage.

That night woke me up and I knew that this lifestyle had to change. I was hopeful that I would get good news from New Paltz and get back in school. In the meantime I continued to look for work in the Sunday classifieds. There were always a lot of restaurant jobs available and that was something I had some experience in. I applied at a few places and finally got a job bussing tables at a place called Daltz, which was owned by TGI Friday's. This job gave me some legitimate experience and I was quickly promoted to waiter. The money was decent and I enjoyed the instant gratification of earning money based on the quality of service I provided.

Servers at The Waldorf Astoria

Mal was home for the summer and heard about a big Hilton Hotel strike in New York City. He suggested that we go to the city and cross the picket line to get jobs. Now being a scab, as it's called, was very dangerous. The picketing union employees would try to deter anyone from filling their jobs while they tried to settle their disputes. We were young and knew that this was the only way any of these quality hotels would ever hire us. We took a chance and jumped on the train to Manhattan. Mal and I were dressed to impress. We both wore tan khaki slacks, white dress shirts, and ties, with tweed blazers and brown shoes. We blended well on the streets of mid-town Manhattan and were ready to interview. The first hotel we went to was the world famous Waldorf Astoria. At Human Resources we filled out applications for restaurant jobs. They interviewed us together and we were offered jobs in Peacock Alley, their formal dining room. This was a four-star, five-diamond restaurant that featured Cole Porter's piano in the lounge. The money was ridiculous and the benefits were outstanding. After hiring us, they asked a question we didn't really understand at the time. They asked if we had any other friends who looked like us, and if so, could we send them in. Now we took this to mean clean-cut, articulate, etc. We couldn't be more wrong and would soon find out exactly what they meant. In any event we did send some friends and family to interview for jobs. Mal's twin sister Lindy got a job in the Cocktail Terrace along with our high school friend Hazel. Our homeboy Brian was hired too and placed in Peacock Alley with us.

First day of training was a lot to take in and was a little intense. This was fine dining at the highest level and we were learning French service. There were so many steps to remember and everyone played a specific part in the dining experience. You had a maître d', captain, sommelier, servers, and busboys. I went to this job like a fish to water. My preparation as the dining-room supervisor at the Ewald dining room at The Republic had given me some basics skills. The perks at The Waldorf were great and they even gave us a dinner break every night in the employee cafeteria. It had everything you could ever want to eat there and best of all, was free. As I looked around at all the uniformed employees enjoying their meals I started to notice something. All of the dark-skinned employees seemed to be working in the laundry, kitchen, and other back-of-the-house positions. All the light-skinned and white employees worked in guest services, housekeeping, bars, lounges, and dining rooms. This was a modern day house nigger/field nigger situation. During slavery, the dark-skinned slaves worked the fields, while the light-skinned slaves worked in the main house. Hence the terms house nigger and field nigger. This is why they asked if we had any more friends who looked like us. They meant light-skinned with white features.

Apart from the blatant caste system, it was still one of the greatest jobs I'd ever had. We were paid $4.60 an hour plus tips, which was considered top pay in the '80s. We usually served around four tables each per evening. People sat and enjoyed their meals and weren't in a rush like nowadays. We would walk with over $150 per night plus our salary, which was a lot of money for young guys like us. We car pooled from Long Island to Queens and parked in a municipal parking lot, then took the subway into the city. This became a lot to deal with, especially when you factor in traffic and having to cross the picket line every day. We told our boss about our commute and he got rooms in the hotel for us so we wouldn't have to make the daily drive. This was a dream come true to actually live in the Waldorf Astoria.

The Waldorf=Astoria

A Hilton Hotel

CERTIFICATE OF ACHIEVEMENT

OUR CONGRATULATIONS TO

MALCOLM PUCKERING

OF THE

FOOD AND BEVERAGE DEPARTMENT

FOR SUCCESSFULLY COMPLETING

PEACOCK ALLEY

TRAINING PROGRAM

FREDERICK J. KLEISNER
VICE PRESIDENT AND
GENERAL MANAGER

DEPARTMENT HEAD

Waldorf Certificate of Training

With all the money we were making Mal, Brian, and I bought some nice suits. We would get dressed up after work and roam the hotel like guests. When people would ask our occupation we would lie and say real estate. We were living the dream, but eventually everyone has to wake up. One day after work we were told that the strike was settled and the union employees would be returning. They thanked us for our service and gave us a bonus plus a certificate of training from the Waldorf Astoria. That certificate would be worth its weight in gold when added to my new résumé. I had enough money saved to pay my rent and portion of the phone bill for several months. It was a great summer!

CHAPTER 23
Hell on Wheels

Shortly after leaving the Waldorf I finally received a response from SUNY New Paltz. They told me that my application for admission to the university had been denied. I really thought I was going to get in but it wasn't to be. At that point I didn't know what my next move was, but I needed another job and fast. Once again I hit up Man Power and they found another temp job for me. This time it was at Fortunoff's, a high-end department store in Westbury. I was assigned to the hollowware department stockroom. When an item was purchased on the showroom floor they would send a message to the stockroom and we would locate the piece then send it down to the cashiers desk. It wasn't nearly as easy as it sounds, because the stockroom was gigantic and had thousands of items on the shelves. Picture a huge storage space where every item has a stock number that you needed to memorize in order to find it. This job was far from convenient but paid the bills while I plotted my next move.

My brother had bought a brand new BMW 325i and I inherited his old Hyundai Excel, which was paid off. It was in good condition and I drove the wheels off that sucker. A couple of years later I was in need of a new car, but didn't have any money or credit. I asked my mother if she would co-sign and she did me one better. My mother told me to drive her to the bank. When we went inside she pulled out a bankbook with my name on it. Then she told me that all of the rent money I'd given her over the years was in this account. She never needed my $40 a week and was just trying to teach me how to be responsible. Then she withdrew the balance and told me to go get my car. All the time I bitched about paying rent made me feel like a real jackass. This was one lesson that I could only hope to pass onto my own kids, should I ever have any.

After the summer break, most of the fellas were gone. Mal went back to college, Joe was in the Navy, Rich the Air force, Brian at Rutgers, while Dave, Claude, and I were home, working. Mal's sister Lindy went to Nassau Community, a local college and we started hanging out. Their father didn't like Lindy going out at night alone and would make me accompany her. Everyone thought we were cousins, so being with her didn't hurt my game with the ladies. Rap music was really growing in mainstream popularity and Lindy knew a lot of famous rappers as well as drug dealers. I mention the two in the same sentence because in New York, the drug kingpins, successful rappers, and sports figures usually hung together. I guess it's because they all had money, were flashy, and were considered local celebrities. We would go to so many industry parties during the week that we became part of their inner circle. We hung with everyone in hip-hop, like Scorpio from Grandmaster Flash and the Furious Five, Jam Master Jay from Run DMC, Biz Markie, Nice & Smooth, MC Serch, Teddy Riley, Dana Dane, Salt-N-Pepa, Hurby Luv Bug, Doug E. Fresh, Dr. Dre from *Yo! MTV Raps*, and even heavyweight champ, Mike Tyson. We also became friends with some really hard-core drug dealers from the "40 Projects" in South Side, Jamaica Queens, and Azie Faison from Harlem who the movie *Paid in Full* was based on. We would always party at different celebrities' homes after the club. They treated us like we were one of them and that's when it hit us that we should start a group of our own. A year earlier, manager and producer Hurby "Luv Bug" Azor asked Lindy to be the DJ for his new group Salt-N-Pepa. That invite was vetoed by group member Salt, who was in a relationship with Hurby at the time. This worked out for us because now Lindy could be the DJ for me and Mal, and Hurby would help with the production. We called our group 911 and our raps were mostly about positivity. Mal and I started writing songs over the phone. Anytime I wasn't at work we were on the phone comparing lyrics. The University of New Haven

911 Rap Group

wasn't that far from New York, so Mal would come home from college on the weekends and we'd hit it hard. On Sundays we'd go to Hurby's house in Queens to work on our songs. Afterward we would all drive Mal back to school and Hurby would help with gas and even treat us to McDonalds with money he'd just made from shows with the girls.

At the time Hurby was working primarily with Salt-N-Pepa and a young rapper named Dana Dane. He was making money with them so we completely understood when we couldn't get together. As his groups got bigger, he had less and less time so we started looking for another person to help us. One of our childhood friends, Daryl Higgins aka DJ Big Hig, knew everyone in the area. He wanted to help and took us to Cassad Rehearsal Studio in West Hempstead. It was a small building and their studio was on the bottom floor. Upstairs was a group called Spectrum City, which would later become the iconic group Public Enemy. The two musicians that ran Cassad were Charles Cassius and Eric Sadler. We became good friends, especially with Eric, and he helped us work on a lot of different ideas for our group. We wrote several songs but nothing seemed to get any traction and we became frustrated. Making matters worse, my mother was on my ass about going back to school. Just then I had a heavy conversation that would temporarily sidetrack my musical aspirations. Big Hig had gotten a job at Def Jam Records, so we went to their offices to hang with him. While there I ran into a guy who managed a recording artist named Tank. We were talking about the business and I expressed how frustrated I was with our progress and that I needed financial security. He suggested that I take a break and join the military. He said the business would still be there when I got back and I'd have money saved plus benefits. His words must have really resonated with me because the following day I went to a recruiting office and enlisted. When I told my mother what I'd done she was a little scared but felt it might be good for me. Five days later I was at Fort Hamilton in Brooklyn for processing. Next stop Fort Dix, New Jersey for my first day of boot camp as a private in the United States Army.

I found boot camp to be a bit comical. All of the sleep deprivation and overzealous drill sergeants yelling at us seemed a little over the top. I came to realize that this was going to be more mental than physical and went about it like a game. The majority of the other recruits were from the Midwest and Southern states. I was the only one in my unit from New York and I figured that most New Yorkers follow other career choices first before considering the military. The fact that I was joining the Army after a short stint in college was a little backward, too. Most enlisted men join the service to get the GI Bill to help pay for school when they get out, that is unless you already have a degree and come in as an officer. Either way, being a street-wise kid was an advantage and helped me to deal with all the lunacy. I remember lying in bed the first night listening to all the cries of fresh trainees wishing they were back home. This just fueled me to be stronger and the days flew by. Boot camp was six weeks long and it didn't take long for me to find my way into some mischief. For that month and a half we weren't allowed to smoke cigarettes or drink alcohol. All we did was train, train, and more training from dusk to dawn. A few of us were really tired and wanted a night of recreation to ease the stress. We knew this was a risk but felt it would be worth it. After lights out there would only be one drill instructor, who usually sat at a desk half asleep, watching a small TV. Our bunks were on the second floor and we thought if we stayed quiet enough he wouldn't hear us. So two of my fellow privates and I snuck off base to the local town. There we found a liquor store and purchased a bottle of Everclear grain alcohol and a pack of Newport cigarettes. Once the package was secured we snuck back onto base and into our barracks. Now Everclear is probably the strongest liquor you can legally purchase at 190 proof, which is 95% alcohol by volume. You can actually start a car with this stuff and we were about to put it into our bodies. We needed a chaser and got a few cans of Coke from the soda machine. We used our Army-issued metal canteen cups to mix our high-powered cocktail. The Everclear was so strong that no amount of Coke could dilute it and it was like drinking fire. It didn't take long for us to get drunk and without noticing, we were getting pretty loud. We unintentionally woke up a fellow soldier, who snuck downstairs and ratted us out to the drill instructor. I guess he thought this would garner some brownie points but instead labeled him a snitch, which wasn't a good reputation to have. The drill instructor made his way upstairs and busted in on our little party. He was furious that we'd pulled this shit on his watch. I thought for sure we were going to get kicked out of basic but he had other plans for us. He chose to punish us physically. He made us do push ups, sit ups, bear crawls, duck walks, and other extreme exercises until we were totally exhausted and throwing up. These drills were hard enough when we were sober but being drunk made them unbearable. Once he was satisfied we'd learned our lesson we had to clean up and then hit our bunks. He never told the commander what happened and we thought we were in the clear. The same trainee that dropped the dime on us decided to also tell the company commander the following morning. We were immediately summoned to his office, where he chewed our asses and gave us all Article 15s. An Article 15 is non-judicial punishment and permits commanders to administratively discipline troops without a court-martial. This stays on your military record and we also received a dock in pay. This was not a good way to start our military career and we stayed out of trouble for the rest of basic training.

When I graduated, my mother attended the ceremony. Fort Dix was a two-and-a-half hour drive and my mother didn't drive all that well, so she got a ride from Richard Screws, a man she was dating at the time. Although she said they were only friends, I knew that it was more. Richard was originally from Indiana and cousins with Katherine Screws, the mother of Michael Jackson and the famous Jackson family. This made Richard one of Michael Jackson's uncles, which was kind of cool. He was a truck driver and a real country boy. He spoke with a heavy Southern accent and had a hard time saying Malcolm and would call me Mike, which never sat well with me. I had a love/hate relationship with him because he would often try to act like a father figure and I resented that. I had one father and although he was gone, I felt no one else could or should try to take his place. I'd heard Richard was married, too, which also made me lose some respect for him. At graduation my mother seemed proud and I felt like I had made the right choice enlisting. I was happy she had come, but our reunion was short-lived because the following day I began AIT (Advanced Individual Training) so we said our goodbyes.

My job classification was Sixty Four Charlie, transportation specialist. In layman terms, a truck driver. I learned to drive everything from five-ton cargo trucks to fourteen-ton tractors with forty-foot trailers. This part of training was fun and a lot easier than the previous time spent in boot camp. We got some time off on weekends for R&R to blow off steam, which was a nice perk. The last week of AIT they lined us up in formation to tell us the duty station we would be going to after training was finished. The Instructor called my name "Puckering" and I answered, "Yes, drill sergeant." Then he said, "Do you want to know where you're going?" Again I said, "Yes, drill sergeant." Then he said, "Germany." I could feel all the blood rush from my face and I was devastated. When I spoke with the recruiter I specifically mentioned that I didn't want to leave the country. He had deceived me, and I was going to a foreign land, and wasn't happy about it.

After training was finished I got a couple weeks off before having to board a plane for Frankfurt. This was a long flight and when we landed I still had another six-hour bus ride to base. I was stationed at Garlstedt, which is in Northern Germany about twelve kilometers

2nd Armored Division Forward

from Bremen where they make Beck's beer. I was placed in a tank battalion called the 2nd Armored Division Forward. This was the division that the famous General Patton once commanded and our motto was "Hell on Wheels". I was assigned to the 498th Support Battalion and we were called handlers because anything that came up, we could "handle" it!

We were a field unit and spent almost seven months out of the year off-base, sleeping in tents. In the field we would train and play war games to keep us sharp, should we need to be activated. At first I drove a five-ton cargo truck and transported simple supplies and troops. Later I graduated to a thirty-six-foot stake and platform tractor-trailer. With this truck I transported weapons and hazardous material. I liked being in transportation, because this allowed me to get a break from the field. During the exercises I would regularly be sent back to base to pick up supplies. Going to base during a field exercise was wild. Picture being the only man on an island full of beautiful women. All the men were in the field, so I would pretty much be the only male on base and took full advantage of this exclusivity. There were three social clubs on base, the Enlisted Men's, NCO, and Officers. I preferred the NCO (non-commissioned officers) club although I was only a PFC (private first class). They had a nice bar and played great music. During field exercises, the place would be packed with women. In full disclosure, it could get dangerous being the only guy in the club. I remember going home with a girl and waking up the next morning to a picture on the nightstand of a sergeant in my platoon. I had just slept with his wife, whom I thought was single. There were a lot of married women cheating on their husbands in the military. Some of these women had either gotten pregnant or were looking to marry a man with financial stability and benefits, but weren't really in love.

Another time I was sleeping with a girl who worked in the mess hall. She had a child and told me she was the dependent of another soldier on base. Sometimes she would bring her son with her when we hung out. I believed her story about being an Army Brat until one day I saw her son walking hand in hand with some man at the PX. The boy pointed at me and yelled, "Hi Malcolm." I heard the guy ask the kid how he knew me, and he told him that me and mommy were friends and played together when he was away. Come to find out, this was no random guy but her husband and that was his kid. This could have gotten me in a lot of trouble and maybe even killed. That was some scary shit, so I started vetting all the women I met from that point on.

I made a lot of friends in Germany and we partied hard. We were off on weekends and every Friday started with a visit to the base liquor store. Everyone on base was issued a ration card for cigarettes, liquor, and coffee. You were allowed four cartons of cigarettes per month and fifty single packs per year. There was a certain amount of coffee and liquor you could purchase each month as well. Every time you bought one of these items your card was punched. These items were really expensive in Germany, so the ration cards helped to deter us from selling these things on the black market. Four cartons of cigarettes was only $18 for us. On the black market you could get $150 US. Occasionally I would sell my monthly rations on the economy, which could get you thrown in military prison if caught. Luckily I never got busted and enjoyed the extra income.

Social drinking was a big part of the German culture. The drinking age was only sixteen and you could even buy beer in some of the coin-operated vending machines. Just think about that for a minute. A vending machine can't check ID, so pretty much anyone with some loose change could buy a beer. We would regularly drink from the end of work on Friday through Sunday night.

One Saturday afternoon, after returning from a month in the field, we threw a little party in the barracks. My platoon leader bought most of the booze and snacks to show his appreciation for a successful exercise. We got pretty hammered and it felt great to let loose after a month of roughing it. When the party winded down, my platoon leader left to go home. He was married with a brand new baby and lived in off-base housing. He shouldn't have been driving, but said he was cool, so no one stopped him. Germany had a zero-tolerance policy when it came to drinking and driving. This was understandable when you see how they drive over there. A lot of the roads, especially on the autobahn, didn't have speed limits. You could literally drive a fast as you and your car could handle. When they had accidents at those speeds there wasn't much left and they would joke that everything could be cleaned up with a hose. If you were pulled over by the polizei (German police) and suspected of drunk driving, you were issued a mandatory blood test right there on the side of the road. If you refused to take the blood test, they would crack you in the nose with their baton and get it that way. You had agreed to be blood tested when you were issued a European driver's license. Unfortunately, my platoon leader never got the chance to take a blood test that day until it was too late. While driving home to his wife and child he fell asleep and crashed head on into another car. He survived with minimal injuries but the other driver was killed instantly. We were all at fault and should have stopped him from getting behind the wheel. It was a tragic incident and ruined that generous man's life. I wish I could say that we learned a lesson about excessive drinking, but we were too simpleminded to slow down. We continued to work hard and play even harder.

I was in Germany from 1987 to 1989 and there were no cell phones or internet available to us. The only way to stay in contact was to use a pay phone or find a calling center, which was really pricey. Germany was a six-hour time difference from New York so I rarely got to speak with my friends and family. Although I was surrounded by people all the time, I still felt lonely. I missed being back in the States with the people I cared about. Every Christmas I made sure to put in a leave request and luckily my vacations were always approved. One Christmas I booked my flight from Frankfurt to Kennedy Airport and was scheduled to leave on December 21st. I let my family know my itinerary beforehand so they could pick me up from the airport. The day before I was scheduled to leave, my company commander told me that I needed to do a run and wouldn't be able to leave the following day as scheduled. She said they would help reschedule a flight for the day after my mission. Unfortunately I never got a chance to let my family know about the change in plans. The original plane that I was forced to miss was Pan Am flight 103. That flight was destroyed by a bomb, killing all 243 passengers and sixteen crew, in what became known as the Lockerbie bombing. The flight went down in Lockerbie, Scotland, killing eleven more people on the ground. My company commander's decision to change my orders had spared my life. That night I received a call from the Red Cross. My family had called them hysterical, thinking I was on that plane and had died. When I finally made it home the following day, I received the tightest hugs. I couldn't even start to imagine what they could have been going through, hearing the devastating news about Pan Am flight 103. I thought to myself that it just wasn't my time and maybe I had a special purpose and needed to stick around for a while.

Being in the Army had its share of hard times. Everything from your job to relationships was based on rank. Officers weren't supposed to fraternize with non-commissioned officers, and non-commissioned officers weren't supposed to fraternize with enlisted men, so forth and so on. My unit had gotten a new platoon leader that I happened to known from basic training. He was one of the guys I got the Article 15 with after the Everclear fiasco. After basic I went to AIT and he headed to OCS (Officer Candidate School). I was a SP4 or specialist E4 by now and he was a second lieutenant. We had been boys back in the day, but weren't supposed to have any kind of friendship because he was an officer and I was enlisted. We kept our previous friendship quiet and he pulled some strings to get me out of the motor pool to become his personal driver. This had a lot of advantages and we shared our friendship in secret to avoid any military scrutiny. He lived off-base and invited me to spend Thanksgiving with him and his family. I accepted and had a great time, enjoying the holiday with my friend. He lived off-base and the community was filled with other officers and their families. We should have given this a little more thought, because someone saw me leave his home and reported us to the company commander. My friend was confronted about having me to his home and explained he'd invited me over for the holiday. They said that it was against military policy to have any fraternization between officers and enlisted men and he was moved to another company. I lost my job as his driver and was sent back to the motor pool. I never understood this practice in the Army. I always felt that as long as you did your job and showed respect for rank it should be fine to hang out after work. They didn't see it that way, so my friendship with my boy was finished.

Living in Europe was a lot different from living in the States. Things that we considered taboo were normal there. Sex wasn't demonized and you could see naked woman on television at any given time. Prostitution was legal and considered an honest profession. In fact, it was overseen by the government, and it wasn't rare to see a husband drop his wife off at the red-light district for work. Drinking age was only sixteen and you could drive as fast as you wanted on most roads. You would think with all this accessibility to things like this there'd be a lot of abuse, but it was just the opposite. Condom machines were everywhere and they practiced safe sex. This was causing their population to shrink and the government even offered incentives to entice people to have children. STDs and rapes were low, especially when compared to the US. There's something to be said about implementing too much regulation. At the end of the day I guess people just don't like to be told they can't do something.

CHAPTER 24
HIP HOP

I had a first sergeant who was a genuine redneck. He'd done three tours in Vietnam and was a real hard-ass. He talked like a hick and we all thought he had to be in the Klan. I say that because he seemed to be harder on the brothers than anyone else. Maybe he wasn't a racist, but that's how I felt at the time. I had two roommates, Leon who was a huge, crazy black guy from Atlanta and Rodney, a skinny, quiet brother from Louisiana. One day first sergeant had a room inspection and was ripping us a new one. He nitpicked everything, and nothing was clean enough. When he went into the bathroom to inspect the shower, my roommate Leon followed him in and closed the door behind him. I had no idea what was going on but about a minute later they both emerged and the first sergeant quickly left without saying a word. Afterward Leon told us that he had grabbed the first sergeant by the collar and told him if he didn't stop fucking with us that he was gonna beat his ass and then tell everyone he called him a nigger. It must have worked because after that inspection he left us alone. The crazy thing was although Leon looked really mean he was actually the nicest guy you could ever know. This was the one time when judging a book by its cover was a good thing.

My orders for Germany were for thirty months or two-and-a-half years, and I was nearing the end of that tour. I had fun overseas but was excited to get back to the States. My obligation to the Army was for three years total, so this left me with six months before I got out for good. Four weeks before I was scheduled to leave I received a disappointing letter from the Army. It stated that since I only had six months left in service I would stay in Germany for the remainder of my time and be discharged from there. The explanation was with only six months left it wouldn't be cost-effective to relocate me to a new base in the US. However, if I were to extend my service a minimum of six more months, bumping me up to a year, they would send me back as scheduled. Staying in Germany another six months was not an option for me, so I extended an additional six months and was sent back to the States. My new duty station was Fort Polk, Louisiana, also known as Little Vietnam. I packed my things and went home for a couple weeks' vacation before having to sign onto Fort Polk. I wanted out of my forced extension and that's when I started thinking about my mother. She was always going to doctors for all sorts of neurological issues. Our neighbor was in local politics and I explained what had happened in Germany and that I needed to be home to help my mother. He said he couldn't do anything, but could get me in contact with my congressman. I wrote my congressman and mentioned that my mother was not well and how the Army had pushed me to extend. My request for help went unanswered and I had no other choice than to make the trip to Louisiana as scheduled. About a month into my contract at Fort Polk I got a message to see my company commander. When I walked into his office I could tell he was pissed. He said that a congressional package had come in on me and I was to be processed out immediately. My congressman had gotten my letter and that afternoon I was processed out of the Army with an honorable discharge. I had served my three years and was finally going home. I had good memories of my service in the Army but it was time to move on.

Things had changed a lot in New York during the three years I was gone. For one, the music business had blown up. Hip-hop and rap music was a novelty when I left but was now big business. A lot of the friends I had worked with were now major players in the recording industry. Hurby Azor, who worked with us early on, was not only having huge success with Salt-N-Pepa and Dana Dane but was also producing a new rap duo named Kid 'n Play. Kid 'n Play (Chris & Chris) were a lot like Mal & Mal and not only made records but

Working in the studio

movies, too. All I could think was, "This should have been us!" Our friend Eric Sadler now called himself Eric "Vietnam" Sadler and was a member of a hit production team "The Bomb Squad". They were the producers for Public Enemy, Vanessa Williams, Bel Biv Devoe, Ice Cube, and so many more. When I met Eric he was living in his parents' house and now had a loft in Times Square. My buddy Daryl "Big Hig" Higgins little brother was in a group called The Leaders of the New School featuring a young rapper named Busta Rhymes. Seemed like my little break from the business may not have been the best choice after all. All of my friends in the business were living large and I was starting back at square one. Nonetheless, I was determined to get our group back together and work on a record.

Another thing that had changed in New York was illegal drugs. The mid-'80s was the height of the crack epidemic and it seemed like everyone was either using or dealing. Before I joined the Army powder cocaine was still considered a rich man's drug. It was expensive and usually done socially on the club scene. With the arrival of crack, the high society persona of powder cocaine quickly faded. Crack was also cheaper than powder and brought a whole new element to the game. This made my drug use even more secretive. Two of my close friends were now dealing part-time and since it was free I started getting high much more frequently. They still had regular jobs, but were selling coke to other friends to sustain our habit. The friends and co-workers they sold to were mostly white and too afraid to venture into the hood and get their own drugs. I went on some of these runs to pick up from their suppliers and these were some seedy-ass places. I could see why these white kids didn't want to get their own shit. This was a really reckless time in my life but at that moment I didn't realize the danger I was putting myself in.

The goal was still for Mal, Lindy, and me to get a recording contract. First, we needed to cut a demo tape that we could shop around to the record labels. Staying with my mom would pose some problems because she wasn't going to let me just work on songs all day without contributing to the bills. I had developed some high-end restaurant skills while working at the Waldorf Astoria and was ready to put them to use. With the training certificate they gave me I was sure to get a server position in a nice place, or so it would seem. I applied at the Garden City Hotel, a very expensive and classy place. A friend's girlfriend was working there and suggested I come in and apply. I got on my suit and tie, along with my freshly typed résumé and headed on over. I thought the interview went well and felt positive that they were going to offer me a position. After some waiting I was called back in and told that they had other candidates more experienced and would not be offering me the job. The following day I spoke with my friend's girlfriend who worked at the hotel. She told me that she had gone down to Human Resources and got a peek at my application. The interviewer had scribbled some notes in the margin that I felt were offensive. She had written, "Black but well-groomed". It took me back to the Waldorf when they asked if I had any other friends that looked like me. I would have called Al Sharpton, but didn't want to get my friend's girl in trouble for snooping, so I let it pass.

I continued to hit the pavement and eventually got hired at a familiar place from the past. I found myself back at Fortunoff's, the high-end department store I worked at temporarily before joining the Army. This time around I was hired to be a waiter in a small restaurant inside the store called Clara's Cafe. Although it was tiny they had a vast menu and were always packed with rich housewives. I enjoyed working there and was offered a promotion only months after starting. The general manager asked if I would like to be the restaurant manager. I jumped at the chance to learn the business

Waiting tables at Clara's Cafe

side of food service. As the manager I was expected to wear a suit and tie to work. I only had one suit and not a lot of money to buy new ones. I didn't want to lose this opportunity because of my limited closet so I came up with a plan. My friend Dave was dating a cute Puerto Rican girl whose mother was a professional booster. She looked like a rich white woman and used her wealthy appearance to shoplift in high-end stores. Everyone called her Go Go and she was going to be my ticket to a new wardrobe. Go Go didn't drive and would ask me and my friends to take her to the mall. Our job was to drop her off and leave the car parked with the trunk unlocked and then roam the mall for an hour or so while she did her thing. While I walked around she would steal expensive things and then make multiple trips to the car to unload. Her system was crazy! First she would steal a large designer handbag. She used her belt to remove the security tag from the clothes. Then whatever she stole got stuffed into the bag until it was full. She'd empty the bag at the car and make her way back for another load. Before heading to the store, she usually took orders so she wouldn't end up with things she couldn't get rid of. She was like a ghetto Amazon Prime. After a couple of hours we would meet back at the car and I'd drive her home. For my taxi skills she would pay me $100 cash, which was cool for a couple hours of window shopping at the mall. This time, however, I didn't want the money because I needed clothes. I gave her my measurements and Go Go snatched three designer suits, along with some shirts and ties for me.

Things didn't always go as planned and every once in a while she would get caught. She had quite a reputation in the department stores and was constantly on their radar. One time the store that caught her offered to let her go if she would agree to be a consultant and help them catch people like her. She refused, stating she could make more money stealing from them. She was great and had a lot of energy for an older lady, hence the name Go Go. She died some years later but I'll never forget her.

Now that I looked the part with my expensive attire, I was ready to learn all about restaurant management. The hours at the Cafe were morning till early afternoon, which gave me plenty of time to work on my music in the evenings. We also continued to attend the music industry parties, rubbing elbows with anyone who could possibly help propel our musical aspirations. Around that time Lindy started dating an up-and-coming music producer named Damon Dash. Damon lived in Harlem and was first cousins with actress Stacy Dash. He was a street-smart guy and very focused on being a success. He had two groups at the time along with an unknown solo rapper named Jay Z. We asked Damon to help us out and he let us use some of his recording time at Firehouse Studios. This was the first time we'd worked in a fully equipped recording studio with an engineer. The songs we did at Firehouse sounded really professional and we felt good about them.

Damon and Lindy's relationship grew and they had a son, Damon Jr. Mal and I spent a lot of time babysitting and were proud uncles. Unfortunately Lindy and Big Damon's relationship fell apart and the custody battles were brutal. This was even harder on Little Damon as he watched his parents fighting, with him stuck in the middle. Along with their relationship ending so did our free time in the studio. Damon and Jay Z went on to start Roc-A-Fella Records and the Rocawear clothing line, among other successful entrepreneurial ventures. Mal, Lindy, and I were becoming the Forrest Gumps of hip-hop!

Our group started working with a friend I had met while at George Jr. Republic. His name was Frank Franklin and he had come into some money, which he used to start a small record label and production company called LSR Records and Management. We had stayed in touch over the years and when I mentioned that I had a group he offered to help. He lived in Louisiana but was originally from Freeport where Mal lived. He flew up and listened to the demos we had cut in the studio with Damon. He liked what he heard and loved the concept of our group. He signed us to a contract where he would put up all the capital. His percentage was really high, but we were cool with it because studio time was expensive and no one else was showing any interest. He booked us into the studio we worked at years earlier in Hempstead with Eric Sadler. Eric was no longer there and it was run by another friend named Dave, aka B Hop. Public Enemy, who were really big now, still occupied the studio upstairs. We went there two to three days a week to work on our tracks. Some of the songs were good and some needed a lot of work. Aside from working in the studio, Frank also wanted us to get used to performing. He rented a hall in the neighboring town and put together a showcase that we would be featured on. Aside from us he had Chief Groovy Loo and the Chosen Tribe, Scoob Lover from Big Daddy Kane, Jay Z, a few other groups, and then us. This would be our chance to see how the general public would respond to our music and we were excited.

Mal and I did most of the work putting the venue together because Frank was back in Louisiana. He was scheduled to drive up the day before the showcase and put on the finishing touches. The night before the gig I got a call from Frank's family with some devastating news. On his drive up from Louisiana a drunk driver jumped the median and slammed head on into his car. He was critically injured and died on the scene. That night I not only lost a music producer but also a very good friend. This was awful and we questioned whether to still have the event. After speaking with Frank's family, we decided to still put on the showcase as a memorial in Frank's honor. We would donate all of the profits after expenses to his family. Mal and I decided not to perform but the event went well and the money helped his family with some of the burial expenses. Frank's passing was really hard and our future dreams of becoming rap stars died along with him. The music business was just too fickle and cutthroat for us. The ride was over and now I needed a new dream and didn't have a clue what that was going to be.

CHAPTER 25
THE MAGIC SHOP

The hours were long as the manager at Clara's Cafe and I wanted the flexibility I had back when I was just a server. I started looking and found a job at the Huntington Hilton, a really nice hotel in Suffolk County. I was hired as a breakfast and lunch waiter and did very well there. I worked from 5:30 a.m. - 1:00 p.m., Monday through Friday, which coincidently meant more free time to get in trouble. On the weekends me and my friends would hit the clubs. The majority of my time was spent running the streets getting drunk, high, and having sex. I was a mess and without music to keep me busy had nothing to strive for. I fell into depression and started screwing up at work. I was coming in late and hung over from the night before. I was treating the guests like shit and being confrontational with management. Everything was falling apart and I didn't know what the hell to do with my life. The Hilton got tired of my attitude and eventually let me go. Getting fired felt like the end of the world but turned out to be just the push I needed.

While I was at the Hilton my mother was dating a really nice guy named Hastin Dobson. He was from Jamaica and had a bright spirit about him. He owned several businesses in Brooklyn and had recently bought a home in Port Charlotte, Florida. My mother, now retired, spent a lot of time with him down South leaving me home alone. In hindsight, this was probably not the smartest thing, considering my lack of maturity and reckless lifestyle. In any event she trusted me and I was trying not to let her down. If you had just met me it looked like I really had my shit together. I had recently taken over the payments on my brother's BMW and was living alone in a beautiful home. In reality I was unemployed and dead broke with absolutely no direction. My friends took me out one night for some drinks, trying to cheer me up. That evening I met a very attractive girl named Karen Dean. She was an exotic mix of white, black, and American Indian. I was in the parking lot of the bar sitting in my BMW smoking a cigarette when she passed by with some girlfriends. Me and my boys started talking to them and she and I had a connection. She would later admit that seeing me in that BMW didn't hurt my chances. At the time I never let on that I was a no-job-having loser and one missed car payments away from the repo man. Karen and I started dating and I had to tell her about my being in between jobs. She was very supportive and took care of me until I could get back on my feet. Eventually I did get another job at a theme restaurant called 56th Fighter Group. It was on a private airstrip and was decorated like a World War II Army bunker. With a beautiful girl by my side and a new job I was slowly getting my mojo back. One day while watching television Karen asked me what I wanted to do with my life. I had never had anyone my age ask me that before and didn't know the answer. I was twenty-seven years old and still living at home. I had dropped out of college and had no concrete plans for the future. What did I want to do with my life? Then she asked the question that would make my destiny appear as if by magic. She said, "What did you want to be when you were a kid? Did you have any hobbies or interests?" Just like that I knew what I wanted to do. It hit me like an anvil and I said, "I wanted to be a magician." She asked me to bring over the Yellow Pages and she looked up all the listings under magic and novelty stores. She found a place that was close by called The Magic Shop in Hicksville and off we went. When we pulled up I could see some magic props artistically displayed in the glass storefront. All of a sudden my heart started racing. We went inside and I was in awe of how large this place was. There was a guy behind the counter that looked more like a biker then a magician. He was a skinny, long-haired, white guy with a black leather vest and his name was Dean. I told him I used to do some magic when I was a kid but had been away from the scene for a very long time.

He proceeded to show me something that blew me away. He took a small, red silk handkerchief and made it come to life. It danced all around his hands with no visible means of support. When it stopped dancing he handed it to me and it was just a plain handkerchief with absolutely nothing fishy about it. I had to have that trick and he said it was $40. I was pretty broke so Karen offered to put it on her credit card for me. I appreciated her generosity and was very gracious. As soon as I got to the car I ripped the box open to learn the secret of this wonderful mystery. The gimmick was like something out of a James Bond movie and worth every penny. It wasn't easy to do and was gonna take a lot of practice to learn but I was determined to master this dancing handkerchief trick.

For the next several months after all my bills were paid I took any extra cash to The Magic Shop. I bought books, tricks, and supplies in hopes of building a show. I was there almost three days a week just hanging out and listening to the staff and visiting magicians. I knew this was what I was searching for and exactly where I needed to be. I became so obsessed with magic that it took all of my time and I started to neglect my relationship with Karen. Although she respected my drive, the lack of attention ultimately killed us and she left me. I couldn't fault her and knew deep down it was for the best. Magic was my only relationship now and I was in love!

When I was a kid I saw a magician on television who did an act with birds. He was from Japan and his name was Shimada. He made birds appear and disappear like a real wizard. I had no idea how any of this was done and began to research this style of magic. I bought *The Encyclopedia of Dove Magic* by Benny Chavez, which detailed everything on the subject. This opened me up to all the secret apparatus and methods of the dove magician. I learned a few tricks but needed to find some doves to try them out. At The Magic Shop I asked Dean where I could buy some of the white doves that I saw Shimada use. He referred me to a guy named Bill White, who raised doves at his home not too far from the shop. I called and introduced myself and told him I was in the market for some doves. He invited me over and in his basement he had a huge chicken-wire aviary filled with white Java doves. They were absolutely breathtaking and had an elegance to them as they flew around the cage. He said I could have a couple and wouldn't charge me a dime. All I had to do was promise to follow his express instructions and I could have them. First he made a list of seed needed to make the special diet blend they lived on, along with some vitamins and sand grit. Next I had to promise to never do any outdoor shows with the birds. He said if one got away it wouldn't have the natural ability to survive on its own. Lastly, he said that they were pets and should be given all the love and care that I would a dog or cat. I swore to uphold all of those rules and left Bill's home with my first two doves. I did everything he told me and trained these doves to be in my new act.

Everything was going good with work and magic practice, but my family was going through some issues, mainly my brother. He had graduated from pharmacy school at Northeastern University and took a job with People's Pharmacy in Northern Virginia. We thought with all the success he was doing well. He had a large salary in a great profession and was the ultimate bachelor. He had always stayed in touch and came home to New York quite regularly but we started to hear from him less and less, which was not typical. My mother had an idea what was wrong but never explained to him or me what she thought the problem was. She told me that I needed to take off from work and drive her to Virginia for an unannounced visit to check in on him. We made the drive to my brother's new condo and when he answered the door I could tell in an instant something was off. He was in desperate need of a haircut and looked really skinny, as if he wasn't eating regularly. He had a beautiful condominium but didn't have any furniture, with the exception of a bed and a couple nightstands. His living room, dining room, and extra bedroom were bare. Even more bizarre, in the middle of his bedroom floor was a pile of unopened mail. Upon further inspection we noticed they were mostly unpaid bills. I couldn't understand why he hadn't paid his bills, considering he was making more money than my mother's pension and mine combined. He showed all the signs of someone in deep depression and from what I could see, he had nothing to be depressed about. We stayed a few days and got him to eat and pay some of the overdue bills. We looked at his bank statement and he had a ton of money in his account but just wasn't motivated to pay his bills. My mother knew that Andre was suffering from the same bipolar ailment my father had. She never said a word, as if it was some horrible family secret that needed to be kept in the dark. Seeing how Andre was living I offered to relocate to Virginia and help out. I thought about what I had going on in New York and for the most part it was mostly negative. I knew that leaving my current situation of drugs and bullshit would be a good thing. I had nothing to hold me in New York and could pursue my aspirations of becoming a magician anywhere and Virginia was as good a place as any. Upon returning home I put in my two weeks' notice and packed my things. I looked forward to starting a new chapter, in a new state, with a new attitude.

My brother had bought his condo pre-construction. It was built to order and had all the modern upgrades. There were cathedral ceilings, huge walk-in closets, a double shower, and even a remote-controlled gas fireplace. This was a great bachelor pad! As soon as I got myself settled, my brother gave me his credit card and I went shopping for furniture. I purchased some leather sofas, modern lamps, a dining room set, throw rugs, and some artwork. It felt like the more furniture we got, the more Andre's spirit seemed to brighten up. I began to think he got depressed because he was away from friends and family and my being there gave him the spark he needed to snap out of it. Soon we were going out to nice dinners and barhopping like the single young men we were. Things were looking up!

I needed a job and hit the ground running. The place where I ended up working was called the Monocle, which was a family-owned, fine-dining restaurant on Capitol Hill. The Monocle was the only privately owned restaurant on Federal property in the US. They had purchased the building before the Senate parking lot was there so the government ended up building around them. It was owned by a nice Greek family named Valonos. I interviewed with the maître d', Nick Selimos. Nick was a tall, thin guy with dark hair and olive skin. He spoke with a thick Greek accent and was a real character. He knew all the customers by name and treated everyone as though he was there just for them. Very knowledgeable about the business and a pretty funny guy. I don't know if it's a Greek thing or not, but he also had a quick temper. On a good note, Nick's bark was way worse than his bite and he never stayed mad. The Monocle had been around for over thirty years when I worked there and was a haven for all the big shots on The Hill. From the Senate to the House and the Lobbyists to the Supreme Court. Everyday I waited on these heavy hitters and got to know them on a personal basis. I'd see Ted Kennedy, Bob Dole, Diane Feinstein, Orrin Hatch, Dan Rostenkowski, Justice William Rehnquist, and even Clarence Thomas on a daily basis. We were a union house and the waiters had been there forever. I was the newest and youngest and learned a lot from these career waiters.

One of the bartenders had developed diabetes and I started filling in for him. I didn't know a lot about bartending, but this was Capitol Hill and there were no foo foo drinks or blenders to deal with. Everyone drank wine, martinis, straight liquor, or basic mixed drinks. One night when it was slow I started doing some tricks for John Valanos, while working behind the bar. He really dug what I did and started bringing guests over and asking me to show them. Eventually word got around and I was doing magic behind the bar on the regular. This was a good training ground for me and helped to build confidence and a performing persona. As soon as someone sat down I'd be secretly setting them up for a miracle. I'd sneak things under their cocktail napkins to be revealed moments later as though it was impromptu. It was so cool having such control and being one step ahead of the spectators. Another perk was all the extra tips since I was offering more than just libations. My signature trick was the classic "Card on Ceiling". I would spot an attractive, single girl as well as a good-looking, single guy sitting at my bar. After doing a few tricks to get warmed up I'd bring everyone's attention to the single guy and girl. In a joking way I would ask the guy if he'd like to get the young lady's phone number and what would it be worth to him? Then I would bring out a deck of cards and ask the girl to pick one and put her name and number on it. Next I would tell the guy he could have the number but it would cost him and then ask for the largest bill he had. Nine times out of ten I'd get a $100 bill. I would have him sign his name on the bill in order to recognize it later. Once this was done I'd get the chosen card back from the young lady and lose it in the deck. To make sure I couldn't manipulate the cards I wrapped two rubber bands around the deck. I retrieved the bill from the guy and wrapped that around the bound deck, completing the package. I grabbed a thumbtack from under the bar and threw everything into the air. The only thing that came down was the deck, still wrapped in the rubber bands but no bill or thumbtack. I'd gesture to the ceiling and when everyone looked up they saw the signed card with phone number and autographed bill stuck to the ceiling with a single thumbtack. They had just witnessed something incredible and the response was always sustained applause. Now, for the best part. After witnessing this feat of magic I would tell the guy I needed to get a ladder to retrieve his bill. More times than not he would tell me to just keep it. At the end of my shift I'd get the ladder and take down all my extra tips. This worked great and was the most requested of all the tricks I did behind the bar.

The Monocle also did a lot of private functions in their banquet room and John would sometimes offer my magical services to his clients. This exposure in front of a real audience was invaluable to my development as an entertainer. The Monocle was right on time and exactly what I needed. I read in a motivational book once that "If you want to be a millionaire, you need to surround yourself with people who have millions." I never forgot that and began searching for a mentor who could help me get to the next level.

CHAPTER 26
PATISSIER

Although my job at the Monocle was good I still needed to make more money. Washington DC was full of luxury hotels and restaurants for me to pick from. I applied and was hired at the Ritz Carlton Hotel in Pentagon City. The dining room was beautiful and the epitome of class and elegance. My training was very extensive and lent itself well to my detail-oriented personality. I thrived and quickly became one of their top earners. The kitchen was large and had a lot of different cooks and chefs. There was the chef de cuisine, sous chef, saucier, garde manger, and my favorite, the patissier or pastry chef. The reason the latter was my favorite had less to do with the type of food they made and more to do with one of the pastry chefs who made it. This pastry chef was Kecia Reyes and I had a crush on her from the moment I picked up my first dessert. She was a mix of Filipino, Spanish, and American Indian. This hodgepodge of ethnicities gave her a look that was easy on the eyes. She was smart, too, and a graduate of the CIA, the Culinary Institute of America in New York. I didn't know how to approach her because she always seemed so serious and rarely smiled. For some reason I felt there wasn't a chance in hell she would be interested in someone like me. One of her girlfriends who worked in the kitchen noticed I was always staring and asked why I didn't just ask her out. I never had a problem approaching women before but she was different. I felt intimidated when I was around her and could never muster the courage to speak. Well, this went on for months and then I heard she was going to be moving to New York. Right then I realized that my chances of dating her were finished. The kitchen staff planned a going-away party for her at one of the local restaurants and we were all invited. Up to this point the only words I had ever uttered to her were a cordial "hello" in passing or when I placed a dessert order. Even though we barely knew each other I attended the party anyway. Some of my co-workers who knew I was an aspiring magician asked if I would do something. I hated being put on the spot like that but everyone was looking at me and I couldn't back out. I did a few sleight-of-hand tricks and used Kecia for the final effect. This was the longest we'd ever stood face to face and I felt a spark between us. After I finished we started talking about my magic and also her upcoming move to New York. She told me that her girlfriend mentioned I was always checking her out and asked why it took me so long to speak. I could have kicked myself for procrastinating because now she was moving and I was too late. We ended up talking for the rest of the party and then I asked her to dinner the following night. To my surprise she accepted and I looked forward to being around her even if it was only for a short time.

The date went better than I could have anticipated and neither of us wanted it to end. We had more in common than I would have guessed. She had lived in New York before, we enjoyed the arts, and both loved jazz. With only a couple days until her move, we went on another date to Blues Alley, a jazz club in Georgetown. We ate, drank, talked, and laughed the entire night. I knew it was idiotic to fall for someone who was about to move but couldn't help myself. At the end of the date we walked to our cars and kissed for the first time. There was something special happening and I didn't want her to leave and unbeknownst to me she was feeling the same way. The next day she called and told me that she decided to put off her move to New York. She was curious to see where our friendship would go and I couldn't have been happier.

I was still living with my brother in Alexandria and Kecia lived with her mother in Rockville, Maryland. This was a fairly long ride, so as our relationship evolved she began to stay over at my place. At first, my brother was cool with it but after a while he started expressing his displeasure with our cohabitation. We weren't disrespectful and he seemed to like her but for whatever reason he suggested that maybe we should get our own place. He didn't have to tell me twice and the following week we moved in together. This was the first time I'd ever lived with a woman aside from my mother and there was a slight learning curve. We were both pretty clean and organized so that was easy. The hard part was learning to be financially responsible like she was. I had never been very good with money and had horrible credit. I had defaulted on student loans, and incurred a court judgment from an unpaid hospital bill years earlier. Kecia told me that if I didn't get my money issues together we couldn't be together. At first I thought it was wrong for her to think that way, but after further consideration, I realized I wouldn't want to carry my partner, either. From that point forward I began to work on repairing my credit. I called the hospital and made a settlement payment to satisfy the judgment. I worked out an affordable payment plan with the student loan people. Slowly my credit was getting better and I owed it all to Kecia. She bought a computer and I began to use it to market my magic shows. The World Wide Web was still pretty new and we had the standard dial-up connection. This was really slow but I was learning new skills to build my business.

With Kecia at my side I began to focus attention back on my magic. I found two magic shops that were close by, Al's in DC and Barry's in Wheaton, Maryland. I frequented both regularly and bought a ton of tricks and props for my show. Al was known as the World's Greatest Demonstrator. He had a way of performing a trick that made you have to have it. There was nothing he couldn't do and I learned a lot watching him work. Barry's shop was nice, too, and he always had the newest tricks and books. Barry and I became good friends and I would sometimes tag along when he performed locally. It was awesome to see a real magician performing up close and personal. Once he got a call from the Xerox corporation asking if it was possible to customize a trick designed to fool their senior engineers. Barry needed a crew to pull it off and asked me to help out. Xerox was a sponsor of that year's Olympic Games and wanted something really specific for their two-night event at the annual convention.

The first night they wanted us to levitate a three-foot-wide basketball right over the heads of the audience. It would then float to the stage where it would bounce off into the wings. The following night we needed to float another three-foot ball but this time the ball was all-white. This one had to float from the back of the theater to the stage where it would land on a large Roman column. Then they would project an image of the world revolving onto it as a voice-over said, "Xerox, taking over the world."

We had no idea how we were going to do this but acted like we did. Because we had never done this before we way underpriced ourselves. I think we asked for $3,500 but didn't anticipate how much work or money it would take to accomplish. We had to pay for research and development, supplies, and a four-man crew to operate it. I think we all walked with a little over $500 each for two weeks of practice and two nights onstage. If that wasn't enough the illusion never completely worked in rehearsals. There's a show business saying that goes, "Bad rehearsal, good show!" Luckily it worked flawlessly when it counted and the two nights of performances were a success.

Meanwhile the dove act I'd been working on desperately needed a finish. The most popular finalé for bird magic was "The Vanishing Dove Cage". I believe the inventor was magician/actor Channing Pollock and he used it to close his legendary act. Picture a large metal cage filled with doves sitting on a table. The magician covers the cage with a large cloth. He lifts the covered cage off the table and then tosses the entire thing into the air. The cage and doves instantly disappear, leaving just the cloth that flutters to the floor. I needed that trick in my show. I started asking Barry about it and he looked in some of the magic catalogs to see how much they cost. I couldn't believe when he said they were around $1,500. Then he told me about a professional magician who had semi-retired from performing and converted his rehearsal studio into a magic shop. He suggested I give him a call and see if he had what I was looking for. Following up on Barry's suggestion I called the Denny & Lee Magic Studio in Baltimore and spoke with the owner, Denny Haney.

Denny had quite the career in magic. There is a prestigious course for magicians called The Chavez School of Manuel Dexterity. Its graduates are some of the most respected and famous magicians of

Denny Haney

the past fifty years. Denny was the youngest graduate to ever complete that course. He later became a linguist in the United States Army and went to Vietnam, where he fell in love with their customs and culture. There he met and married a beautiful Vietnamese woman named Lee. After his tour he and Lee came back to the States and put together a very successful illusion act they called The Denny & Lee Show. After a decade of performing as a team they divorced. Denny searched for a replacement and hired another Vietnamese girl named Mihn. Mihn toured with him for over sixteen years before he retired the big show. At one time Denny was doing over 200 shows a year in the college and corporate markets. He decided that he wanted to give back to the magic community and that's when he opened the magic shop. Everyone from Michael Jackson to David Copperfield has shopped at his magic studio. Hands down, Denny is one of the most knowledgeable magicians alive.

I called Denny's shop and asked if he had a Vanishing Dove Cage. To my excitement he did and although it was a less sophisticated model then the one in the catalog, he said it would be good for a beginner like myself. Best part, it was only $400, and that I could afford. He gave me directions to the shop and I made plans to go by later that evening to check it out. Denny's shop was over an hour's drive and

I was so excited about seeing the trick I could barely contain myself. I finally pulled up and saw the big sign in front of the shop. The logo was a white rabbit peeking out of a black top hat and the sign read The Denny & Lee Magic Studio. There was no way to prepare for what I was about to encounter, and upon opening the door was shocked at what I saw. There was glass showcase to the right of the entrance and on top was a paper plate with a huge serving of spaghetti and meatballs. Standing on a chair directly over the plate was a large white man with his back to me. His pants were down to his knees and in the crack of his hairy ass was a small plastic fork, which he was maneuvering over the pasta in an attempt to spear a meatball. All I could think was what kind of people did Barry send me to? Should I turn and leave before they tie me up? I collected my thoughts for a second and decided I wanted that cage too much to walk away, regardless of how crazy these white folks were. Denny introduced himself and invited me in as if nothing strange was going on. After some uncomfortable silence they explained what the deal was. The guy with his ass out was Steve Myers and he worked at the shop. They had bet him that he couldn't pick up a meatball using just his ass and a fork. That explanation didn't make me feel any more comfortable but they seemed nice enough, so I stayed.

Denny asked what kind of magic I did and then showed me some of what he was known for. He took a deck of cards and made beautiful fans with them. Then the cards disappeared and reappeared one at a time at his fingertips. He showed both sides of his hands empty, but continued to produce more cards. Then he grabbed some billiard balls and did a bunch of flourishes, which showcased his dexterity. He made these balls multiply from one, to two, to three, and finally four right in front of my nose. He was like Merlin and I was in awe. He told me the style of magic he specialized in was called manipulation and everything he had just showed me was in the books. He stressed how books were the best way to learn magic. Next he showed me what I had come for, the Vanishing Dove Cage. After demonstrating how it worked I bought it and also grabbed some of the books he suggested. I hung for a while and then headed home. Denny's shop was strictly for professionals and I would make that drive once a month to hang with Denny and soak up as much knowledge as I could.

While working on my act, I would occasionally ask Kecia to watch me practice. She had a good eye and would let me know if I was exposing any of the secrets. She would tell me what she liked and what she didn't like. She would help me so much that I eventually asked her to join me and we became a duo like Denny & Lee except we were Puck & Kecia and not nearly as good. Putting a show together by yourself is hard but as a team became more fun. She looked great

Puck & Kecia

and best of all took it seriously. We developed an eleven-minute dove act, done completely in pantomime to a jazz soundtrack. The act was raw but it felt like we were heading in the right direction. I would film our practices and then show them to Denny who would critique them and give us notes. This was invaluable and we appreciated his expert opinion.

We wanted a more original finish for the dove act other than just the "Vanishing Dove Cage". I decided that we would get a large parrot to add to the finalé. I did a lot of research about everything parrots, from their habits and diet to their temperament. I concluded the perfect bird for us would be a cockatoo. I checked with some of the local pet stores but none of them sold these large birds. Once again I got out the Yellow Pages and found an aviary that raised cockatoos a couple hours' drive in Salisbury, Maryland. We got to the shop and met the owner who began to educate us about cockatoos. She told us that having a cockatoo would take a lot of work and was kinda like raising a child. They are super smart and garnered a lot of attention. In fact if they don't receive enough attention they can get depressed and self-mutilate by pulling out their feathers. Kecia and I had a brief conference and decided it was worth the commitment. As we were walking through the aviary one of the birds jumped from his

Hoppy

perch and landed on my shoulder. I didn't realize how big they were and was a little intimidated. Then the bird started giving me kisses and that was that. She said this particular bird was a boy and his name was Hoppy. I asked why the crazy name and she told me to put him on the floor. When I did he started hopping around like a bunny rabbit and my question was quickly answered. Hoppy was a six-month-old sulfur-crested cockatoo and looked just like the one on that TV show Baretta. He was all-white with a beautiful bright yellow crest. Cockatoos usually live to be anywhere between 60 and 100 years old, so there was a good chance he'd be doing the show without me one day. Hoppy and I became fast friends and I was looking forward to putting him in the show.

CHAPTER 27
CHILDREN'S INN

I had befriended a fellow black magician named Rahaan Jackson at a magic convention in Washington DC. He called one day and told me that Denny's long-time assistant was going to be performing his own show in Atlantic City and Denny was in the market for a new helper. He wanted to do it but didn't have a car and suggested I give him a call. Denny was now semi-retired and only did a few gigs a year. I asked about the position and he told me to come by the shop later that night. When I got to the shop he took me to the basement for an audition. I had to help him lift his daughter Dawn then lay her down and balance her on the tips of three vertical swords. Once she was balanced, we both let go and she stayed there all by herself completely suspended. I won't divulge the secret but this illusion is usually done with three men. The fact he did it with only two made this even more difficult and impressive. I must have passed the test because the following morning at 6:00 a.m. I left for my first gig with The Denny & Lee Show.

The next morning I met Denny and his female assistant, Mihn, at the shop. We had a long drive to the venue and I utilized that time to learn the show. He explained everything I would be responsible for and to be honest I felt a bit overwhelmed. A lot of what he said fell on deaf ears because I had never seen his show and wasn't very knowledgeable about magic. This made me very nervous and my inexperience showed. I asked a lot of questions and was afraid of

Assisting Denny

being perceived as annoying. Denny and Mihn were very patient with me and that helped some. To say I did a great job would be stretching it and in fact it was just the opposite. I thought for sure this would be my last performance with Denny. During the program I broke one of the swords used for the Sword Suspension Illusion we'd rehearsed in his basement the night before. It broke clean off the handle right in front of the audience. As if that wasn't enough when a leg fell off of a table onstage I tried to run out and fix it not knowing it was part of the show. On the ride home, Denny assured me that I had done well and he would continue to use me if I still wanted the job. My formal education in the art of magic and show business began that night with The Denny & Lee Show. Denny told me that show business is only about 20% show and 80% business. A mediocre act with good business and marketing skills can get gigs. Keep in mind, though, to get repeat business and referrals you do need to have a decent show. Every show we did gave me another opportunity to pick Denny's brain. He pointed me in the right direction and suggested magic books and biographies for me to read. Denny always had the audience in the palm of his hand and knew how to equally mix humor and magic. Every stage performer seeks a standing ovation to validate their performance. I watched night after night as Denny received unsolicited, full-house, standing ovations. I wanted this kind of audience admiration and appreciation for myself. I was learning the craft from one of the best and with hard work hoped my day would eventually come.

Denny was one of the most unique people I ever had the honor to spend time with. First off he's the whitest guy I'd ever met. I would say that he was so white you could see his heart light. This is an *ET* reference for those of you old enough to remember that movie. Political correctness had no place in his world. He chain-smoked non-filter Pall Mall cigarettes, farted in public, and no subject matter was off limits. I really enjoyed his sick sense of humor while we were on the road and was very lucky to be one of his assistants. When I started doing some small shows I emulated a lot of what I saw him do before eventually coming into my own. If I'm being honest I still do a few routines in the "Denny style" but now consider it more of a tribute to my friend and mentor.

I felt my dove act was decent enough for the public to see it. Since I had no experience or name for myself it was difficult finding places to work. I asked Denny for some advice and he suggested I solicit old folks' homes and hospitals to hone the act. I would offer my show as a donation and receive some much-needed performing experience. Since I wasn't charging a fee the establishment and audiences would be very appreciative, which always made for a receptive crowd.

The first place we worked was The National Institutes of Health, Children's Inn. This was a wonderful place for kids with terminal cancer. At The Children's Inn terminally ill kids were showered with games, food, and entertainment to help ease the last weeks and months of their lives. To open the show, Kecia and I performed the new bird act. During the performance one of the doves flew up really high and landed on a light fixture over forty feet above us. I just ignored it and kept performing. We did several illusions but I noticed that no one was watching because all their attention was on the dove that flew away. At one point, some of the kids were heaving pillows up in the air in an attempt to spook the dove into flying back to the ground. When we finally finished with the show our dove made his way back down as if he knew the performance was over. Everyone cheered for us and although it wasn't perfect made us feel really good. All the kids were coming up to us as we packed up. They were so full of joy and gave us lots of kind words and hugs. As we drove off it hit me and that's when I broke down. I was sobbing uncontrollably thinking about those wonderful children and how they had been dealt such a horrible hand. Knowing we added a little excitement in their short lives should have felt good but sadness for them was all I could feel.

Next show was at a hospital for children with pediatric AIDS. Again these were terminally ill kids who needed to be distracted from their treatments and failing health. The day of the show I received a call asking if we used any animals in our act. I told them we had birds and they asked if we could leave them at home. They also had us wear surgical masks as we performed. These kids were highly susceptible to bacteria and we had to be very careful not to make them sicker. One routine we did that day really sticks out in my mind. I performed the "20th-Century Silks", where I would tie two blue silk handkerchiefs together with a knot. Then I'd place the knot down a young boy's shirt, leaving just the ends hanging out in full view. Next I'd take a red silk and make it vanish in a cloth bag. For the finale I would grab the end of each blue silk and pull them out of the kid's shirt, revealing the red silk had reappeared tied between the two blue ones. The reason this trick really stayed with me was because of the kid I used. As I was placing the blue silks in his shirt I noticed he had open lesions all over his neck and chest. At first glance I was reluctant to touch him. Then I said to myself that this is a beautiful, innocent child. I didn't want him to feel like he was different so I placed the silks down his shirt without hesitation. The look of surprise on his face as the red silk reappeared from down his shirt was priceless. He hugged me before rejoining the rest of the group and I never forgot that. I still do the "20th-Century Silks" in my show and the memory of that young boy is always fresh in my mind.

We also performed at a retirement home for the old folks. In the dove act I did several tricks with lit candles. I made them appear, disappear, and multiply all throughout that act. The candles must have let off too much smoke because halfway through the show a fire alarm went off and the building had to be evacuated. Talk about a showstopper! When we were finally cleared to return, Kecia and I continued where we left off. When we made Hoppy appear at the end of the dove act, you could hear the audible gasps from the crowd. As we were packing up, a woman asked if she could pet Hoppy. I brought him out and she quickly took him from me and started stroking his feathers. She said that she had a parrot when she was younger and this brought back some great memories. When she was finished another resident asked to hold him. This continued for almost an hour and became more like a petting zoo then a magic show. I didn't mind and Hoppy was loving all the extra attention. It was nice to give those folks some well-deserved enjoyment in their old age.

We did a lot of free shows and were gaining more and more confidence with each performance. We felt like it was time to start making some money, but wanted to try one more thing before we did. Denny was really well-known amongst magicians and was often invited to perform at their conventions. Magic conventions featured some of the most talented and well-known acts in the world. They usually had a magic contest with a cash prize and that really interested us. We wanted to make a name for ourselves and gain some marketable credits in the process. This was a lot harder than we thought because there were a lot of talented magicians in these competitions. We entered a few and found out that getting first place wasn't the only prize to be won.

CHAPTER 28
WATERGATE

There was a big magic convention held annually in Washington, DC called The World Magic Summit and was sponsored by three magic shops. This was the place to be for anyone who loved magic. They had lectures, social mixers, shows, contests, and my favorite, the dealers room. I could spend the entire day in the dealers room alone. That room featured magic shops from around the world showcasing all the latest effects. Dealers would demonstrate the newest magic to reel you in and the only way to learn the secret was to purchase it. They even had a saying, "The secret is told when the trick is sold!"

Magic conventions exposed me to all styles of magic. I saw close-up guys, comedy magicians, escape artists, mentalists, and grand illusionists. I gained an appreciation for all genres of prestidigitation. I also got to meet a lot of the magicians I'd watched on television, which was exciting, too. I made many lifelong friends at these gatherings. One friendship was with an owner of the convention, Nick Ruggerio. He was also co-owner of Collectors Workshop, a manufacturer of fine magical apparatus. When he was younger, Nick was an assistant to the famous Harry Blackstone Sr. As one of the owners of this large convention he put me on the list to compete in the stage competition. This wasn't like most magic contests where anyone could join. You had to send in a tape of your act and be selected by a panel and then be invited to compete. Being a friend of Nick got us a spot that most likely wouldn't have been offered had we not known him. One day while watching our practice, Nick gave me some valuable advice. I always looked really serious and nervous while performing. I guess it had to do with concentrating too hard on not screwing up. Nick told me I should look like I was enjoying myself. He said the audience doesn't want you to fail and failure only makes them uncomfortable. They want you to win and with that advice I worked to keep a smile on my face, even if I screwed up.

We practiced day and night for the upcoming contest. We had the birds trained and the act seemed to be getting tighter. That year there were six other stage acts in the competition. When they introduced us I remembered Nick's words and put a big-ass smile on my face and tried to enjoy every minute of the eleven we spent onstage. At the end the audience gave us a huge ovation and I felt pretty good about our performance. Later that night, before the evening show, they announced the winners of the contests. When they got to the stage magic category I could feel my heart beating out of my chest. They said the winner of first place was Puck & Kecia and everyone started cheering. We had been recognized for all the hard work we put in and it felt great. After winning, we got several offers to work other magic conventions as a featured act. We also got plenty of valuable constructive criticism, which we welcomed. Committing to the competition gave us the motivation we needed to work harder on the act. We had set a realistic, short-term, obtainable goal and were better for it.

By now I had moved from the Ritz Carlton to the Four Seasons Hotel in Georgetown. This was another fine dining establishment, where I was a server for breakfast and lunch. This was the only four-star, five-diamond hotel in the area and attracted the rich and famous. For instance, King Hussein of Jordan literally lived in the hotel. Secretary of State Warren Christopher was there every Sunday. Larry King came in a couple times a week. It was a who's who from Hollywood to Capitol Hill. I served Bill Clinton, James Caan, Danny Glover, Anthony Hopkins, Whitney Houston, Denzel Washington, Chris Rock, Richard Gere, Meg Ryan, Bruce Willis, Lou Rawls, and many more too numerous to mention. I had a lot of stories working there and was even approached by a publisher, asking if I'd be interested in putting them into a book. I declined the offer and always wondered if I'd made the right choice.

One of our regular customers was a young girl who would come in with who I believe was her mother and grandmother. They lived at the famous Watergate, which was around the corner. I could tell they had money but lacked any sophistication or class. One morning I actually caught the grandmother shoving fat-free apple muffins into her purse. Well on this particular visit the young girl called me back to the table after I'd dropped the check. She began to read me the riot act over the high price of sparkling water. After complaining, she suggested if I wanted a tip to delete the expensive water from the check and use the balance as my gratuity. For Christ's sakes, this was the freakin' Four Seasons and everything was expensive. She's lucky I needed the job or I would have shown her my street side. Her final words before parting were, "You'll see me again, I come here all the time". Then she jumped on her broom and was gone.

About a month later I was taking an order for Jon Ledecky, founder of US Office Products and Senator Bill Bradley. From behind, I received a tap on my shoulder and turned to find it was none other than that trashy girl from the Watergate. She wanted to let me know she was in the building and reiterated her parting statement from our previous meeting: "I come here all the time," and then walked away. Jon Ledecky who I'd known for several years asked, "Who the hell was that?" Well, turns out, her name was Monica Lewinsky and this was before the whole cigar and blue dress incident. This chick had balls and seemed to have it out for me. Later that year I saw the news about President Clinton's transgressions and when they showed the girl he had been involved with I couldn't believe my eyes. It was that mean-ass girl from the Watergate. I wish I could say that I never saw her again but she continued to come in. She showed up several times after the news was out, which made some of the regulars uneasy. Vernon Jordan, who was President Clinton's best friend at the time was also a regular. I remember him leaving one time without even finishing his meal upon her arrival. This chick was bad news and in my opinion deserved all the insults and bad press she received.

Magic was still my part-time gig while The Four Seasons was my main source of income. After our win at the magic convention we were invited to perform at Monday Night Magic in New York City. This was a weekly show that featured magicians, jugglers, and other variety artists. It started at The Sullivan Street Playhouse in The Village on Monday nights. The other days of the week the Sullivan Street was home to *The Fantasticks*, the longest running off-Broadway musical ever.

We drove to Manhattan and stayed at the Pierre Hotel, across from Central Park. The Pierre was a Four Sea-

The bird act

sons Hotel and since I was an employee of the company, everything was comped. This really helped out considering Monday Night Magic paid close to nothing. It was more of a labor of love and the exposure and camaraderie were our paycheck. The Sullivan Street was an extremely small theater and not conducive to an angle-sensitive act like ours. Everything that could have gone wrong that night did. First off, our music didn't start when we were introduced. Music was an intricate part of the act because we performed in pantomime and didn't speak. I looked at our minidisc music player and could see that the audio cord had become unplugged from the house system. I bent over to plug it back in which turned out to be a huge mistake. As I bent over, one of the doves fell out of its secret hiding place and landed on the floor right in front of everyone. I quickly plugged the cord in and grabbed the bird, placing him back and then soldiered on with the act. It was humiliating and all I wanted to do was pack up and go home. Everyone told me that it happens to the best but I knew we'd blown it. That was a painful lesson and made for a long, silent ride back home to Maryland. We needed a lot more practice if we were going to go full-time. For the next year that's exactly what we did. PRACTICE!

CHAPTER 29
HYPNOTIST

One day I received a call from a guy named Curtis Carroll who said he'd gotten my number from Denny. He had just moved to the area from Seattle and was looking for someone to help in an illusion show he was putting together. I was a little put off that Denny would loan me out to another magician but I figured there had to be a good reason. He asked if we could meet at his warehouse in Annapolis so he could show me the props and talk about my helping out. I agreed to meet and we made plans for the following weekend. Before we met, I called Denny to ask who this guy was as I'd never heard of him. Denny said he was a full-time performer and worked mostly cruise ships. Denny knew I wanted to work on ships one day and said the best way to learn would be to work with Curtis. I got to the warehouse and we met outside. He was a heavy-set, white man pushing at least 350 pounds. We went inside and he showed me all the props and illusions he had recently purchased. We sat around and he told me all about his show-business accomplishments. He had made his career performing as a comedy magician and also as a hypnotist. His stage name was "Alexander" which was his middle name and his show was tagged "Alexander, America's Funniest Hypnotist." He mentioned that he had recently gotten married and moved to Maryland, where his new bride lived. He told me that the majority of his gigs were on luxury cruise ships and he had made a lot of money on the high seas. His goal was to put together a big illusion show and market it strictly to Fortune 500 companies. The more time we spent talking, the more I liked him. He was very warm and we seemed to hit it off. When we parted he gave me a really big hug. This wasn't one of those pat you on the back, homeboy kind of hugs but a real genuine embrace. Then he gave me a key to his warehouse and said if I needed to use anything there to just let myself in and take it. To have that kind of trust on a first meet-

ALEXANDER

AMERICA'S FUNNIEST HYPNOTIST

Curtis "Alexander" Carroll

ing was crazy to me. That was just the kind of person he was and our friendship blossomed from there.

Aside from getting the key to the warehouse, Curtis offered to get me and Kecia on cruise ships. He said this without even seeing our act. We could have really sucked and truthfully we pretty much did at the time. I knew we had potential, but felt we lacked the real-world experience needed to compete in the cruise market. Curtis's offer started a fire in us and we had to make sure we would be ready should the call come. Aside from working on the act we started purchasing road cases for all the props. Curtis got us a gig at his Elks Lodge to perform the show we would do should we get a chance to work on a ship. We did well, which made him feel better about his endorsement. Curtis was working exclusively for Princess Cruise Lines and had a good relationship with the booker. As promised, he made the call and we were offered a six-week contract on The Sun Princess, sailing the Panama Canal. We had a lot of preparation to do with very little time. First we spoke with our jobs and got the time off. Next we needed passports and a shitload of paperwork to bring the birds with us. We had seven doves, five parakeets, and Hoppy. There was Fish and Wildlife, Department of Agriculture, Health

Certificates, and CITES permits to acquire. Luckily we lived close to DC where all the government offices were located. After a week of running around, we boarded a plane for Los Angeles and joined our first cruise ship as guest entertainers. We had to perform the same 45-minute show twice in the same evening one night per week. After watching some of the other performers' shows I felt like we were in a little over our heads. Our show went OK but didn't have the polish or power of the other acts. They didn't kick us off and allowed us to finish the six weeks, so I guess we weren't too bad. We made some great friends and received lots of advice and critiques, which really helped. On the downside, there were some problems starting to arise in my working relationship with Kecia. She was upset with the lack of recognition she received from the guests. She didn't want to just be my assistant, she wanted to be my partner. In most of the illusions she did the majority of the work but it was hidden in order to maintain the secret. She also did multiple costume changes and a lot of things behind the scenes while I received all the applause and praise. After the show some of the guests would give me compliments or ask to take pictures and never include Kecia. This really pissed her off and in private she was very vocal about it. We would get in huge arguments in our cabin and then be forced to act like the perfect couple while out and about the ship. It was putting a strain on our relationship, so I decided to create some solo routines just for her. This seemed to make her happy and made working together much better. We learned a lot on that contract and were ready to turn those six weeks into a career performing at sea.

Upon returning, we went back to our regular jobs while hoping to get the call to go back out. That call didn't come right away so we found some local gigs and kept our day jobs. Our relationship at home had a lot of ups and downs with the emphasis on downs. Kecia was way more settled than I was and very opinionated when it came to my lack of financial security. This would become the source of many disagreements. We did get a few more contracts on ships, but her heart didn't seem to be in it anymore. One day after living together for seven years, she brought up the subject of marriage. To that point she had always said that we didn't need a piece of paper to prove our commitment. I guess her views changed, so I began looking for an engagement ring. A month later I proposed, she accepted, and we were married shortly after. Once we were married she started talking about having children. This was a subject I wanted to avoid because my focus was on our career. Point blank, she wanted out of show business and into motherhood. At dinner one night with Curtis and his wife Susan he told us that he was considering retiring soon and wanted to pass his hypnosis show on to me. I had no desire to be a hypnotist and was completely happy being a magician. Kecia said that if I learned

Hypnosis promotional picture

his show it would afford me the flexibility to work without her so we could finally have kids. Against my initial reservations, I took Curtis up on the offer to become his apprentice.

To begin, I had to get certified. This sounded a lot harder than it actually was. I found a school that did certification courses in my area. This whole process would only take a weekend and Curtis would bring me on the road and teach me the real work firsthand. After I got my certificate, we worked fairs, resorts, corporate events, amusement parks, and even cruise ships. After a year of being his onstage assistant, he got me a solo show. It was a corporate event in Baltimore at a ritzy hotel in the Inner Harbor. Curtis wasn't there and I was on my own and literally shaking in my boots. I did the induction he taught me verbatim and to my surprise it worked. I made suggestions and created scenarios, which became the volunteers' reality. They bent to my every will and the audience erupted in laughter. I'll never forget the awesome feeling of power with a little fear, as well. To have that kind of influence over someone's mind just didn't feel right. I could see how a Hitler, Mussolini, or Jim Jones could easily influence so many. I would be using these skills for good and not evil so the world was safe from me.

Once I had the confidence to do the show, Curtis began managing me. The first major contract he booked was at the Six Flags Amusement Park in Maryland. I worked the Fright Fest season from the middle of September through the end of October. My schedule was five shows a weekend and the money was sick. I shared the theater with an illusionist named Joe Romano who had been performing there for eleven years. When he wasn't doing the Fright Fest season he performed school assembly programs, which sounded really boring to me. He tried to explain how fulfilling it was to perform these type of shows and said they were quite lucrative as well, but I just didn't see it. We became good friends during the run and he invited me over when the season wrapped. He lived in a really affluent area of Virginia and as I drove through his neighborhood, I couldn't help notice the size of the houses. As I pulled up to his home I was impressed. He gave me a tour and it was just as beautiful inside as it was out. He even had a movie theater downstairs with a marquee and everything. I quickly asked him to tell me more about the school assembly show thing again. He explained that I needed to put together a show that was educational, without skimping on the entertainment. He did two shows at the time that he rotated in and out. One was about reading and the other was a math show. I didn't want to do either of those, so we brainstormed about something that would be personal to me and what we came up with was a magic show that taught about African American History. Right there "Magical Moments in the Lives of Great African Americans" was born.

CHAPTER 30
SINATRA

Putting together an assembly program would take some serious thought and creativity. The magic needed to fit the stories and couldn't be fabricated or forced. Although the majority of the audience would be children, they could tell if you were being disingenuous. This was the first thing Joe advised me when I began creating my program. He said that once I had a good show put together he would act as my agent using his numerous contacts and connections to get me booked. I was on a time schedule because Black History Month was right around the corner and we felt that would be the best time to launch it. The show featured stories about famous civil rights leaders like Frederick Douglass and Martin Luther King Jr. to sports icons like Jackie Robinson and Michael Jordan. The routines I was most proud of showcased the unsung black inventors. These were the men and women who had had a major impact on industry in America, but were left out of the history books. I spoke about Garrett Morgan, who invented the traffic light and George Washington Carver who came up with 300 industrial uses for the peanut including soap, glue, and paper. I even spoke about Richard Potter, the first documented American magician, who just happened to be black. The show had something for everyone. "Magical Moments" was booked and paid for by the local Parent Teacher Association. My goal was to make sure they left the assembly just as informed and entertained as the kids. One of the

Magical Moments Post Card

best compliments I received was from a teacher who told me one of her students had wet himself because he didn't want to go to the bathroom and miss any of the magic. That's one hell of an endorsement—a show so good you'll wet yourself! Although it went very well there was one slight hiccup. We booked schools mainly in Virginia, Washington D.C., and Maryland. The show was offered all year long, but February seemed to be the only month it sold. There's a ton of snow up North that time of year and a lot of the shows had to be shuffled or rescheduled due to bad weather. I never understood why it wouldn't sell any other month except February. We even had a small blurb on the postcard mailers that said, "Celebrate Black History all year long in a unique and entertaining way". It didn't seem to matter because the phone still only rang with requests for Black History Month. After three successful years I retired that show but was really proud of what I had created.

I still had a good job at the Four Seasons, along with the periodic magic and hypnosis show and was feeling pretty optimistic about the future. My marriage had its problems but being with Kecia seemed to keep me out of trouble. While we were together I didn't do any drugs and wasn't running the streets. Now that we were married and she was no longer in the show the talk about kids seemed to come more frequently. I truly didn't feel I was ready to be a father. Call me selfish, but I wanted to have my career first and kids second. I never wanted to look back at my life and spite my kids for keeping me from achieving my goals because I needed to provide for them. Every time she brought up having kids, I found a way to divert the conversation. A few months later I got a ship contract and went out solo. When I got on the ship and unpacked my bag I found a beautiful book on the life and career of Frank Sinatra inside. Kecia knew I loved Ol' Blue Eyes and had snuck it into my bag. When I thumbed through it, I found a short note inside the cover. I assumed it was some nice letter about our relationship or my drive as an entertainer, but was dead wrong and a bit surprised at what it said. In a nutshell the note expressed her disappointment in our marriage and with me personally. I was oblivious that things were that bad and didn't know what to expect when I got back home. Upon returning, Kecia picked me up from the airport and told me that she had moved all her things to her mother's and wanted a divorce. Being so driven in my quest to become a great entertainer I never saw it coming. I was laser-focused and didn't think about anyone else's needs. We got legally separated for one year and when the twelve months were up, our divorce was finalized. I wish I could say it was easy but losing someone you've spent that many years with really sucked. Even if you know it was the right choice it's never easy starting over. To numb the pain I resorted to my old ways and that included alcohol and cocaine. I made frequent trips to New York to perform at Monday Night Magic, which was really an excuse to hang with my friends and get high. This was so counterproductive, considering how hard I had worked to escape that toxic environment. This was a dark period for me and then one day I woke up and decided I wanted better and threw myself into becoming the best magician possible and enlisting a team to help me.

The first person I studied with was Peter White. Peter was a chain-smoking hippie who had a company called P&A Silks. He made the finest silk scarves for magicians and although they were expensive, his quality was unmatched. Peter had a wealth of knowledge when it came to bird magic. He taught me how to train the birds to fly back to me and built original custom props for my show. He could be abrasive but I never complained because I was on a mission for greatness and he was an expert in the field. He never charged me like he did his other protégés, and I never questioned it. Maybe helping me was his way of giving back to the art that had given him so much joy.

My other teacher was Vito Lupo, a highly regarded multi-award-winning magician. He was a big star in the world of magic and performed all over the world. He'd done a lot of television and was a regular at the famous Crazy Horse and Lido in Paris. Everyone in the magic community looked up to Vito and I was lucky to get personal instruction from this master. He taught me about natural movement, colors, deceptiveness, and stagecraft. Vito was known for being an expensive teacher yet he didn't charge me either. Maybe, like Peter, he saw something in me and wanted to be a part of helping to develop it.

Lastly, was my long-time mentor and friend Denny Haney. As a performer you can only do but so much on your own. Eventually you hit a wall and need an outside set of eyes to act as a director. These three were the best directors I could have ever dreamed of and I was getting closer to leaving the security of my day job but still needed a little push to make the leap. That push would come from Curtis, my hypnosis teacher and manager. Curtis always spoke about having his own theater. He said that he only wanted to be the owner and perform from time to time but wanted me to be the main attraction. In other words, I would be the headliner and he would provide the financing and know how to make it a profitable venture for all involved. We started looking for show rooms in Ocean City, Maryland but couldn't find anything big enough, plus it's a seasonal town and most places close down for the fall and winter. Then Curtis called and told me he found a place in Orlando, Florida. This was the last place on earth I would ever consider moving to. My mother and brother had both migrated to Florida and tried many times to get me down there. I would fly down for holidays, but felt Florida was way too slow for the direction I was headed. Then he made me an offer I couldn't refuse. He offered to pay me $1,500 per week plus a really nice condo to live, and even take care of groceries. All of this plus I'd be headlining a beautiful theater on International Drive in Orlando. Preparation had met opportunity and I said, "YES!" After twenty years as a professional server I finally discarded my security blanket to become a full-time magician.

CHAPTER 31
Magic & Mischief

I had recently purchased a town home in Baltimore when Curtis asked me to make the move to Florida. I chose to keep my house just in case the theater flopped and I needed somewhere to come back to. Next I got a leave of absence from the restaurant, then loaded my SUV and headed down South. This took a huge leap of faith and I put all my trust in Curtis and his wife Susan who would now be my employers.

Curtis taught himself hypnosis from a book titled *The Encyclopedia of Stage Hypnosis* by Ormond McGill. He took that knowledge and built a long, successful career for himself. At the time we met Curtis was the most popular and prosperous hypnotist working on cruise ships. His wife Susan was successful, too. She was Dean of the School of Public Policy at the University of Maryland and an aide to US Senator John Danforth, as a foreign service officer in the State Department. She later became The United States Trade Representative under President George W. Bush. Curtis and Susan met while she was on a cruise with her family and he was the comedy magician on board. They fell in love and were married shortly after.

They took their savings along with Curtis's dream and opened The Magic & Mischief Theatre. When I arrived in Orlando, Curtis showed me where I'd be performing and it was phenomenal! There was a huge lobby with glass counters for the magic and gift shop. Inside the showroom he had installed 250 tiered theater seats. The stage was large and had a beautiful decorative proscenium. It was equipped with all the drapes and curtains needed, along with a sound system and intelligent lighting. There were two full dressing rooms, one with a shower and it was perfect! We went outside and he showed me the marquee and lighted poster boxes on the front side of the building. There it was, full-sized posters of my ugly mug on display for everyone to see. I hadn't even done a show yet, but felt like I had already made it. Now I needed to make my show just as professional as the theater.

Puck
Magician & Hypnotist

8815 International Drive
Orlando, FL 32819
407-352-3711

Magic & Mischief business card

Since I would be performing big illusions I was going to need an assistant. Curtis and Susan said they would pay the assistant $350 per week to perform two shows a night. I needed to find a girl but being new to Orlando didn't have the slightest idea of where to look. Then the girl who worked the box office said that one of her friends was looking for work and thought she'd be good in the show. I told her to ask her friend to come by the following day for an audition. Her friend's name was Laura Mae Varner and she was twenty-five-years old. Laura was a cute, slim, white girl and looked the part, even though she had no show-business experience. I escorted her to the stage and pulled out one of the illusions. I showed her the secret space in the box and told her how to position herself to hide in it. This compartment was really small and she didn't think it was possible. I told her it looked smaller than it actually was and this is why they called it an illusion. She was pretty nervous but I got her to lie inside and closed the door behind her. We encountered a problem and the door wouldn't close all the way. To put it bluntly, her boobs were too big. She started laughing and said, "I wouldn't have had this problem a month ago," and that's when I realized those tits weren't factory equipment. Then she said, "Let me try something," and right when she said that the door slammed shut. I asked what she did to make the door close and she said, "I just took a deep breath." Needless to say, she got the job. Next step was to get her a wardrobe and teach her the show.

Curtis told me that there would be two different performers per night. It would be myself and comedy magician, John Ferrentino. John had enjoyed some early success on television in the '80s and early '90s. We really didn't need two acts, but John had helped Curtis find the theater. Also unbeknownst to us, John knew Curtis's weakness and used this knowledge to get in the door.

A year earlier, Curtis decided to have gastric bypass surgery. After the procedure he dropped over a hundred pounds and was on his way to getting healthy. His brother was also obese and Curtis talked him into having the operation, as well. While his brother was in surgery there was a problem and he didn't survive. Curtis was devastated and blamed himself. When he lost his brother, he began drinking heavily. He had always drank, but you never really noticed, because it was usually in social situations. Plus he held his liquor pretty well and was never sloppy or acted drunk. After he lost the weight it became quite noticeable when he was intoxicated. His drinking was getting out of control and John exploited this.

John knew when Curtis drank you could talk him into just about anything. When Curtis was drunk on the ship, John got him to commit to things. First he got Curtis to say he would hire him when he opened the theater in Orlando. Second John got him to hire his girlfriend who was a dancer on the ship and not a US citizen. He wanted to get her into the States and figured if he could get Curtis to hire her she would be able to get a work visa. While he was wasted, Curtis typed up a mock contract that she could use for the visa application. He asked John how much should he put for their weekly salary and John told him to make it six-thousand dollars. Now this was just supposed to be a fake contract just to get his girlfriend into the country and the real one would be drawn up once the theater was open. When the theater opened some months later, John held Curtis to the six-thousand-dollars-a-week salary. He even got a friend of his who was a lawyer to back him up. Curtis and Susan couldn't do anything about it without going to court, so they focused their attention on getting the doors opened and would deal with him later.

The theater was plagued from the start. When the 250 seats were permanently installed Curtis was unaware this would cause a problem with the bathrooms. When you exceed a certain number of seats it increases the number of toilets needed to pass code. We were short and the bathrooms needed to be expanded, which would push the opening back almost two months. Since the theater wasn't open by the start date on John's contract, they were still obligated to pay his astronomical weekly salary. This was devastating since we weren't open yet and there were no profits coming in. The more frustrated Curtis got the more he drank. Curtis was constantly having business meetings with vendors at the Bahama Breeze restaurant, which was located directly next door. The bar was his office and the bartenders were his employees. He'd be three sheets to the wind, making deals with vendors who were eager to take advantage of his inebriated state.

Meanwhile, I was working on the show and training Laura, who was picking up the technical aspects of the act pretty well. As for her stage presence, there was much to be desired. We had a dry run with a test audience and afterward Susan told me Laura was chewing gum the entire time. She also said you could hear her stomping around backstage like a Clydesdale. She needed some polishing, but wasn't that bad. I needed to get her a wardrobe and took her shopping. Curtis gave me a $500 budget so I hit a high-end mall to look for a show dress and ended up at Cache, a really chic store. She tried on several dresses but there was one in particular that seemed to pop. It was a blue off-the-shoulder dress that was sexy, yet elegant. It also matched my blue and black show jacket to a tee. The dress was $350 and within budget, so we got it. Afterward we went to a restaurant and got something to eat. I wanted to take that time for us to get to know each other, which I thought might help with our onstage chemistry. She could really talk and I mostly sat and listened. She told me that she was a single mother with a four-year-old son. There were plans to go to college but that all changed when she got pregnant. She seemed a little naïve, but there was something really genuine about her. I guess it was her age and inexperience but it made her endearing. The more time we spent together working on the show I could tell she was starting to like me. I liked her too but at the time wasn't looking for a relationship. In fact I was casually dating a girl I met in Orlando a short time earlier. When I wasn't with the girl I was seeing I was hanging out with Laura. She was fun to be around and one thing led to another and we broke protocol and started fooling around. Laura was thirteen years my junior and not very worldly, so we didn't have very much in common aside from our physical attraction. Curtis made it clear that he didn't want me to have any sexual relations with the assistants because he didn't want to have issues from outside the theater spilling inside. With this in mind we had to be very secretive about our extracurricular activities. It was obvious she wanted more from me but I was upfront and let her know I wasn't looking for anything serious.

Back at the theater things were progressively getting worse between Curtis and John. John had an ego and would try to tell Curtis how to run the theater. This was OK when Curtis was drunk but on the rare times he was sober caused quite a stir. John was bleeding the theater dry with his forced salary and that caused a lot of fights, too. All of the blowups just made Curtis drink more. When Susan finally confronted him about his drinking he denied there was a problem but after some self-reflection finally admitted he was an alcoholic. He asked for help and at first we thought this was a good sign, and he would be fine. Then he started sneaking around and would disappear for hours at a time. When confronted, he would get confrontational and start fights with us. The next morning when he'd wake up sober, the apologies would begin. With things getting worse Susan told him he needed to go to rehab and no was not an option. She found a facility called Crossroads Rehabilitation Centre in Antigua that was founded by music legend Eric Clapton. The price was substantial, but for Susan this was a non-issue when it came to getting him well. Curtis listened to Susan and went to the Caribbean to dry out.

Susan was traveling between DC and Florida and in Curtis's absence gave me more responsibilities at the theater. I stepped up and started helping to get the theater ready for opening. There was so much to be done, but finally we were ready for the grand opening, which coincidentally was just in time for Curtis's return from rehab. For the opening we had an industry night where all of the local hotel concierges were invited to a complimentary night of hors d'oeuvres, drinks, and magic. We had a good turn out and it was a fabulous evening. This was geared to push business our way and we were excited to start filling seats with paid customers. Unfortunately our celebration was halted with the incoming news of an approaching storm. Welcome Hurricane Charley!

CHAPTER 32
SEA WORLD

On August 13, 2004 Hurricane Charley made landfall in Florida. It was a category four with winds of at least 145 mph. Instead of filling seats after our successful opening night, we were preparing for the storm. A few years earlier my mother and Mr. Dobson had gotten married and built two beautiful homes on the water in Punta Gorda. I was really worried for them because Charley was scheduled to make landfall right there at their homes. My brother had gotten married as well and now had two kids. He made his home in Wellington, which was close to Miami and luckily not in the path of Charley. I, on the other hand, was in Orlando and it was headed our way, too. The hurricane was pretty frightening and we lost power for a couple days. The damage to our condo was minimal but the destruction to my mother and Mr. Dobson's homes was substantial. They lost the pool enclosures, roof tiles, had broken windows, plus water damage. Although their homes were beat up, no one was hurt and that's what mattered most. After Charley, we had two more hurricanes, which had a major impact on Florida. For the next few months I performed regularly to audiences of fifteen to thirty people. Tourism died in Central Florida and it hit us right in the box office. It didn't help either that John was still demanding his extravagant salary. One night it all came to a head when Curtis blew up and kicked John out. John, of course, went to his lawyer friend and filed suit against Curtis and Susan. They ended up settling for an undisclosed amount but I heard through the grapevine it was pretty hefty. Everything was falling apart and we were holding on as best we could. Between the hurricanes, John's salary, the lawsuit, decline in tourism, and Curtis relapsing we shut down short of a year. It was really sad to see Curtis's dream fade so quickly. Banking on the theater's success I had left my restaurant job and sold my home in Baltimore. I had grown to like Florida and decided to make Orlando my new home. We still had the condo, so I didn't have to move right away and Curtis hooked me up with a gig that he'd done for many years but no longer wanted. The client was called Grad Nights and was in Seattle, Washington.

Grad Nights was an all-purpose events company that put together entertainment and activities for post-prom parties. They sometimes call these parties "Lock Ins" because the high school graduates at these events are chaperoned and shuttled from venue to venue. They raised money all year to pay for these extravagant parties and no expense was wasted. They rode a nice bus and went to all kinds of fun places. Some examples were bowling alleys, roller rinks, go-cart tracks, amusement parks, night cruises, dance clubs, trampoline arenas, laser shows, and even the Space Needle. The party also included a hypnosis show, which was the highlight of the night. The hypnotist's schedule could be brutal. I would start at midnight and go through sunrise, which really throws your clock off. You perform all over the place and I did shows in sand on a volleyball court as well as on a go-cart racetrack. Grad Nights was no cakewalk but the money was great and I couldn't turn that down. In two to three weeks I'd do around seventeen to twenty-two shows. The Grad Night parties were designed to keep the kids from drinking and driving after prom. These events worked well and each year helped to save hundreds of teen lives. Although exhausting, it was emotionally and financially rewarding. The money I made helped keep me afloat after the untimely closing of the theater.

When Grad Nights finished I was back home and found myself spending more time with Laura, although we were still not in a relationship. One night after having some drinks at a restaurant I hopped in my SUV and headed to her house for a visit. She lived about thirty minutes away and, still not knowing my way around, missed the exit for her house. This sucked because the next off-ramp was twenty minutes away. Frustrated about missing the exit I didn't notice a car switching lanes beside me and got cut off. I was kind of buzzed and reacted by swerving, which was the wrong thing to do in an SUV. The truck flipped over at 70 mph and I was sliding down the turnpike on my roof. Eventually I hit the guardrail, which brought me to an abrupt stop. Everything seemed to go in slow motion and I was unusually calm. I was wearing my seatbelt, which probably saved my life. I was upside down when I unbuckled the seatbelt and fell right on my head. I crawled out the side window, which was busted and checked myself out on the side of the road. I didn't have a scratch on me, even though my truck was totaled. I crawled back into the vehicle and retrieved my cell phone, but before I could make a call, I heard sirens headed in my direction. Someone passing by must have called the police, who were there within minutes. An ambulance also showed up shortly after. They asked what happened and I explained I'd been cut off and when I swerved to avoid hitting them, my truck flipped over. I was very composed and the subject of alcohol never even came up. I was shocked that they just ruled it an accident and didn't issue any tickets. A tow truck came to get my SUV and I called Laura to pick me up.

When Laura showed up she had her son in the back seat. He was sleeping and this was the first time I had ever seen him. On the ride to her house I told Laura that I was developing feelings for her and we should be in a relationship. Maybe it was the fact I almost lost my life and she was there for me or maybe I was just ready to settle down, but I asked and she accepted. From that night we were in a committed relationship. In the morning I got to interact with her son, who was very attached to her. He was a ball of energy and, from what I could tell, used to getting his way. She and I came from very different times and backgrounds, but she was a good person and I was willing to give it a shot. For the next month we spent a lot more time getting to know each other better. The only places we went were mostly clubs, bars, and her house and then she asked if I would accompany her to a Christmas party. We had a great time at the party and an even better one later on at her house. Not too long after, she invited me to go with her to Sea World. When we got there she was acting a little weird. I had no idea what was up, so I asked her if everything was all right. She sat me down on a bench and told me she was pregnant. Now I was thirty-nine with no kids and a small part of me was scared to death, but the other part was kind of excited. Because I'd been adopted, I had gone my entire life without one true blood connection. There was nobody that I shared any genetic resemblance to. I was alone and for the first time had the opportunity to experience what so many on this earth enjoyed. I told her that I was excited and if she wanted to keep the baby I would be there for her and take part in the child's life. Although our relationship was fairly new, we were going to be bound for life through this child and there was nothing I could have done to prepare myself.

Once the news set in it was time to let my family and friends know. First I told Curtis and Susan, who I still lived with in the condo. They seemed happy for me and Curtis put in a request to be the godfather. My mother, to whom I'd never even mentioned Laura's name, was very understanding and surprisingly happy for me. I thought since Laura and I had only dated a short time and weren't married, she would be upset. I guess at my age she felt some relief that I wouldn't end up living my whole life without a child. On Laura's side, the reactions weren't quite the same. Her parents were totally against her bringing another child into the world without a husband and they both wanted to speak with me. First up was her father, Fred. Fred was in his mid-fifties and worked for himself as a carpenter. When not working, he loved to fish and had a very close bond with his grandson, whom he tagged his grand-buddy. He was kinda country and seemed to be a genuinely nice guy. We met at Laura's house and sat in the living room to talk. He told me that he and his wife were against us having this child without being married. Then he shared that he and his wife got married when she was pregnant with Laura and it was the right thing to do. If we weren't going to get married he suggested we seek out other options. Then he told me how they spoiled Laura and she would now be my responsibility. I began to get the feeling he was trying to discourage me from having this child. I said I would consider everything he said and talk about it with Laura. I thought that was a crazy conversation until I sat down with her mother. The conversation with her mom made the one with Fred seem like child's play. Laurie was an Italian from Buffalo and only eleven years my senior. She had a big personality and I could tell was pretty much the boss at home. She, like Fred, said that having the baby without getting married was not an option. I was damn-near forty and Laura twenty-six and couldn't for the life of me understand why they were so involved. This was a major red flag and I should have taken more notice, but instead I just listened respectfully. I told Laurie the same as Fred, that I would consider their advice and discuss it with Laura.

Laura and I had a lot of long conversations. She didn't want me to be forced into marriage because of the baby. We had spoken about living together and that was as far as we'd gotten. Her son played a part in the decision as well. She wanted to make sure that if we lived together I would treat her son the same as the child that was on the way. I spent some one-on-one time with him and could tell this was going to be work. Her son Cameron was extremely hyper and not used to being told "No". I was a product of the '70s, where a child listened to their parents the first time or risked getting backhanded. Laura, on the other hand, was raised in the '80s and '90s, when kids could mouth off to their parents and live to talk about it. This was going to pose some problems, but I felt in time we would be able to work through them.

Up to this point in my life I had really lived. I'd traveled, had lifelong friendships, dated more than my fill of women, chased my dreams of becoming an entertainer, and was becoming financially stable. The only thing missing was a family of my own. With that in mind, I decided to buy a ring and propose. Now was I head over heels in love with her? No. But I loved her as a friend and felt she had a good heart and would make a great mother and wife. I had a friend at one of the hotels I worked that had an arranged marriage. He and his wife were in love and had a great family. I asked how they went from strangers to such a happily married couple. He told me that they began with a friendship and then learned to love each other. Through that process they built an unbreakable bond. Those were the exact thoughts on my mind when I proposed to Laura. I was going to build a friendship first and then learn to love her.

CHAPTER 33
STARR

Laura lived in a small, two-bedroom rambler in old-town Saint Cloud. Her mother was a realtor and had purchased the home for close to nothing and it carried a $600 a month mortgage. Laura received half of that in child support from Cameron's dad and her mother covered the rest. This was going to be way too small for us so, with her mother's help, I searched for a new home. We found a comfortable home with a nice fenced-in lot for the kids to play. It was a good time for real estate and I got the home at a good price, using my VA loan. I worked with her father to get the house in shape for us to move in. We painted the interior and steam-cleaned the carpets. I needed an office, so we built one in the garage. One side was for my office and the other for storing my magic props and illusions. We put up a wall, put in a window, laid carpet and insulation, and finished by piping in some air conditioning. We worked well together and were really getting along. When all the work was finished I rented a truck and drove to Maryland to get all of my things out of storage. Everything was set for the arrival of my first child.

Curtis was still in the condo in Orlando and Susan had gone back to Annapolis. Once the depression of losing the theater had sunk in, his drinking got worse. I tried to help him but didn't have a lot of time, as I worked to provide for my new family. He told me that he needed to stay in Florida because Susan didn't want him coming back to Maryland until he stopped drinking. His lease was ending at the condo and he asked if he could stay with us until things got better. He had done so much for me there wasn't any way I could say no. Laura wasn't due for four more months, so we set him up in the baby's room. After a week the room started to smell like alcohol, which was leaking from his pores. Curtis would go out for hours and then I'd see his Mercedes parked on our front lawn with him sleeping, mouth open, in the driver's seat. He'd wake up and come inside, trying to avoid everyone. Next he'd shower and then come out in his robe to socialize while trying to act sober. I guess he thought he was fooling us but we knew his routine all too well. In the morning I would catch him shaking terribly with the DTs. He was in really bad shape and there was no way to help him.

Laura wasn't working, so I concentrated on getting my promotional materials together so I could get some gigs to pay the bills. A few blocks down from the now-closed Magic & Mischief Theatre was a place called Wonder Works. The building was an architectural oddity that looked like it fell out of the sky and landed upside down on its roof. Inside was a laser tag arena, 4D motion theater, glow-in-the-dark rope course, educational exhibits, and *The Outta Control Magic Show*. The latter was a dinner show that featured comedian/magicians Tony Brent and Danny Devaney. Their show was a combination of magic, comedy, improv, juggling, impersonations, and straight lunacy! They performed two shows a day, five nights a week. On Mondays and Tuesdays they were off and had other local magicians fill in. One of the substitute magicians knew I was looking for work and recommended that they try me out. They gave me a shot, and since the first night went well I was put into their rotation. This helped tremendously to get me back on my feet.

Back on the home front things weren't going as smoothly. Laura and I had very different ideas when it came to parenting and we clashed quite a bit when it came to her son. His dad was still a big part of his life and the grandparents were very vocal when it came to his upbringing. All I could think about was how it was going to be when the baby was born. I tried to treat him as if he were mine but they constantly told me I was being too tough. I planned on being just as tough with my own child. It was the way I was raised, and I thought

Mikayla Starr

since I was doing OK, it was a good thing. It was obvious that I was unprepared and had a lot to learn about being a father and stepdad.

The next several months went quickly and it was time for me to meet my child. Mikayla Starr Puckering was born on August 27, 2005. Joining us in the delivery room were both our mothers. The second I held her in my arms, the tears started flowing from my eyes. I was finally face to face with my own flesh and blood and the feeling was overwhelming. My mother saw me sobbing and called me a crybaby. She had no idea the symbolism of what I was encountering. To her it was just a baby, but to me it was much, much more. Since birth I'd lacked a genetic connection of family that only this child could fulfill. This beautiful little girl had filled this void and I planned to love her with all my heart.

Now that Mikayla was here Curtis made plans to go back to Annapolis. Susan was appointed the US Trade Representative and became a cabinet member to President George W. Bush. She told Curtis that she couldn't risk problems with her job and the only way he could return was if he went right into a rehabilitation facility. He agreed and went back up North to work on his health and marriage. We asked him to be Mikayla's godfather and hoped it would help with his recovery. At first I checked in on him quite regularly, but with little spare time on my hands we temporarily lost contact.

In November Laura and I flew to Vegas to get married. When you visualize a Vegas wedding you usually think of a small chapel with an Elvis impersonator doing the vows. We, however, had a real ceremony and reception with around fifty of our closest family members and friends. It was at the Aladdin Hotel and Laura's mother took care of mostly everything. Denny was there, too, and performed a show for our guests. They gave us a giant suite and it was the perfect place for a magician to tie the knot.

After our wedding I was back home, learning how to be a father. I had never had to be responsible for anyone other than myself and it wasn't easy. Cameron was in first grade and having some problems adjusting. One day he got suspended for kicking a little girl in the back. I was really upset and felt there was no excuse for that kind of behavior. Laura, his father, and I met up to figure out how to deal with this. Laura and I had offered to host a baby shower for her little sister the coming weekend and asked his father to keep him. He needed to be grounded and felt being in the middle of a baby shower wouldn't be conducive to his punishment. His father already had plans, so we decided that he would stay with us, but be confined to his room and not be allowed to participate in the party. While setting up for our guests, Laura's father told me he had a puzzle that he wanted to give Cameron. I explained that he was on punishment and it wouldn't be a good time for a reward. He agreed and thanked me for being present in helping to raise his grand-buddy.

During the party I went to Cameron's room to check on him and when I popped my head in the door I saw he was playing with the puzzle I asked his grandfather to hold off giving him. When I inquired where he got it he said that his grandfather gave it to him and said it was their secret and not let me know. I was pissed! How was I supposed to have any authority over this child when I was being undermined like this? I called his grandfather to the kitchen and asked why he had given the puzzle to Cameron after we had collectively agreed it was a bad idea. I totally expected some kind of apology but got something completely different. He became enraged and started yelling at me for confronting him. He said before I came around he saw his grandson all the time. Then he said something that really caught me off guard. He said that he really felt like hitting me. At first I thought he was joking because up to that point we had a good relationship. He was dead serious and I couldn't believe what I was hearing. What was going on and where was this rage coming from? By this time people started coming over to see what all the commotion was. Fred left and went outside and I followed him. Outside he kept trying to lunge at me but one of Laura's uncles stepped in and held him back. By now, everyone from the party had poured out onto the driveway to witness the spectacle. This just seemed to get him more riled up and he continued to try to attack me, but couldn't get past Laura's uncle. Finally I had enough of being threatened and said to let him go. When he was free we started fighting, which only lasted a few punches until we were separated. Laura's mother grabbed him and they drove off. Immediately the party was over and my relationship with her parents was, as well. I knew in my heart that he felt bad but once he committed to being upset he just couldn't swallow his pride and reel it back in. Later I found out that he had a few beers in him, which must have also played a part in this unsolicited attack. Laura was upset about the fight, but knew it wasn't my fault. It was very unfortunate and I wouldn't see or speak with her father again for seven years.

CHAPTER 34
OPEN SESAME

I enjoyed being a father, although Laura did most of the child-rearing while I was on the road. I had gotten a cruise ship agent and was back working at sea. The ships weren't very steady, so I picked up some corporate gigs, and the occasional Wonder Works show to make ends meet. This gave me enough money to scrape by, but I needed to come up with a better plan. I received a call from Curtis that he was out of rehab and doing well. He was working a ship out of Los Angeles and said he would be making a stop at the Magic Castle. The Magic Castle is a private club in the Hollywood Hills that features some of the greatest magicians from around the world. Curtis knew the booker and offered to drop him my video for consideration. I was excited because the Magic Castle could give me the exposure I needed to advance my career. A week after he dropped off my tape I got an email from Ron Wilson, the entertainment director. He said that although my act wasn't perfect he could tell I had a good teacher and showed potential. Then he offered me a week's contract in The Palace of Mystery, the main showroom. I couldn't say yes fast enough and a month later I was in LA, standing before a bookshelf in the lobby of the Magic Castle uttering the words "Open Sesame". Upon saying those magic words the bookshelf slid open and became a doorway to this world-famous Mecca of magic.

Goldfinger

The Castle was a playground for magicians, celebrities, and bigwigs of all kinds. Because it's a private club you had to either be a member or know a member to get in. You needed to be twenty-one and the attire was formal and absolutely no picture taking allowed once inside. There were four formal showrooms, as well as other nooks and crannies to watch expert magicians at work. They had several bars and a fine-dining restaurant, too. This place was amazing and I was loving it! During the weekdays I performed two to three shows a night. On weekends I'd do five or six. So, all in all, we're looking at around twenty-two shows for the week. The crowds were great and the week went really fast. I met so many of my magical heroes that had inspired my love for the magical arts.

One of those people was a very well-known magician named Jack Goldfinger. He worked with his wife Dove and the act was fittingly named Goldfinger and Dove. I had first heard of Goldfinger and Dove in the early '70s while thumbing through my parents' monthly subscription of *Ebony* magazine. I came across a picture of a black magician standing in front of the Magic Castle. I read the article and learned who this master magician was. He and his wife were the opening act for Redd Foxx for many years and had performed on numerous television shows. He had a swag and charisma that was unmatched by other magicians. Seeing that spread in *Ebony* is what made me really believe I could do magic as a career and I had to meet this man! Mark Haslam, one of the acts I shared the stage with that week, told me he knew Goldfinger and would give him a call to see if he could get him to come up. When we got to the show the following evening, he said that he called but no one answered and he left a message on his machine. I wasn't sure if he was in town or even checked his messages, so it wasn't looking too good. After my last show that night there was a knock at my dressing-room door. In walked none other than Jack Goldfinger. He said, "My brother, Puck, you have arrived. I told them not to let you know I was here, because if you sucked I didn't want to meet you." Well I guess I didn't suck too bad, because I was face to face with the man himself. We talked for a while and he took a picture of the two of us, then he was gone. The following day when I unlocked my dressing room there was an envelope on the floor that had been slipped under the door. I opened it and there was a picture of me and Jack Goldfinger that he had printed. He superimposed the Magic Castle in the background and it said, "Puck Made It, Jack Goldfinger." It was the best day and best part of getting to work the Magic Castle. Jack and I became good friends and remain so to this day. He's now the entertainment director at the Castle and I've worked there annually ever since.

When I got back home I received a call from an old friend, Scott Alexander, who coincidentally was also a former assistant in The Denny & Lee Show. He had put together a really big magic production show on a ship for Norwegian Cruises. The show was called *Elements of Illusion* and would run for three years on the brand new Pride of Hawaii. He would take off 10 weeks a year, Halloween through New Year's to be with his family and was looking for a magician to cover his vacations. He asked if I'd be interested in being his replacement. I wasn't really sure because Mikayla was still very young and I didn't want to be away from her for that length of time. I asked about the pay and when he told me, I almost passed out. This was by far the largest weekly salary I'd ever been offered to perform magic. I discussed everything with Laura and she reminded me that I would

Elements of Illusion

be spending two and a half months a year in Hawaii while making more money than I had ever earned before and what was there to think about. She also said that as long as I brought her out a couple weeks a year she was cool with it. I accepted Scott's offer and they flew me out to learn the show.

Elements of Illusion was a Cirque-style show with no dialogue, lots of music, dancing, costumes, and, of course, magic. The budget for this production was well over a million dollars and had a cast of ten dancers, myself, and a principal assistant. For my principal I brought in Krystal Davis who assisted me at Magic & Mischief in Laura's absence. She was a trained dancer, actress, and great magic assistant. She and I had a brother and sister type relationship so Laura was cool with it. This was a huge show that had seven large-scale illusions packed into a 45-minute production. I had five costume changes and even did some dance choreography that was created for us by Mark Kanemura, who later became an All-star on the TV show *So You Think You Can Dance*. This was a lot of work and the hardest part for me was learning to eat fire. *Elements of Illusion* was based on the four elements, Earth, Air, Fire, and Water. Eating fire would be an intricate part of the show and was something that scared the life out of me. Scott was quite proficient in fire-eating and coached me through the whole process. He even made me a set of custom training and show torches. He said the only thing you need to remember is never to breathe in. When that part of the show came I was focused and fully concentrated so as not to kill myself.

The next two years on The Pride of Hawaii were great. I was in a fabulous show and thoroughly enjoying the beautiful islands of Hawaii. It wasn't all play and I worked nearly every night. I did twenty minutes in the welcome aboard show, performed in *Elements*, had a late night hypnosis show, a comedy & magic performance, taught a magic class, and was a part of the farewell show. I never complained and felt it helped to justify the paycheck.

During the run I received some devastating news. I got a call from Curtis's sister telling me that he had literally drank himself to death. His organs were shutting down and he was in hospice with very little time left. She told me that he wanted to speak with me and was I okay with it? I told her yes and later that day he called to say goodbye. This was one of the hardest things I ever had to do in my entire life. He tried to make jokes and keep things light, but the reality and awkwardness were hard to disguise. He ended the conversation by saying how proud he was and that he loved me. We never said, "Goodbye" but instead ended with, "I'll see you later." The following day his sister called and said that he had passed. I had a show that night and powered through as best I could. They say the show must go on, and that's exactly what I did. I believe there are no coincidences and everyone comes into your life with a specific purpose. I always felt that my dad had sent him to help me realize my dreams and potential. Curtis did just that, and I am so thankful for the time I had with him.

After Curtis's passing I stayed in close contact with Susan. Curtis was Mikayla's godfather and had generously offered to help pay for her college when she grew up. Susan said that she wanted to fulfill Curtis's promise to do so. I asked Susan to be Mikayla's godmother and in that role she has done so much to expose Mikayla to the arts and culture as well as be a strong role model in her life. Mikayla and Susan became very close and that bond still remains.

Hawaii was one of the high-lights of my career and *Elements* a great experience in my magical life. Educational and profitable, what more could I have asked for? After two years on that ship it was re-flagged and sent to Europe. That was the end of The Pride of Hawaii and the original *Elements of Illusion.* Back to reality and back to grinding for work.

It's often said that when a door closes a window opens. This rang true not soon after leaving the Pride of Hawaii. I went to a party at a friend's

Godmother Susan & Mikayla

home and met a magician named T.C. Tahoe. T.C. was fairly well-known in the industry and had been working for Carnival Cruise Lines for many years. I told him how I had just lost the Pride of Hawaii and was going to have to get with my agent about finding some new ships for me to work. He mentioned how well-connected he was at Carnival and offered to submit me to them. I was really appreciative and immediately got him my promotional video. A couple weeks later I received a call from Virginia Blankfeld, Carnival's entertainment director offering me five contracts over a one month period. Each ship would only be two to three days long. There was one catch, though; she only wanted my hypnosis show. I would be required to do two family shows and one late-night R-rated adult show per cruise. Since I had nothing else in the works I agreed, thinking I'd work my magic in somewhere down the line. Those five weeks turned into over three years, working exclusively for Carnival. I performed five to seven cruises a month, on twenty-two different ships, performing hypnosis and eventually my magic show. Working for Carnival was exactly what I needed at that time in my life. It allowed me to comfortably support my family while gaining a shitload of experience. I got to work every week on phenomenal stages with great tech crews in front of large, enthusiastic audiences. Carnival is where I got to hone my craft, performing over 150 performances a year.

Every hypnosis show is different as the participants in each show are different. Any doubts I had about the power of hypnosis were quickly put to rest after seeing it work week after week. I remember one show, telling the volunteers that they were going to smell the worst thing they'd ever smelled. I said

Magazine Cover

this smell wouldn't make them sick but it would really make their eyes water. One of the guys onstage started reacting in a way that I hadn't seen before. He started crying profusely at the suggestion of a horrible smell. This was not a subtle cry, but a loud sobbing that was starting to make the audience uncomfortable. I approached him off-mic and asked what was the worst thing he'd ever smelled? He told me that when he was in Vietnam he would smell the flesh as the bodies of dead soldiers were burnt. I was in shock and had to think for a minute about just how to handle this. First off, I didn't want to remove that thought from his mind because it was a part of who he was. I did however need to remove it for the duration of the show so he could stop scaring everyone. I told him that the memory of the burnt bodies was gone for now but would return twenty minutes after the show was over. It worked and the show went on without any other issues.

I would always close the show by giving a few volunteers suggestions that they would take back to the audience with them. I'd trigger these later on with a word, number, or phrase. My favorite was telling one person that when they were back in their seat after leaving the stage and heard me say the word "plane" they would jump out of their seat and run back onstage. I would then suggest that they're really scared because Martians had landed on the ship and were taking over. They needed to warn me and everyone in the audience about the alien invasion. This would bring the house down when the volunteer had a good imagination. They would sometimes build a little fort with the chairs onstage and be really jumpy when I pretended to point out these imaginary beings. Well, this one night it went horribly wrong. I used a tall, buff, black guy, thinking it would be funny because he was so macho. When I said the trigger word "plane" this guy got up and started screaming like a woman. Then he ran out of the theater and never came back. Although the audience was laughing, I couldn't stop worrying that this guy would jump overboard in fear. After the show, no one could find him and that's when I really got scared. About an hour later in the back of the ship a crewmember found him in a laundry basket buried under some dirty sheets. They called me and I went and removed the suggestion and woke him up. From that day forward I always added that they would not leave the theater no matter how scared they were. The things you learn along the way.

Another time I received a call from Virginia in the office telling me that I had been requested to entertain on a very special charter. This would be the first full-ship charter of its kind and they wanted me to be a part of it. It was a 1,720 passenger all-swingers cruise out of Tampa. She said they wanted me to do the dirtiest show I could put together. I mentioned that my late night show was pretty tame and mostly innuendo but she said that she had faith I could give the client what they wanted. Now to this point I had done the Bare Necessities Nudist Cruise but that didn't come close to preparing me for these folks.

From the moment I boarded the ship, you could just tell it was going to be a wild experience. I was one of two acts hired to work that cruise. It was myself and a comic who would act as the MC and host. I was only scheduled to be onboard one night and then debark the following day in Mexico. I put together what I felt was a show conducive to the guests' lifestyle and hoped for the best. At one point I made the suggestion that they were on a very hot beach and the temperature was quickly rising. As it got hotter in their minds, the clothes started coming off. Now usually when this happens in my family show, I make it a point to mention that no matter how hot it gets you will keep your clothes on. For this group I just let it go and took my chances. Halfway through the routine more than half of the volunteers were butt-ass naked. Then I abruptly changed the scenario and suggested that now it was extremely cold and getting colder by the second. Then I told them the only thing that was going to keep them alive was body heat and that's when the shit hit the fan. I saw a hot twenty-something girl jump up and straddle a seventy-something man and start having sex. I immediately ran over and broke them apart stating that no one would be having sex on my stage. It was like trying to break apart two dogs in heat, without the luxury of a garden hose. So I got through that routine and was thinking the worst was now behind me, but how wrong I was. For my next bit I told all the women that when I wake them and say the word "hypnosis" they're going to look down at their breasts and realize their nipples are missing. They have no idea where they are, but will thoroughly believe in every fiber of their mind the gentleman seated closest to them has stolen their nipples, and dammit they want them back. I proceed to wake them and casually mention the word "hypnosis". Right at that very moment one of the volunteers, a heavyset, black woman yells out, "This motherfucker stole my chocolate chips!" The audience fell apart and I couldn't stop laughing my damn self. I looked in the wings and saw the comedian and cruise director doubled over. But it didn't stop there. Next a petite, white woman gets up and starts yelling at the guy next to her to get up. When he does she commences to pull his pants down to his knees. She then starts yanking and pulling on his penis really hard, as if trying to rip it off. The whole time yelling, "I know they're in there, I know they're in there!" This poor guy is screaming at the top of his lungs in pain. That was a hell of a show and definitely one for the books.

After the show the cruise director told me that I would not be getting off the ship as scheduled the following day. There had been a break out of H1N1 (swine flu) and we would be skipping all Mexican ports, so I had to stay on board an additional day. For the next twenty-four hours I saw people having sex in every area of the ship, while consistently getting hit on by guys asking me to have sex with their wives. This was the craziest cruise and hypnosis show of my entire career, and one I'll not soon forget.

CHAPTER 35
JADE

I often struggled learning to balance my career and family. I was a good father when I was around, but not as hands-on as I should have been. I also wasn't that great of a husband. Because Laura was so much younger and less worldly I tend to treat her more like a daughter than a wife. I knew this was wrong, but for whatever reason I had a hard time changing. I was performing a lot more on ships, which meant less time home working on my family. I also had other issues that needed my attention outside of our home. My stepfather, Mr. Dobson, had become ill and died on November 4, 2008. I was on a ship when I got the news. I will never forget this date for two reasons in particular. First was Hastin's passing and second it was the election of our first black president, Barack Obama. I wish he could have hung on for one more day to witness that historic achievement for African Americans, but unfortunately he died before the results were announced.

My brother was having major problems, too. He and his wife had separated and his marriage was falling apart. He didn't handle it well and literally went to pieces. He started acting out and became very aggressive. To make matters worse, he started dating a woman with serious addiction problems and she brought him down to the gutter. She fueled his anger with his wife and made divorce inevitable. It was an ugly court battle and after bringing his OxyContin-dependent girlfriend into the home he lost custody of his kids. He was

Mom and Andre

also fired from his job and spent time in and out of jail for domestic battery. We started to notice that he was becoming delusional and very angry. At first we attributed his mood swings to the divorce, but then it became clear the bipolar disorder that plagued my father had been passed down to him. We always knew he showed the signs but he was able to mask them when things were going well, which was most of his life.

I was trying to work on my own family, but was finding less and less time to do so. Dealing with my brother while trying to take care of my twice-widowed mother was consuming me. Add work and paying bills to the mix and I was stretched as far as I could go. I told my brother he needed to realize the drug-addict girlfriend had to go and he should get treatment and medication for his disorder. He did eventually get rid of her, but fought the idea he was sick and felt there was nothing wrong with him. He had gone from being a respected pharmacist with a beautiful family and enormous home in Wellington, Florida to unemployed, living in a foreclosed home, with a criminal record. My mother enabled him, too, which didn't help and I always had to be the voice of reason.

My mother lived almost three hours from me and I needed to get her closer, if I was going to be of any real assistance. I helped sell her home in Punta Gorda and got her a new house in a wonderful retirement community thirty minutes away. It took a lot of work, but she was set up and mortgage-free in a beautiful area with people her age. When in town, I would do her grocery shopping and other errands to help out.

My brother wasn't doing anything to get better and eventually became homeless. Against my better judgment, I picked him up and moved him in with my mother. This ended up being a huge mistake as he fought with her daily. He and I would fight as well, and he'd call me every name in the book, even threatening to kill me. It got so bad that I had to have the police remove him and my mother got an order of protection. I would work so hard to shield my mother from my brother and she would always give in and secretly help him with money and whatever else he needed. One time, while at the house, I asked where her car was. She told me that a friend took it in to the shop for maintenance. A month later the car was still missing and I asked again, receiving the same explanation. Eventually she told me she gave the car to my brother. I realized at that moment there was nothing I could do to help either of them and that was that. I cut off all communication with my brother and stopped speaking with my mother about him. My brother was never going to get better as long as he couldn't admit he was sick and my mother was never going to stop enabling him as long as she continued to feel guilty about his situation. I needed to start worrying about what I could fix and that was my own family.

Although my marriage was rocky, I hadn't thought of quitting. Laura and I had problems but never felt they were marriage-ending. The news I got next would motivate me to be a better father and husband. Laura told me we were having another child. I felt this would be a good thing and help mend our relationship. During the pregnancy, I was on two different tours, which kept me away from the house. This was definitely not the way to work on becoming a better partner. I cut one of the tours short and caught a plane home to be there for the birth of my second child. I made it just in time and was there when Maliah Jade came into the world. I couldn't believe how perfect she was. Usually newborns are all wrinkly and red but she was absolutely gorgeous. This time felt different than when

Mikayla, Cameron, Maliah, Laura

Mikayla was born. I felt more prepared and sure of myself. Now I had two magnificent little girls to protect and take care of. Right there in the delivery room I had an epiphany. Even though I had these two gems in my life, I was still missing something. I realized that I didn't have any kind of faith. I started thinking of everyone in my life who was successful and what they had in common. It was faith in something bigger than themselves. I lived with the philosophy that if I couldn't feel or see it, that it wasn't there. I felt a spirit come over me and this wonderful feeling made me want to be a better person. My boy Joe had been saved, giving himself to Christ and told me how life-changing this had been for him. He never pushed his beliefs on me but said if I ever had any questions he would be there for me. He said that things still weren't perfect but each day was better than the one before. I wanted that feeling in my life and that's when I started praying for guidance. I didn't expect to get an answer, but one came in the form of an opportunity. This opportunity would test my newly found faith while strengthening me in the process. They say God doesn't always give you what you want, but he does give you what you need. I placed my faith in The Lord and it proved to be the missing piece to a truly happy and enriched life.

CHAPTER 36
YOUTUBE

America's Got Talent was a popular television show that featured all kinds of acts from singers to jugglers. It was gaining popularity each year and becoming my generation's *Ed Sullivan Show.* I tuned in every season to see people I knew competing for the chance to be crowned America's top entertainer. On season five a friend of mine, Michael Grasso had become the first magician/ illusionist to make it into the top ten. This was a big deal and made him a featured act on their summer tour. When the season was over his producer asked if he knew of any other magicians that he thought would do well on the show. He and his consultant Rico De La Vega suggested my buddy Scott Alexander. Scott spoke with the producers and sent in a video. They liked what they saw and set up an audition in front of the celebrity judges at the iconic Fox Theater in Atlanta, Georgia. Scott decided to showcase the Water Levitation illusion made famous by Doug Henning and David Copperfield. In this illusion he would make a woman appear out of thin air, floating on a fountain of water. To do this he would need three assistants. One to float, and two to do the backstage operation of the illusion.

He asked if I would assist him and be a consultant. He also said the taping would take nearly ten days out of my life without pay. I thought about it briefly and said yes, because opportunities like this didn't come around all the time and I didn't want to have any regrets. The show flew us out to Atlanta and shipped all the props.

On the set of America's Got Talent

Due to limited space, we rehearsed in the alley behind the theater in less-than-desirable temperatures. It was outright cold and his poor assistant Lisa was freezing her ass off as she floated on a fountain of ice-cold water. It was our turn to audition and the tech crew set us up on the large stage. As soon as the camera light turned red to signal that we were on, something strange happened. From the wings Scott's wife Jenny and I could see him just standing there, frozen like a deer in headlights. We started yelling at him to pick up the cloth and start the trick. After several failed attempts to reach him, he finally snapped out of it on his own and went into his choreography. He caught up with the music and carried out the rest of the illusion without a hitch. The judges not knowing that he had messed up the beginning, gave him good comments and we advanced to the next round in Las Vegas.

For the Vegas round they put us up at the Planet Hollywood Hotel. Coincidentally, this was the same property where I had my second wedding when it was the Aladdin. The room they gave me was insane! It had a drop-down movie screen with projector, washer and dryer, full kitchen, living room, separate bedroom, and a Jacuzzi. I felt like a star and it wasn't even my gig. The Vegas performance was awkward because there was no audience. You had to perform in front of just the three judges, who at the time were Sharon Osborne, How-ie Mandel, and Piers Morgan. They didn't show any expression, so you didn't know if they liked you or not. In the end, Scott advanced and was put through to the quarterfinals. This next round would not be taped as before and was going to be live on TV.

In the live shows, Scott wanted to do something big. I came across an illusion manuscript that I had purchased years before and nev-er used. It was a grand illusion designed to vanished twelve people who would then reappeare moments later in the back of the theater. Scott liked it and came up with the idea of making it a gospel choir instead of just twelve random people. They could be singing right up to the moment they disappeared and start again upon reappearing. He started searching out choirs on YouTube and found the perfect one, The Crenshaw Elite Gospel Choir from Los Angeles. Imagine the whitest man on Earth vanishing twelve black gospel singers. This was either gonna be great or fall completely flat on its ass. The day of the live performance they have a full run-through to block the cameras and troubleshoot. For our rehearsal, things went horribly wrong. The curtain Scott bought to shade the vanish of the choir was treated with flame-retardant chemicals. This was tacky and stuck to the release mechanism therefore, exposing the entire vanish of the singers, making for a not-so-magical performance. We were embar-rassed and devastated, to say the least. The live show was just hours away and we had a defective illusion in need of a quick fix. We took the whole rig into the parking lot of the CBS Studios and started working on it. We didn't have any tools, so we snuck into one of the television show buildings, which I believe was *The Price is Right* and stole, or should I say borrowed, the tools needed to repair the prop. We worked on it right down to the wire and without another rehears-al left it all in God's hands. Once again, a bad rehearsal made for a good show and everything went off without incident and the crowd loved it. The judges' comments were positive with the exception of Howie Mandel. He mentioned being distracted by one of the assis-tants, saying he looked like an accountant. That accountant he spoke about just so happened to be me. Not knowing it then but this would not be the last time I would stand in judgment before Mr. Mandel. Unfortunately for Scott we were eliminated and that was the end of his run. The experience was great and gave us a wealth of knowledge about working live television.

A year passed and I started seeing advertisements
looking for acts to be on
America's Got Talent. I spoke
with Scott and he rec-
ommended me to his old
producer the way Michael
Grasso had done for him a
year earlier. I spoke with his
producer Craig, who told
me that it was too late and
they had already filled all
the slots. He did however
suggest that I upload a video on YouTube for consid-
eration in a special *AGT/*
YouTube submission con-
test. The show would pick

Scott Alexander

the top twelve videos and those acts would compete on a special live
show. Then, after those twelve acts perform, the top four performers
chosen from that show would advance to the semifinals. I took his
advice and uploaded a ninety-second video of me performing the
Dancing Handkerchief. This was a stage version of the trick I saw
performed at The Magic Shop when I first got back into magic. In
my routine an ordinary handkerchief comes to life and dances all
around. It dances on my shoulder, in my pocket, and even in a corked
bottle. I performed a modern one-man version and thought it would
be a good fit for the show. A couple of months later, they announced
who made the top twelve and to my disappointment I was not one of
them. There were three magicians who were chosen, two of which I
knew personally. Although I didn't make the cut I was happy for my
friends. Fast forward two weeks and I get a call from a producer on
AGT who asks if I was still interested in being on the show. Without
giving it any thought I said yes! She proceeded to tell me that one of
the acts that used large tigers in their show had encountered some
problems with the ASPCA and had to drop out of the running. I was
the next magic act on the list and they wanted me for the live You-
Tube show in less than two weeks.

She asked what trick or illusion I would want to perform. I said The Dancing Handkerchief that I had uploaded on YouTube. She tried to tell me that it was a big show and I should do something really big to impress the judges. With such a short time to prepare I said that it would have to be The Dancing Handkerchief or nothing. I didn't want to take a chance and do something I didn't have down with such short notice. Eventually she agreed and I went to join the live shows at

Dancing Handkerchief

the Performing Arts Center in New Jersey. Since I had helped my buddy Scott the year before, he returned the favor and became my assistant and consultant. We worked with the producers to make this small piece of magic look as big and impressive as possible. I had to give them three choices for music so they could submit them for approval to be used on television. The songs I chose were Frank Sinatra's "Young at Heart", "Fireflies" by Owl City, and "Shake, Señora" by Harry Belafonte. When the producer saw "Shake, Señora" he said there was a newer, more modern version done by the artist Pitbull. He played it for me but I felt it was too fast. I said if they could slow the song down I could definitely use it. They agreed and submitted it along with my other suggestions. So now I had to rehearse with all of these songs until I received notice of which one was approved. I also had to do a lot of interviews and B-roll footage, so they could make an interesting video package for me. They pushed the fact I was a husband and father working cruise ships and wanting desperately to be home more with my family. Winning AGT would give me the opportunity to have my own show in one place so I could go home and put my kids to sleep every night. The package made me look like Father of the Year! There was footage of me playing games with the entire family, feeding the baby, swinging Mikayla, etc. In reality, my marriage was falling apart and I was not nearly as present with the kids as they portrayed me to be. That didn't really matter and the producers and editors made me look great!

After watching *AGT* for several years I didn't think my act was strong enough to compete on the show. On a local level my confidence was good, but on a national stage like this felt it was severely lacking. I began to pray like I'd never done before. I remember seeing a movie with Tyler Perry called *Diary of a Mad Black Woman*. In the movie a drug-addict mother and an abusive husband look to Christ to turn their lives around. There's a gospel song that plays when they make the metamorphosis from sinners to believers. This song is called "Father, Can You Hear Me?" I fell in love with the lyrics, melody, and overall message of that song and all that it represented. I found the song and downloaded it to my iPhone. This become my running theme song and helped give me the confidence and strength to have the performance I needed. I listened to it when I woke up, practiced, and went to sleep.

The night of the live performance was stressful and everyone was running around like chickens with their heads cut off. Now I still hadn't been told which song I would be using on the show. They kept saying that they were waiting on permission from the artist. To calm myself, I started watching some of the other acts' performances on the monitors in the green room. Hearing the judges' negative comments was getting to me, so I stopped looking and began to pray again. A short time later, during the commercial break, I was called to the stage. Right before I walked out my producer says, "We just got permission and you're going to be using Pitbull's version of 'Shake, Señora'." I was really happy because out of all my choices his fit the best. When I got out there I remember looking at the judges, who were Howie Mandel, Sharon Osborne, and this year a brand new one, Howard Stern. As mentioned earlier, Howard was from my hometown of Roosevelt and always joked on his radio show about being the only white kid in the neighborhood. I knew he had a reputation of being a smart-ass and was hoping he would take into consideration our common thread and be easy on me. When the commercial was finished the host Nick Cannon introduced me. During his intro he said, "Hey, Howard, he's from Roosevelt, New York," to which Howard looked at me and gave a thumbs up. My music started and I was off. When I did *AGT* with Scott it was at the CBS Studios on a small sound stage. That studio made you hyper-aware of the twenty-two cameras and small audience. My season however was in a proper theater and had a huge audience of over 3,000 people. This made the cameras melt away and hearing the audience's cheers was very calming and felt natural to me. I was in my element and for the following ninety seconds the nerves went away. My set was good and I couldn't ask for it to have gone any better. The

With host Nick Cannon

crowd's applause and screams were deafening and gave me a boost of adrenaline, which felt awesome. Now it was time for the judges' comments. Howard Stern began by acknowledging he too was from Roosevelt and talked about being chased and beaten up many times there. He complimented my act, but said he wanted to see something bigger should I be voted through. Sharon Osborne said I was very professional and confident but wanted bigger, as well. Howie Mandel's comments were pretty much the same. They loved it but felt that I should do something more grand if I made it to the next round.

The following day is judgment when the votes are calculated and the best acts advance to the next show. They called me out for the results with two other acts. It was myself, a female comic, and my good friend, Eric Buss, who is also a magician. They play that really dramatic music and dim the lights to create a tense environment. After a long, uncomfortable pause Nick said, "The act going through and coming one step closer to a million dollars is ... The Magic of Puck." When he called my name I let out a huge sigh of relief. I felt an enormous debt of gratitude to all those who had helped me and also to God for this fabulous blessing.

The second I left the stage I was shuttled into a room with the executive producer, my producer, and some of the tech staff. They wanted to know what I had planned now that I had made it into the semifinals. I didn't even get a chance to soak it all in and went right into creative mode. I had one illusion in mind that was in my show when I worked at Curtis and Susan's theater in Orlando. It was called Asrah, and was invented by a magician named Servais Le Roy in the early 1900s. Here's the basic effect. A woman lies on a couch and is covered with a cloth. She rises and floats high in the air. The cloth covering her is whisked away and she instantly vanishes as the cloth falls to the floor. The illusion regularly stops there, but I added a reappearance of the woman in a glass box that was shown empty just moments before. The executive producer was familiar with the mechanics of this illusion and had reservations it could be pulled off on their stage. I assured them that it could be done, but was asked what else I had, in case it couldn't. I told them I could do the same vanish and reappearance but instead of floating her, she would be seated in a chair before the vanish. I was told to prepare both illusions and they would choose which one I would do. Most performers on the show practice just one ninety-second bit, but I had to practice two. This sucked, but there was nothing I could do about it.

I needed a team and called in Scott's wife, Jenny, as well as my longtime assistant and friend Krystal who was now living in LA. I no longer had the Asrah illusion I used in Orlando and called an illusionist friend John Bundy to see if he had what I needed. He did have one in his warehouse and generously said I could borrow it. We had everything we needed and began preparing both illusions for the semifinals. My producer suggested that I figure out a way to somehow incorporate the Dancing Handkerchief from the previous round. She said it would be a nice callback and give the illusion more personality. I thought it was a brilliant idea and needed to figure out a way to work it in. I spoke with my friend Sean Bogunia, who built the gimmick for the Dancing Handkerchief I used in the quarterfinals. I told him that I wanted to have one of the judges sign a handkerchief and then have that same handkerchief fly from the judges' table to me onstage around twenty feet away. He said he had the perfect solution. He was about to market a gimmick that would do exactly what I needed. A few days later I got the gimmick in the mail and it couldn't

Krystal's reappearance

have been more perfect. I couldn't wait to see the judges' reactions when that silk handkerchief flew off their table. Team Puck worked diligently on both illusions until we felt they were good to go. We had one final rehearsal with just the producers, where we presented the two illusions. They were completely fooled by both and left it up to me as to which one we wanted to present. My final decision was to perform the Asrah.

For my video package this round, they ramped up the good husband and dad premise. They showed me doing magic in Central Park and other spots around New York City. For the live shows they put a lot more time and money into making the act look big. We got pyro, costumes, hair, makeup, and a highly trained tech crew to help with staging. For a moment I got to see what it was like to be in the big time. They wanted us to look the best we could and spared no expense in doing so.

After ten days of preparation and rehearsals it was time to show and prove. For the second time in just a few short weeks, I was on television in front of fourteen millions viewers in a live performance. If something major goes wrong you just suck it up and hope for the best. Again, I prayed! This time Nick's intro spoke about how I had

Flying Silk

amazed the judges in the last round with a handkerchief but was told
to go bigger. He finished by saying, "Let's see what he's got lined up
for tonight. From Roosevelt, New York, it's The Magic of Puck!" I
began by speaking directly to Howard Stern asking him to sign the
handkerchief that was displayed in front of him. When he was done
I told everyone to keep their eyes on the handkerchief and when I
finished that sentence, the hank flew from Howard to me as if willed
by telekinesis. I could see the look of astonishment on their faces. For
the next ninety seconds, everything fell into place. That night exceed-
ed my expectations and everyone on my team did an outstanding
job. Jenny and Krystal were flawless, while Scott made the levitation
look like real magic. I knew that God had shined his light on me that
evening and it was awesome.

As the judges gave their comments I felt like I was going to bust.
They were so complimentary and I have to say, it felt amazing. Even
though I was in front of such a large audience I found myself overcome with a calming sense of intimacy. It was almost like an out-of-
body experience and I was becoming reflective.

CHAPTER 37
PASTEBOARDS

To this point, my life could best be described as a card game and I humbly played the hand I was dealt. My cards at times really sucked, but I stayed the course and always looked forward to getting another chance. With every new hand came more choices and better opportunities to win. In my late teens I looked up the definition of "magician" and found out it was a person with exceptional skill in a particular area. I also looked up the word "illusionist", which read, a person who performs tricks that deceive the eye. I guess when you combine the two you get a master of deception. Now, the word deception usually carries a negative connotation, but in the world of the magician it's much more innocent. In order to turn a bad hand into a good one I had to become an honest liar. The twentieth-century magician Karl Germain said, "Conjuring is the only absolutely honest profession. The conjuror promises to deceive and does." In laymen terms, the magician says he's going to trick you and then fools you badly. Blurring the lines between perception and reality is how I had to play my cards. This became my go-to tool when the deck was stacked against me. If you look in some of the old magic books, playing cards are sometimes referred to as pasteboards. They say playing the pasteboards is more luck than skill. Being a magician, I learned to use my skill to help tip the scale in my favor. Although considered a game of chance, I studied and practiced to manipulate those cards into doing my bidding.

I'd like to think I played the game like a long-distance runner. Along the route I dealt with all the hills, curves, potholes, ditches, and inclement weather. I started out slow and then relied on my endurance and tenacity to scratch and fight for the win. When I was young, my father told me I was really strong and I was beginning to truly understand just what that meant.

Standing onstage in front of America that night got me thinking of just how far I had come. This wasn't supposed to happen. Abandoned at birth, I was set up for failure. In my adolescence I was different and always felt as though I didn't fit in. I never did well in school and stayed in trouble. Losing my father, the one person who I felt truly understood me, was crushing. Court placement in detention homes should have kept me on the wrong path. In my late teens and early adulthood I gravitated toward a life of crime and drugs. Failed marriages and estranged family ties should have broken me. But there was always one constant in my life from age six, and that was magic! Magic pointed me in the right direction. Magic gave me a place to belong and feel accepted. Magic gave me my beautiful children. Magic brought me to God and helped me to find the faith I so desperately needed to succeed. Magic saved my life and I am eternally blessed. I found magic!

CHAPTER 38
CONTINUATION

The previous chapter "Pasteboards" was meant to be the last in this memoir and then the unforeseen happened. A purely by-chance occurrence resulted in a chain reaction that would forever change the very fabric of who I thought I was, and where I thought I came from. I'd like to begin where we left off.

Although I was having public success from my appearances on *America's Got Talent*, my personal life was in disarray. When I submerged myself into the routines I prepared for the television show I was inadvertently neglecting my wife and kids. This only helped to deteriorate an already frail and putrefying marriage. Laura had confided in friends and family that she was no longer happy in our marriage. She felt we were living more like roommates than husband and wife and realized she was no longer in love with me. To be honest I couldn't really slight her for feeling that way. Our substantial age difference, background, and overall take on life were dissimilar. This became a major issue, especially when it came to how we wanted to raise our kids. I was brought up with an old-school approach when it came to parenting whereas Laura practiced a newer mentality. In simple terms when the kids acted out she liked to utilize the occasional "time out" where as I leaned more toward the discipline of "knock out!"

We were growing apart but I wasn't ready to just give up and be alone. I thought long and hard about how difficult it would be for me to start over again. I was in my late forties, had small children, and traveled for a living. Any woman my age had grandkids my children's age. Why would they want to start over again after finally getting their kid out of the house? Also, the amount of trust it would take for someone to comfortably deal with my constant travel and career felt damn near impossible. With that in mind I said to myself that Laura wasn't a bad person, and I was still attracted to her, so why give up my family. We talked and truly tried to work out our marriage but once a woman decides she's done there's little anyone can do to reel her back in. Once I realized it probably wasn't gonna happen I moved out and left Laura and the kids the house. Without involving the courts we came up with an amount that I would pay monthly in child support and then split custody. At first we still had thoughts of reconciliation but the more time that passed, the more we came to the realization we were better off as friends. After almost two years of living apart we finally divorced. We kept our agreement with the kids and just filed papers at the courthouse without contention. Because we split amicably the kids never felt any emotional strain. We became co-parents and continue to do so on very good terms.

Now a single man, I continued to perform and travel the world while still carving out time for my kids. Who would have known, but being a single dad really beefed up my parenting skills. I was finally learning what it meant to be a father. When I was home with them we spent quality time and it was terrific! For the first year I mostly concentrated on work and the girls. By year two I was ready to try my hand at dating. With a busy schedule I decided to go the internet dating route. I was on match.com and a variety of other popular sites, hoping to find that one true love. Unfortunately all I found were a lot of crazies and catfish artists. I remember meeting one woman who, from her profile, was quite attractive and seemed very smart. We chatted for a while and then decided to meet up for dinner. I got to the restaurant and was walking all over looking for the girl from the profile picture. After pacing back and forth an older woman called my name. I must have walked past her five times not knowing she was the same person from the dating site. This woman looked at least twenty years older than her picture and could have been my mother. While seated at the table for dinner I casually asked how long ago it was that she took her profile picture and was surprised when she stated it was new. "New, my ass!" was what my inside voice shouted! Needless to say that was our one and only date. On another occasion I met a woman who was very pretty and after chatting online, we realized we grew up in the same neighborhood and went to the same high school in New York. She was younger but graduated with my best friend Malcom's little brother. I immediately called his brother Chris and asked if he remembered her. He said yes and that she was really hot. So at this point we took our text chats to the phone line and were really hitting it off. She was easy to speak with and we had a neighborhood connection to fall back on. Her profile picture was only a headshot so I asked for a full pic in order to see more. Every time I asked she would come up with some excuse as to why she couldn't send one. She did however describe her body and it sounded sexy. I naively believed her and we continued getting to know each other on the phone. This went on for almost two weeks and then I asked for us to meet. The day before we were set to see each other she finally sent a full head to toe picture. Now I don't want to sound shallow or disrespectful but what she described to me was far from what was pictured. She was probably around 200 plus pounds and not the curvy, shapely physique she previously described. I wasn't disappointed that she was a plus-size woman, that I was alright with. I was disappointed that she had misrepresented herself. Her deceit left a bad taste in my mouth. Looks aren't everything but you have to have an attraction both mentally and physically and these two women had cheated me out of the ability to make a fully informed decision before becoming emotionally involved. My buddy Malcolm suggested that moving forward I should ask for proof of life like in those ransom movies. I could request a recent picture with the woman holding that day's *Wall Street Journal* under her chin! Anyway, I decided that internet dating wasn't for me and maybe I should first learn to love myself and just be happy with my career and children for a while.

Still riding the wave from *AGT*, my career was doing great. I was thoroughly enjoying time with my girls and felt life was good but something was still missing, and that's when the tides turned. Watching an episode of the TV show *Shark Tank* would have an unexpected effect on my life. Two of the contestants asking the millionaire investors for money to make their dream business come true were a couple of Asian woman starting a dating app. They called it "Coffee Meets Bagel." What a crazy name for a dating app, I thought. The women said they wanted to name it something that didn't scream "I'm single and desperately looking for a partner" so "Coffee Meets Bagel" was conceived. This app was like nothing else out there. First off, you didn't search through tons of profiles swiping left and right. Using your Facebook

Coffee Meets Bagel profile pic

friends list as a guide, every day at noon they sent you one profile and picture of who they thought you might like. You can either like that profile or decline it. If you like the person then you are a mutual match and go to a chat room to meet. After being on this app for a couple of months I received my regular noon match and liked what I saw. On my computer screen was a gorgeous Latin woman around ten years my junior who was an educator. I accepted the match and she and I were sent to a private chat room. After my past experiences with dating sites I quickly asked to meet as to not waste time if her profile was bogus. To my disappointment she was in the middle of moving and couldn't meet up. I was scheduled to join a ship in Alaska that week and would be gone for one month. With her move and my schedule we never got the face-to-face meeting I wanted but continued to chat on the site. Our chats evolved to the phone and I got to hear her voice and vibrant personality. We hit it off immediately and were even poking fun at each other right off the bat. Her name was Johana and she was from Puerto Rico but raised in the Bronx, New York and worked as a high school assistant principal.

My soul mate

Super smart and could be very funny and playful at times. She was seven years divorced from her high school sweetheart and they had two sons, 17 & 19. When I told her about my young girls I expected the worse but was pleasantly surprised when she mentioned she always wanted a daughter. I also told her about my career and travel. She said it would be a bit of an adjustment but welcomed the alone time it would permit. So for thirty days on a cruise ship in Alaska we spoke everyday via phone and also on FaceTime. This was the first time I'd ever got to know someone without the distractions of being in the same physical space. It turned out to be a good thing as it eliminated all of the pressures that dinner dates and early intimacy can cause. We just talked and absorbed each other through casual, and sometimes deep, but always playful conversation. I never imagined it would happen but I met the woman I had been waiting my entire life for, and fell in love. Upon returning from my contract we finally met in person and it was as though we had known each other for years. I also introduced her to my girls, something I had never done with any other woman before. She fell in love with them almost instantly and they fell for her, as well.

We dated for a year and decided why waste any more time. Johana and I jumped in with both feet and got married, bought a home, and blended our families. It's crazy how when you learn to like yourself, have faith, and stop aggressively searching for love that it falls right in your lap. This was marriage number three for me and the old adage, "The third times the charm" was beyond fitting. I believe Johana was heaven-sent to be my one true soul mate. God may not come when you want him, but he's always right on time.

CHAPTER 39
20/20

I was in bed one night with my wife and fast-forwarding through an episode of the prime-time news magazine program *20/20*. An image on the screen caught my attention and I felt a strong urge to hit rewind on my remote. The image was a graphic that read, "Louise Wise Agency". I knew that name from the letter I received as a teen when inquiring about my adoption. I quickly hit play to find out what it was about. The narrator said Louise Wise was the premier agency to adopt Jewish children in the sixties. What I learned next was very disturbing and had my heart beating double time. Louise Wise had been secretly splitting up newborn twins and triplets, sending them to live in separate adoptive homes. They never told the new parents that the child they had taken into their family had an identical sibling or siblings. In this one particular case a set of triplet boys were sent to three different homes. One with a wealthy family, one middle class, and the other poor. They were trying to see how these children would develop being raised in different styles and classes of homes. It was the ultimate experiment in nature verses nurture. They had psychologists visit these children regularly and evaluate them from newborn to age ten. They were being tested and even observed on film. The whole case study was finally exposed when the three boys accidentally found each other in their late teens. This *20/20* episode was to promote the documentary about these particular boys titled *Three Identical Strangers*.

This brought up a bunch of feelings from the past and I began to tear up. Once when I was a teen my mother and I had gotten into a battle of words. She would often throw daggers and slide in tidbits from my adoption in retaliation. This one instance she told me if I ever meet a girl whose last name is Feldman to be careful not to sleep with her, as she could be my sister. I never understood exactly what she meant but assumed my birth mother's name was Feldman and it was possible she had other children and was simply a warning. Watching this show that statement took on a whole different interpretation as I contemplated was I a twin or triplet?

Louise Wise had been closed for some years but the journalists did find some of the people that participated in these home visits. They asked if they felt any remorse for splitting up these children and to my surprise the answer was, "No." One even tried to justify their behavior stating that back then there was a shortage of white, Jewish children and separating them gave more families the opportunity to adopt. When I heard this it all started to make sense. That was probably the reason I had seen so many of the other children get adopted while I remained in the foster home; I was Jewish but not the desired color.

At the end of the program they said if you were adopted through the Louise Wise Agency in the sixties to write the address shown to find out if you were part of this highly unethical experiment. Without hesitation I wrote down the address and the following day sent an e-mail.

I started getting e-mails from a company called Spence-Chapin. They had acquired all of the adoption records from Louise Wise upon their closing and would be handling my inquiry. They told me to be patient as they searched for my records and prepared them. It took nearly six months and then I received a phone call from a gentleman in their office letting me know that my paperwork had been prepared and would be in my e-mail shortly. He called personally to explain a little about some of the emotions I may be dealing with after reading what they found. This started to scare me a bit and I began to worry. He told me to reach out to him should I have any questions or concerns. He also told me about some support groups that I could join as well as professionals to speak with should what I learn become too heavy for me to handle. I was now bracing myself for the worse as I waited nervously for the report to show up in my inbox.

Within twenty minutes the report arrived. I was in the car with my wife when it came in and immediately pulled over. I was all over the place emotionally so Johana read it to me and this is what it said.

SPENCE-CHAPIN

Prepared by Joeseph M Hall, MSW

Provided on June 29, 2018

Introduction

Spence-Chapin is the legal custodian of your Louise Wise adoption records. When Louise Wise closed, Spence-Chapin, as an approved adoption agency agreed to maintain Louise Wise files in perpetuity in accordance with New York law. In response to your request for adoption record information we have reviewed your file and we are happy to provide you with a summary of the information contained therein. Please note that this Personal Adoption History narrative is based on what your birth mother chose to disclose during the planning for your adoption. The information cannot be verified. Please understand that the language used in your record may reflect societal and professional norms of the time period in which your adoption was planned.

Spence-Chapin is bound by law with regards to the information we can provide. New York State law only permits the release of non-identifying information.

Birth Mother and Maternal Birth Family

Your birth mother was born in the Northeast region of the United States, and that is the region where she was residing at the time of your birth. She was twenty-one years old when you were born. It was reported that her race was White, and she practiced the Jewish faith. She stood approximately five feet and five inches tall, and she was of "average" weight. She was described as having long, straight light-brown hair, greenish-blue eyes, and a fair complexion. She was said to be quite friendly," "attractive," "rebellious," and "of good intelligence." Your birth mother discontinued her school in her senior year of high school. After high school she left home and held various jobs including as a

waitress, a typist, and as an assistant for a commercial artist. She en-
joyed painting and aspired to become a painter. She was also interested
in sports, and it was indicated that she had received some instruction
in pet grooming.

Regarding your birth mother's physical health history the following in-
formation was reported. Your birth mother was diagnosed with a mild
seizure disorder called "petit mal," symptoms of which began when she
was twelve years old. The disorder, which she managed with medica-
tion involved attacks about twice per year involving hand twitches and
numbness of the mouth. It was stated that she fainted a couple of times
during adulthood due to pressure on the right side of her brain for which
she was hospitalized. It was noted that about two years before you were
born your mother was in an automobile accident that resulted in about
a three month hospital stay.

Regarding your birth mother's mental heath history it was reported that
during a time of significant stress in her early adulthood she experienced
an hysterical episode which resulted in a brief stay in a psychiatric
center. It was also reported that your birth mother was a heroine addict,
a condition for which she voluntarily engaged in psychiatric treatment.
It was stated that she began using heroine about three years before you
were born.

Your birth mother was the oldest of three siblings, including her younger
sister and brother, who are your maternal birth aunt and uncle. Both of
your maternal birth aunt and uncle were residing with your maternal
birth grandparents in the Northeast region of the United States at the
time of your birth. Your maternal aunt was seventeen while your mater-
nal birth uncle was fourteen at the time.

About three years before you were born your birth mother gave birth to a
son who does not share a birth father with you and therefore he is your
biological half-brother.

Birth Father and Paternal Birth Family

Your birth mother reported the following about your birth father. He was
forty years old when you were born. His place of birth and his place of
residence at the time of your birth were unspecified. It was reported that
he was Black. It was indicated that he may have practiced the Prot-
estant faith, although your birthmother stated she was not sure of his

religion. He was said to be tall with a slender build. He was described as having dark hair that was closely cropped, and dark eyes that were intense and he had a medium complexion. He was further described as attractive and it mentioned that he had a goatee. Your birth father's education was unspecified. He was a jazz musician who composed musical scores for films, and he played the piano for a band. He was said to be well known in his profession. No health history information was provided for your birth father.

At the time of your birth your father was married to a woman who was not your birth mother. However he and his wife had been maritally separated for approximately two years before you were born. Your birth father and his wife had two children together by the time of your birth. Their children are your biological half siblings whose ages and genders were unspecified in the record. It was stated that the biological half siblings of yours were residing with their mother in the Northeast region of the United States at the time of your birth. Nothing further was reported about your birth fathers family.

Prenatal, Birth and Adoption

It was noted that your birth parents had known each other for over one year prior to the time of your birth and they resided together for part of that time. Together they left the Northeast region of the United States and relocated to Europe. When your birth mother learned that she was pregnant with you she informed your birth father who was happy to know she was pregnant. However he reportedly began dating another woman while in Europe at which point your birth mother ended their relationship and returned to the Northeast region of the US. Your birth mother stated that she had not seen or communicated with your birth father for about six months before your birth. She had heard that he had also returned to the United States but she was unable to locate him.

Requesting assistance in planning your adoption your birth mother was in communication with Louise Wise about six moths before your birth. Your birth mother expressed a desire to parent you. However, she also expressed that she was currently without resources and had no definite place of residence or means of support. In consideration of those factors and under the circumstances of her relationship with your birth father she felt she would be unable to provide you with the security and stability in life that she felt you deserved. She believed that adoption would

be in your best interest. Your adoption planning occurred in conjunc-
tion with a governmental child welfare agency who conducted a diligent
search for your birthfather to no avail. Your birth father was therefore not
informed when you were born and he did not participate in the planning
of your adoption.

About three months before you were born your birth mother married a
man who was not your birth father. Your birth mother did not report
this to Louise Wise until after you were born and therefore not much is
known about your birth mother's husband or their relationship.

It was reported that your birth mother took barbiturates and used her-
oine while she was pregnant with you. It was stated that your birth
mother was arrested and taken temporarily to a detention center about
two months before your birth. In her final months of pregnancy your
birth mother was hospitalized for her petit mal condition as well as for
drug detoxification. Your birth mother received prenatal medical care.

On June 17, 1966 you were born in a hospital in the Northeast region
of the Untied States. Your delivery was normal and spontaneous. You
were born weighing seven pounds and eight ounces and you were twenty
and one half inches long. You were said to be a healthy newborn who
did not have any withdrawal symptoms. You were described as a hand-
some child with a mass of very curly hair and brown eyes. You were
also described as having an oval face and pleasant facial features.

You remained in the hospital for about two and one half moths fol-
lowing your birth due to a condition of hypospadias. The condition
reportedly was considered not serious. When you were discharged from
the hospital at about two and one half months of age you joined a
private home of a foster family which had been arranged in conjunction
between Louise Wise and the governmental child welfare agency.

Following your birth your birth mother came in and out of communi-
cation with Louise Wise and the governmental child welfare agency. It
was indicated that your birth mother was conflicted between her desire to
parent you and her understanding that she would not be able to provide
you with adequate care. It was believed that this conflict would become
overwhelming for your birth mother rendering her unable to efficiently
communicate with the workers who were making adoption arrangements
for you. Additionally, the fact that your birth mother was married to her

husband at the time of your birth further complicated your adoption planning. Even though her husband is not your biological father, because of his marriage to your birth mother he was considered to be your legal father. Legal fathers are required to provide consent to the adoption of their spouse's children. Your birth mother and her husband divorced about fourteen months after your birth. Following their divorce your legal father's whereabouts were difficult to track and it became a prolonged process to locate him for the purpose of obtaining his signature on documents consenting to your legal adoption.

When you were about two years old your foster family could not continue their child care commitments for reasons unrelated to you. It was therefore arranged for you to join another private home of a foster family. When you were almost three years old your birth mother requested a visit with you which was permitted. It was unspecified in the record where the visit took place though most often birth parents visits occurred at the Louise Wise office. It was observed that you and your birth mother played and interacted well together and your birth mother expressed that she was genuinely pleased with the fine progress that you were making in your development.

Following the visit with your birth mother she expressed a desire to parent you. However she subsequently had trouble maintaining communication with Louise Wise and the governmental child welfare agency and she continuously was unable to demonstrate that she was taking steps toward readiness for parenthood. Therefore Louise Wise and the child welfare agency believed that it was in your best interest to move ahead in the planning of your adoption.

When you were about four years old your foster family was temporarily unable to continue their child care commitments for reasons unrelated to you. You therefore began residing in the third private home of a foster family for a period of about five months. When you were a few months shy of your fifth birthday you returned under the care of your second foster family. Louise Wise had been monitoring your health and development since your birth and it was reported that you had grown into a healthy and well developed child.

When you were approximately five years old a judge ordered that your birth mother's parental rights be terminated and you then became eligible for legal adoption. On December 6, 1971 when you were five and *one half years old you joined the home of your adoptive family. Your adoptive paternal grandparents resided near your second foster family and therefore your adoptive parents reported to Louise Wise that they were fond of you and knew you very well. Your adoptive parents had expressed an interest not only in adoption but specifically in adopting you. Prior to your legal adoption finalization Louise Wise continued to monitor your progress while in the home of your adoptive parents. It was concluded that you were doing very well in the care of your new parents and Louise Wise formally recommended your legal adoption. On November 28, 1972 when you were almost six and one half years old your adoption was legally finalized in the Family Court of Queens County, New York.*

When Johana finished reading we both just sat there in the car with tears in our eyes. It was like being dropped off of a tall building. I was a ball of emotions and trying feverishly to process all that I had just heard. When I wrote to Louise Wise at fourteen while in George Jr. they had sent a very tame and select portion of what was in my file. I guess they didn't feel I could handle the full story at such a young age, especially considering my juvenile situation at the time. What a crazy ordeal I went through at such an early age but the one saving grace was that I wasn't a twin or triplet.

I started to fantasize about what famous jazz musician and composer my birth father could be. Maybe Quincy Jones? My adoption report mentioned my birth father composed for films and I knew that Quincy scored the iconic television mini series "Roots" and movie "The Color Purple", not to mention he had an affinity for white woman. I jokingly thought about all the back child support coming my way. I had always tinkered on the family piano in my home and was starting to understand where my musical interest may have stemmed from. At a young age I gravitated toward jazz music and played drums in the improv class at my junior high school. My oldest daughter taught herself to play piano and it came so naturally to her. Was this all a coincidence, or just in our blood? The fibers of my life were starting to come together.

Hearing that my birth mother had met with me and pondered the possibilities of keeping me was a little hard to take. I had always believed the reason for not getting adopted until I was five had to do with my not being as desirable as the newborns. To hear that my birth mother didn't relinquish her parental rights until they were snatched away by a judge in the child welfare department changed everything. I wasn't undesirable and unwanted. The mere thought of that had always weighed heavy on my heart. A little over fifty years old and I was finally learning my origins. What came next was an unexpected twist in my life story all thanks to a little spit in a tube.

CHAPTER 40
BLOOD

For my birthday Johana gave me a present that would bring me closer to the answer of who am I, and where did I come from. This very thoughtful gift was a personal DNA kit from Ancestry.com. I sent in my tube of DNA and waited the six to eight weeks to receive my results. When I got the e-mail that my kit findings were ready to be viewed my heart began to race. I logged onto the site and saw that my background was split down the middle between European Jewish and African with a touch of Caribbean thrown in for flavor. This information verified that the nationality Spence-Chaplin had sent was correct. Then they have a page that shows all of your DNA matches. These are people that share your DNA and are your relatives categorized from very close to distant. My matches showed two hits, a very close match as well as a second cousin. I sent them both messages stating who I was and that I would like to speak with them if they were up for it. I quickly received a response from both with contact info and an available time for me to call.

The first person I spoke with was the very close match. It was a man named Marc Ressler who lived not to far from me in Jacksonville, Florida. When he answered I could tell from his voice that he was white. He sounded very pleasant but I could tell was a bit confused of how we were related. When I asked about his family background he told me he was adopted and knew very little of his birth family. Then I asked how old he was and he answered "Fifty-four".

That's only three years my senior and then it hit me. In the report Spence-Chapin sent it stated my birth mother had another son from a man who was not my birth father just three years before having me. I was talking to my half brother. I let him know I was adopted too and about the adoption report. Between my file and the very close DNA match on Ancestry there was no question we were half siblings. He seemed just as stunned as I was to learn about this revelation. Marc told me that

My half brother Marc

he owned several businesses and was married with a young child close in age to my youngest. For the next forty or so minutes we chatted and familiarized ourselves with each other. He told me that he was raised with Jewish parents in Queens, and I mentioned that I grew up there, too. I told him the story about how I started this journey toward my biological family after seeing the *20/20* episode about The Louise Wise Agency. He said that he was going to write Spence-Chapin and inquire if he went through Louise Wise, too. He asked about our birth mother and I hated having to tell him that she was a troubled woman. He was a little caught off guard to learn of her heroin and barbiturates addictions. However, from my report it said she didn't start using until after Marc was born. He was relived to hear that and we joked about how I drew the short straw since she was using heavily during her pregnancy with me. We exchanged social media pages so we could put a face with the voice on the other end of the phone. From his pictures I could see that his father was white and the only physical characteristic we seemed to share was our dimples. I felt a calm, familiar connection to this man that I had only known for less than an hour. We were strangers joined by blood.

Cousin Martee

My biological mother Michele Feldman

Next I spoke with the second cousin match, which turned out to be the key to unlocking my entire family tree. Her name was Martee Shabsin and she lived in Laguna Beach, California. Martee sounded older and seemed intelligent as well as very sweet. As I told her who I was and about my adoption she seemed intrigued and asked a lot of questions. When I told her about my file from the adoption agency she wanted to know what they said about my parents. I was open about my birth mother's addiction as well as the seizures and poor mental health. She said without hesitation I know who your mother is, she's my cousin Michele. She said Michele Feldman is your mother! I knew she had to be right because of the comment my mother had made some time back about me being careful should I meet a girl with the last name Feldman. I had found my birth mom and was feeling an array of emotions. What I felt was short-lived when Martee continued and told me that Michele had passed away seventeen years earlier. She said that my birth mother's sister and brother were still alive and she would reach out so I could meet them. Martee hadn't seen my birth mom since they were very young but sent all the pictures she could find of them from that time period. Although these old black and white pictures depicted my birth mother as a child it was fascinating nonetheless. I was looking to see if we shared any similarities at that age. I couldn't believe I was looking at the woman that gave me life. I was saddened to know we would never meet and talk so I could ask the thousands of questions that were ricocheting throughout my head. I would never get to see her face and tell her that I held no animosity

My biological father Mal Waldron

or resentment toward her and in fact would like to thank her for being strong enough to let me go and be raised by a family that could give me the life she was not capable of providing. This meeting was not going to happen, but Martee would continue to fill in all the blanks of my biological family. Martee told me that my maternal aunt lived in Virginia but didn't know where my uncle lived at the time. My aunt's name was Honi Feldman Lacy and my uncle was Jesse Feldman. After some detective work, Martee was able to contact Honi and tell her about me. From their conversation Honi mentioned she was aware of me and had even seen a picture Michele showed her from when we visited during my stay in the foster homes. Then she asked Honi if she knew who my birth father was. Without skipping a beat Honi said, "Yes" and proceeded to tell her his name.

I was laying in bed with Johana when I heard my phone vibrate. It was around 4 a.m. and since I was having a hard time sleeping decided to check it out. I had received an e-mail from Martee and the first line read "I know who you father is!" I couldn't move and just sat up in my bed temporarily paralyzed for thirty seconds. I finally brought myself to continue reading what Martee had sent. She said while talking with my aunt Honi she learned that my father was a man named Mal Waldron. Below this sentence was a Wikipedia link with the name Malcolm Earl "Mal" Waldron. His name was Malcolm! I had always heard that my birth mother named me and I thought it had something to do with Malcolm X, who was murdered while I was growing in her stomach. I couldn't have been more off the mark. It was way more significant than that, she named me after my birth father. So I guess in a roundabout way, I was a Junior. My head was going to explode and I had to see more. Hesitantly I touched the link and couldn't believe all that was popping up on my phone screen. His Wikipedia page was tremendous and said that he was a legendary American jazz pianist, composer, and arranger. He had more than 100 albums under his own name and seventy for other band leaders. The little blurb about him in my first adoption report from Louise Wise didn't even scratch the surface of who this man was in the jazz world. He was a *giant!* Then I did a Google image search for Mal Waldron and found a vast amount of pictures posted there. The resemblance was very similar. Through the tears that were steadily streaming from my eyes I was looking at a darker-skinned me. My sobbing unintentionally woke Johana. She was worried that I received some bad news or something but that wasn't it at all. I told her I found my father and proceeded to show her all that I had been viewing. I put in a search on YouTube to see if I could find some video of him, and boy did I! There were so many videos of his music and then I struck gold. There right in front of me was a full documentary on my birth father titled *A Portrait of Mal Waldron*. This was a film by Tom Van Overberghe that was released in 1997. It examined Mal's life and there were appearances by many jazz legends all speaking in admiration about his illustrious career. I got to see Max Roach, Steve Lacy, Jeanne Lee, and others raving about the man that fathered me. The most wonderful thing about the documentary was being able to see the man himself playing music and talking candidly about his work and life. At one point Johana had fallen back to sleep and when she briefly awoke asked why I was watching videos of myself. She heard Mal's voice in the film and thought it was me. I closed my eyes and listened for a minute. She was absolutely right, we sounded very much alike. This gave me a proud, yet eerie, feeling.

I learned that he was the one and only Billie Holiday's accompanist for the last three years of her life. They wrote a song together called "Left Alone" that she never got to record as she passed away shortly after. It would later be recorded by Abbey Lincoln and a host of other prominent jazz singers. It was released again in 1993 by Joe

Left Alone written by Mal & Billie Holiday

Satriani, reaching #21 on Billboard's Mainstream Rock charts and received a nomination for Best Rock Instrumental Performance at the 1995 Grammy Awards. Mal spoke of how "Lady Day" became like an older sister to him and helped develop his talent. When I was with my first wife we both shared a love of jazz. As stated earlier, I played drums which coincidently I learned from my adopted father and she had played tenor saxophone when she was younger. As a kid I remembered seeing Diana Ross portray Billie Holiday in *Lady Sings the Blues* and fell in love with her music. Kecia also loved Billie and we started listening to her music around the house and on long drives. I had no idea at the time that my birth father was playing on some of those very recordings that were flowing so melodiously throughout my ears. Looking back I believe it was a genetic connection to Mal, matched with the introduction I received from my adopted father that drew me to Billie and the appreciation I had for the world of improvisational jazz music. It was the perfect balance.

Mal's most well-known composition was a song he titled "Soul Eyes." It was recorded by John Coltrane, whom he had worked with shortly after John left Miles Davis's band. This sultry ballad became a jazz standard and has since been recorded hundreds of times by

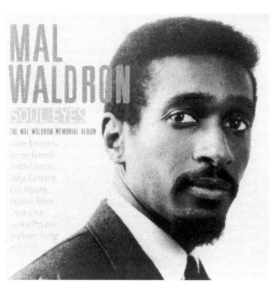

Mal's famous jazz standard Soul Eyes

a host of artists riding the rhythm and lyrics he composed. I did a search of his classic song and the list of recordings went on for pages. There was even a current artist named Kandace Springs, a protégé of Prince that recorded it and even titled her album "Soul Eyes." The song and album with collaborator Terence Blanchard shot her to prominence scoring appearances on David Letterman, Jimmy Kimmel, and *The Tonight Show* with Jimmy Fallon. Unfortunately he never got to see these newer artists interpreting his work as he passed away in December of 2002 at the age of 77 in Brussels, Belgium. Again I found myself with that full, yet empty, feeling. Another birth parent I will never get to sit with and share life's journey. I couldn't stop there and needed to know more. At that point I decided to dive in and learn as much as I could about the people who birthed me.

CHAPTER 41
HALF DOZEN

I spoke with Martee and asked for my maternal aunt's phone number. I needed to speak with her myself and ask about my birth mother. I thought if anyone would know who she really was it would be her younger sister. I took a couple days to think on it and then called my maternal aunt. When she answered the phone I asked if this was Honi and pronounced it Ho-knee in which she corrected me saying it was pronounced Honey. I felt pretty stupid butchering her name like that but she made me feel at ease and we began to converse. Honi knew who I was even before I said my name. She had received a heads up from Martee and was expecting my call. I asked her to tell me about my birth mother and she didn't pull any punches. She basically said that her sister Michele was a pain in the ass! I chuckled to myself that she was being so raw. Then she explained how her sister had put their family though the wringer. She was always doing bizarre things that would end with the family having to bail her out. She said Michele became pregnant with Marc as the result of a fling in her senior year of high school. She mentioned the family was unaware since she was not living home at the time and wore loose-fitting clothes to hide her baby bump. When she finally came clean, the family helped her with the adoption process since the father denied any involvement and she was in no position to raise a child alone. When Michele was pregnant with me, the family was aware and her father was dead set against Michele hav-

My maternal aunt Honi

Michele the free spirit

ing me. I asked if it had anything to do with it being "The sixties" and she was a white Jewish woman having a black child to which she replied, "No, it was because she was a screw up and they knew she couldn't take care of me." I told Honi that my adoption report had mentioned my birth parents lived together in Europe until Mal started seeing another woman. She explained that this was incorrect. Mal was living in Paris at the time and didn't know that Michele was pregnant. At a concert in California Michele befriended singer Peter Yarrow of the American folk group Peter, Paul, and Mary. She told him she was pregnant with Mal Waldron's child and wanted to go to Paris and let him know personally. She didn't have the means to fly so Peter gave her money for a one-way ticket to Europe. Upon meeting up with Mal to give him the news he had some news for her as well; he was living with another woman. I asked Honi if this was hard on my birth mom, but she said her sister wasn't the jealous type and in fact wouldn't mind sharing if you get what I'm saying. This was 1965 and still the time of free love so I'm guessing this attitude wasn't uncommon. Michele decided to return to the US and was depending on a government program at the time that offered cost free flights back for certain US citizens but unfortunately it had ended so she again relied on her family who helped get her home.

My birth mom had been married several times but a couple of these were sham unions to acquire US citizenship. That explains why they couldn't find the man she married right before I was born so he could sign off on my adoption. Honi sent several pictures of my birth mom at different ages throughout her life. There was even a photo with one of her sham husbands named Dan from Thailand as well as another with Eddie Mormando who was a legitimate husband she was with for many years until his death. I can truly see how she was a strain on her family. It's probably a good thing that Marc and I were her only children.

When she was younger Michele was diagnosed with epilepsy but this prognosis was incorrect. What she really had was a condition called arteriovenous malformation or AVM, and it was considered fatal without treatment. This causes a tangle of abnormal blood vessels connecting arteries and veins in the brain. The Arteries are responsible for taking oxygen-rich blood from the heart to the brain. Veins carry the oxygen-depleted blood back to the lungs and heart. A brain AVM disrupts this vital process. AVMs are rare and affect less than one percent of the population. Around 1983, world renowned neuroradiologist Dr. Alex Bernstein, who pioneered embolization of AVMs, operated successfully on Michele and she survived another eighteen years before the symptoms returned. She died in New York City in August 2001, a month before 9/11.

Now that I knew my parents' names it was a natural progression for me to search for any other siblings. I had already met my half brother Marc from my birth mother and knew she had no other children. I then focused my attention on my birth father, Mal Waldron. Spence-Chapin's report mentioned that Mal had two children from his wife but didn't state their ages or genders. I took to Google in a fevered search for more information. Eventually I found what I was looking for, a page that had a small biography documenting Mal's family tree. Mentioned in the text was the wife he was separated from while with my birth mother. Her name was Elaine and she occasionally sang on his recordings. They had two daughters, one of which was Billie Holiday's goddaughter. It didn't say how old they were but I knew they had to be much older than me, since Billie Holiday had died in 1959, seven years before my birth. I used my detective skills or lack thereof to check Facebook. I thought how common could the name Waldron be? I searched mainly for females, hoping something would stand out and sure as the day is bright I found something. One of the names on the list of Waldrons was a woman named Mala. I said to myself that has to be it. I went to her page and knew in an instant she had to be my half sister. Her photos were an array of album covers and live concert pictures. Upon further examination I read she was a jazz singer,

He's my father album cover

pianist, and composer like her dad. There was one cover in particular that made me start to imagine a life that could have been. It was an album with her and Mal together. They had a recording titled "He's My Father." Seeing them on a project together made me feel like I had missed out on something. Don't get me wrong, the father who adopted and raised me until his early passing was my number one fan and I loved him beyond words. It's just that looking at them together like that made me feel a little hollow inside. I guess it's something that's just fathomless.

Just like with Mal I searched YouTube to see if she had any music or videos I could watch. There were several concerts listed and I clicked on one with Mala and her band performing live at the Kennedy Center in Washington, D.C. I was beyond impressed with her skills as a singer, songwriter, and pianist. She was awesome and there was no doubt her father's talent had trickled down.

I noticed that Mala and I had a mutual Facebook friend named Ivy. I had no idea how she knew Mala but I sent her a message to inquire about the connection. After some time passed my friend Ivy responded and said she knew Mala from the neighborhood and was friends with her younger sister Lauren. The neighborhood she referred to was Malverne. This was the same place I lived while in Mr. Brown's foster detention home as a troubled teen. Could I have been that close to my siblings and not have known it? This story just kept getting better and better. Ivy asked how I knew Mala and I told her that I didn't. Next, I brought her up to speed on what I did know and told her that I was thinking Mala could be my half sister. Ivy expressed how deep that was and asked what I planned to do with this information. I asked if she thought Mala would be receptive to me approaching her with all of this and she answered very honestly, saying she didn't really know. Again, she had been friends with the younger sister and didn't know Mala well enough to give a definitive answer. Taking a leap into the midst I decided to send Mala a message and hoped for the best. Thinking about writing and actually finding the right words took a couple of days. I wanted to let her know who I was but not scare her away thinking I was some kind of kook or guy trying to gnaw his way into their already established family. This was so damn tricky and was driving me nuts. I would write something, then second guess myself and erase it, all to write something else equally worthy of deletion. Finally I settled on the mindset of less is more. I would send a simple note asking for a phone call and then drop the bomb on her later. My message to Mala read, "Hi Mala, my name is Malcolm Puckering and I would like to speak with you about your father if at all possible. Please let me know if this would be OK? Thank you." A few days later a response, "Hello Malcolm, I'm out of the country at the moment. Perhaps we can speak when I return home on Sept 3. Thanks, Mala."

It was August 16th when I received her message and September 3rd couldn't come fast enough. It seemed like forever as I waited impatiently to learn if I'd found another sibling. I took this time to think about what I really wanted to learn about this man and the family that knew him. I didn't want just the usual questions answered, I wanted the unusual ones too. I had a desire to learn everything, while at the same time searching for clues to my own identity. The wait was over and I sent Mala a follow up message to establish a day and time to connect. We settled on the following day at noon and I was to initiate the call. Right on time I dialed her number, which had a New York area code. She answered within a couple of rings and our conversation began. I told her that I was adopted and had recently come into possession of my adoption file with detailed descriptions of my birth parents, minus the identifying material. I explained that according to the records my birth father was a 40-year-old black man and was a talented jazz pianist and composer who also scored films. It was also stated that he was well known in his profession. At the time of my birth he was married but separated from his wife. I then told her about my DNA results from Ancestry and how it led me to a maternal aunt that knew who my birth father was. She said his name was Mal Waldron. I further detailed that after researching Mal's Wikipedia page I learned his date of birth was exactly 40 years before I was born, just as my records had documented. She was silent for a moment and then kind of chuckled and said, "The time line seems right and it's surely possible." Then she followed with, "He did love women and dated a lot." That previous statement was just the right mix of humor and certitude, allowing the tension created by my opening monologue to slowly disappear. Speaking with Mala didn't feel as uncomfortable and awkward as I'd anticipated. She was very warm and seemed open to what I was suggesting. If the shoe had been on the other foot I would have probably been a lot more guarded. I asked if anyone else had ever approached her family with the same claim and she said I was the first that she'd heard of. That was comforting to know he wasn't some serial sperm donor with hundreds of illegitimate children scattered all around the world. She asked me to tell her once again about my adoption and how I came upon this information. At times there were brief moments of silence and I could tell Mala was slightly shaken as she strove to ingest all I was conveying. It was obvious she was caught off guard and not prepared for this conversation. Evidently Mala thought when I messaged wanting to speak about her father that I was a writer, musician, or journalist of some sort and was solely calling to talk about her dad and his body of work. We spoke for around an hour and I was learning so much in such a short time. As I talked she mentioned that Mal and I sounded very much alike. I guess my wife was dead on in making that same analogy.

Mala and I had some surprising similarities. We were both born in June and our astrological sign was Gemini. She joked how Geminis are very indecisive and could be a handful when it came to making plans, something I could definitely relate to. We were both performers and notably comfortable in front of large audiences, a trait we more than likely inherited from our shared father. Mala had been

Mala Waldron

married multiple times and was in a fairly new marriage as well. She also had two daughters from a pervious marriage. Then it became even more incredible. We had grown up in Queens and not just the borough, but the same small towns. I started out in St Albans and so did her family. I was relocated to Springfield Gardens after my adoption and they lived there, too. My parents moved us to Roosevelt, a town where the Waldrons had also resided. Lastly, I was sent by the courts to live in Malverne and she and her sister both went to Malverne High School. What are the odds that I would be within a stone's throw of my paternal family all throughout my early life? This was uncanny and the thought of living in such close proximity was simply astonishing.

Her father's side of the family was from Jamaica, something I found to be a humorous connection since my adopted mom and dad were also from the West Indies. So, basically no matter which family raised me there was no way to avoid a strict Caribbean upbringing.

I then started in with questions on who Mal was as a father and person in general? Mala said when her parents divorced Mal was living in Europe. That meant her mother did a majority of the parenting and Mal got to see them on school breaks, usually overseas and on the few occasions he performed in the States. Their family time together was said to be enjoyable and they got to travel and watch him perform. Mala said Mal was a chain smoker and was rarely seen without a non-filter cigarette hanging from his lips. She said they would sometimes laugh as he played piano with a lit cigarette in his mouth that sported a two-inch-long ash that never seemed to break off. On occasion, she and Lauren would get burnt by the cherry red ember as they received hugs from their dad. Mal could have a lurid

An older Mal

sense of humor and would call at odd hours just to share a joke. She said he didn't speak a lot, so much so that he rarely did any verbal intros for his compositions. During concerts he would play one song, then another, all without the usual backstories and overly dramatized facts. He just did what he did, and that was play music! I guess that's where his love of telling jokes came into play, they were his comfort zone when it came to socializing. He spoke four languages, English, French, German, and Japanese, which is sort of ironic for a man of so few words.

Early in his career he had used heroin, like my birth mother. Mala said that he hid this very well and not even his closest friends, family, or fellow artists knew. In an interview I found online he talked openly about how a lot of musicians back then used heroin, believing it help to advance their music. In 1963 he had a major breakdown caused by an overdose. He said it was so bad that he couldn't remember his own name or how to play piano. He received shock treatments and a spinal tap to bring him back. It took over two years for him to regain his motor skills and return to playing piano regularly. Some say that when he relearned to play music it was then that he developed the distinct style which would later define him. Whether that is true or not, he didn't use heroin again.

Mal re-married and started another family on the other side of the ocean. His second wife was a Japanese singer named Hiromi who had two children when they met. They had three kids together whose names were Sara, Michael, and believe it or not, "Malcolm". Malcolm was his oldest with Hiromi, which led me to the reality that my birth father was probably unaware that Michele gave birth to a boy and had named him Malcolm. If Mal had known about me it was unlikely he would have had another namesake. I was overcome with sadness to learn my birth father most likely didn't even know I existed. I thought how could this be since my birth mother had flown all the way to Paris to inform him? Did he just not care to follow up and find out if she'd had his child? Maybe he thought she decided to terminate the pregnancy? I didn't know what to think and will probably never learn the answer. This is something I would have to come to terms with and be content with all the pieces of the puzzle that I was able to connect. One uplifting thing to come from this new revelation was the fact I had another three half siblings. This new information brought my count to six, or should I say one half dozen.

CHAPTER 42
FAMILY

Learning you have a half sibling with only presumptive evidence can be hard to swallow, and before you can fully commit to the situation more proof is required. Mala never said this was the case but I completely understood if she needed more convincers to be sure. Knowing that I was on Ancestry.com, Mala decided to have a search done with them, as well. This would be all the confirmation needed to know the absolute truth. While we waited to get her results our conversations continued. I told Mala that I felt a connection with her that couldn't really be put into words and she acknowledged the same feeling. We decided if our DNA did not match it was OK because at least we got to meet each other and that was still a good thing. I so enjoyed our talks and was not only getting to know her but also about my paternal grandparents, half sister Lauren, and of, course, Mal. Mala said that Lauren worked in the film industry as a script supervisor and also wrote some herself. She lived in Los Angeles and kept very busy. I asked if she had told Lauren about me and her answer was, "Yes." She mentioned that her sister was very laid back and wasn't the excitable type but seemed interested in my story. I asked if she could set up an introduction and a few days later she sent me Lauren's phone number. When we spoke Lauren was very nice but definitely not as much of a conversationalist as her older sister. We had a very good talk and she told me a lot of great stories about my birth father. Between my two half sisters, I felt as though I was really getting to know the man who for so long had been a mystery. I mentioned that I performed regularly at The Magic Castle in LA and would love to meet her on my next trip to Hollywood. She said that would be great and then asked something really funny before we hung up. She said that she always wanted a younger brother and asked if she could beat me up when we eventually meet. I thought that was hilarious and heartwarming at the same time. After we spoke Lauren sent me some pictures of everyone we had talked about. I got to see their mom Elaine, Mal's second wife Hiromi, their kids Malcolm, Sara, and Michael, as well as Mala's two daughters. There were some promotion pictures and a couple black and white photos of Mal when he was a child. It was awesome to see everyone I had been hearing so much about.

Well the time was quickly approaching to learn if Mal was truly my birth father. To this point I believed that he was, especially due to the timeline and seeing our resemblance, but I still wasn't certain. If I'm being completely honest I was really nervous. Who's to say for sure my birth mother had told her sister Honi the truth? Again, it was the sixties and there were a lot of drugs involved. I also contemplated that if Mal wasn't my birth father then I would probably never learn who was. Well the day finally came and I received a text from Mala that said, "It's official bro, we're related!" She got her results back and my name showed up as her closest DNA match. My search was over and I now knew for certain who my parents were. I also knew for sure that I had three half brothers, and three half sisters. I was relieved and elated!

My oldest daughter, Mikayla's godmother Susan, planned a trip for us all to meet in New York City for Thanksgiving. She put us up at The Marriott Marquis in Times Square. I let Mala know I planned to be in Manhattan and it would be a great time for us to meet if her schedule permitted, and was ecstatic to hear she was free. That Thanksgiving weekend was one of the coldest in the city's history and I was happy she was willing to make the drive from her home in Queens. We met in the lobby and I recognized her immediately from the pictures. She had brought her husband Silvain and I had Johana with me. We sat in the lounge for drinks and appetizers and I was thoroughly enjoying this long overdue meeting. She had some

Me and Mala in NYC

more pictures for me to see and it was a very nice evening getting to know each other better. To cap the night off, Silvain, who was a professional photographer took some pictures of us together to commemorate this special occasion.

When she got home Mala sent me a couple of her jazz albums to listen to. Her music was contagious and I fell in love with one song in particular. It was titled "Ellie" and she had written it for her mother Elaine, who was now deceased. It had an uptempo rhythm with an Ella Fitzgerald style of scat singing that was very infectious. I also began listening to Mal's music, too. All I had to do was say, "Alexa play songs by Mal Waldron" and his music flowed continually through the evening. His catalog was so large I could listen for hours and never hear the same song twice. I was becoming closer to my birth father solely through the melody of his music. What a blessing it was to have so much of him out there for me to view and listen to anytime I pleased.

I was booked to work The Magic Castle in April and sent Lauren a message asking to meet up. Luckily she was going to be in town so we set on a day to do lunch. We met up at a very cool cafeteria-style restaurant in Hollywood. Lauren came across as very personable but kind of quiet. It's hard to be completely comfortable with someone

The entire Waldron clan

you share DNA with but in all reality is still a stranger. There were times when it was silent, which could feel a little awkward but was normal and to be expected. When we talked about her love of movies she really began to open up. She also told me how one summer Mal had brought the entire family out for one of his tours. He flew her, Mala, their mom (Mal's ex wife), and Mala's daughters all to Japan to meet up with his current wife Hiromi and all their children. It was one big family gathering and she said it was a lot of fun being with Mal and their extended family. I was hoping Lauren would get to see one of my shows before I headed back but it was her birthday weekend and she was going out of town. All in all it was an informative and delightful visit.

The weeks that followed I found myself pondering just how all of this information about my biological family had come to light. Had my new bride not been a fan of the television show *20/20*, I would have probably never seen the piece on the *Three Identical Strangers* documentary. That same evening I would not have been fast-forwarding through the opening segment allowing me to catch the name of The Louise Wise Agency, compelling me to hit rewind. I would have never seen the closing credits where they appealed to anyone who had come through Louise Wise's doors to follow up with Spence-Chapin for adoption files. All of this leading to receiving my personal report with all the clues to my birth family that would have never passed before my eyes. Johana would have never felt the compulsion to give me the Ancestry.com kit that started the DNA dominos to fall. I now knew without any diffidence the lineage of my existence. With this knowledge I went from a self-imposed perception of pity to the understanding of just how charmed a life I was blessed to be living. God gave me the genetics and upbringing specifically designed to develop and hone my life's purpose. I had two earthly fathers, one in blood and one in love. One gave me the chromosomes to follow the path of entertainment and the other helped nurture and develop that talent. I often wondered why it took so long to learn my truth? I found the answer in a single Bible verse from Corinthians 10:13 KJV.

> *"There hath no temptation taken you but such as is common to man: but God is faithful, who will not suffer you to be tempted above that ye are able; but will with the temptation also make a way to escape, that ye may be able to bear it."*

Simply stated, God won't give you more than you can handle. To uncover my reason for being I needed to be mentally and spiritually ready. All of my research into Finding Magic had inadvertently led to the hunt for my natural family, and I had found both. My life feels much more complete, and with my purpose now realized, the true journey begins. Sharing Magic!

DEDICATION

Six months after he wrote the foreword to this book my former boss, mentor, and friend, Denny Haney passed away. He suffered a very brief battle with cancer and was 73 years old when he transitioned quietly in his sleep at the shop he so tirelessly built to help elevate the art of magic.

I had heard from friends that Denny was not doing well and that I should come up to Baltimore and see him. It's crazy how things fall into place at times of need. Not shortly after hearing the news I received a last minute contract from my agent to join a cruise ship the following week in, of all places, Baltimore. I would even be staying overnight in a hotel which would give me more time to spend with Denny. When I arrived at his shop it was obvious Denny was very sick. He had lost a ton of weight and was very weak. He was too tired to speak with me that night and was happy I would be back the following morning when he hoped to have more energy. When I came back the next day he was at his computer working. His voice was almost gone and it was a little hard to understand him. He called me over using the nickname he'd given me years earlier, "Puckity Puck." We talked and it was evident he was most likely not going to survive his disease. I found myself in the worse possible situation having to say goodbye to someone who had helped so much to mold me personally and professionally. I told Denny that I was going to pray for him since I knew he didn't pray. He quickly corrected me and said that he did pray. He also mentioned that his son Denny Jr. had brought a priest to the shop and was asked to confess his sins. He then said something that really stuck with me. Denny said that he thought long and hard about his life but couldn't come up with anything he had done that was truly horrible. He said that his life for the most part was really good and that's not a bad way to go out. I agreed and we parted with that last thought and in less then two weeks he was gone

Denny was cremated and, as per his request, was buried in Colon, Michigan which is considered the Magic Capital of the World. The famous Lakeside Cemetery is the final resting place for many well-known magicians and now Dennis John Haney.

Denny was famous for doing absolutely anything to get a laugh and I would like to close this dedication with one of those times that still makes me chuckle. Denny had a pet pot belly pig that lived in his magic shop. The pig's name was Baby and she could be a real handful. I was working at Denny's shop in Essex, Maryland which was around a fifty-minute drive for me. One morning upon arriving at work I noticed that Baby had pooped all over the carpet in front of a display counter. Now pig poop is very distinct as it's hard and perfectly round. I called for Denny and told him what Baby had done. He immediately started to yell at Baby for pooping inside the shop. Then he does the unimaginable. Denny bent down and picked up one of the poop balls with his bare hand. Not stopping there he then pops the pig poop into his mouth. He's chewing and laughing at the same time and I'm disgusted and close to tossing my cookies. Then he smiles and there's brown poop all over his teeth. He literally was staring at me with a shit-eating grin! Then he goes behind the counter and I'm hoping he's getting something to clean it up but instead comes back with a box of Dunkin Doughnut's Munchkins. He had set me up bad. Before I came into work he scattered some of these chocolate doughnut holes all over the floor and then waited patiently for me to arrive. Who does that, I thought, but that was Denny's sick sense of humor in full form. Anything for a laugh and that's what I will miss the most. See you on the other side, my friend.

THANKS TO:

Denny Haney, for your invaluable guidance and mentorship.

Scott Alexander, for bringing out my creativity and being my "magic wife".

Curtis "Alexander" Carroll, for pushing me to do what I love as a career.

Susan Schwab, for your friendship and generosity.

Malcolm Williams, Richard Levy, and Joseph Murray, for always having my back and taking this crazy ride with me.

Rodney Johnson, for inspiring me to put my story on paper.

Leonard Andre Puckering, for picking me to be your little brother.

Evelyn Puckering, for showing me what love is.

Elsie Puckering, for teaching me to be a man.

Martee Shabsin for helping to put the puzzle pieces together.

Johana Santiago-Puckering, for being my God-given soul mate. I love you.

Learmond Graham Puckering, for your unconditional love and support. I miss you every day.

God, for allowing me to see that it's never too late to believe!

In Memory of Claude James

Claude, Mal, Rich, Me, Joe

CPSIA information can be obtained
at www.ICGtesting.com
Printed in the USA
BVHW041911171019
561398BV00009B/383/P